# REEL
# HISTORY

## CultureAmerica

Karal Ann Marling

Erika Doss

SERIES EDITORS

# REEL HISTORY

## In Defense of Hollywood

Robert Brent Toplin

University Press of Kansas

Published by the
University Press of
Kansas (Lawrence,
Kansas 66049),
which was organized
by the Kansas Board
of Regents and is
operated and funded
by Emporia State
University, Fort Hays
State University,
Kansas State
University, Pittsburg
State University, the
University of
Kansas, and Wichita
State University

© 2002
by the University Press of Kansas

Library of Congress Cataloging-in-Publication Data
Toplin, Robert Brent, 1940–
    Reel history : in defense of Hollywood / Robert Brent Toplin.
        p.   cm. — (CultureAmerica)
Includes bibliographical references and index.
    ISBN 0-7006-1199-1 (alk. paper) — ISBN 0-7006-1200-9 (pbk. : alk. paper)
    1. Historical films—United States—History and criticism.  2. United States—In motion pictures.  3. Motion pictures and history.  I. Title. II. Series.
PN1995.9.H5 T67 2002
791.43'658—dc21          2002005421

British Library Cataloguing in Publication Data is available.

Printed in the United States of America

10  9  8  7  6  5  4  3  2

# Contents

# Illustrations

# Introduction

Recently, while traveling on a train out of New York City, I introduced myself to a businessman sitting next to me. When I indicated that I was a university professor who conducted research on Hollywood's treatment of history, the traveler smiled and rolled his eyes. Communicating a cynical view of Hollywood's portrayals, he suggested there was "plenty to complain about." The man assumed I agreed with him, expecting that a professional historian would be eager to decry Hollywood's preference for fiction over fact, entertainment over education. "Why can't moviemakers portray the truth?" the businessman asked. Answering his own question, he claimed that *real* history was much more interesting than the "reel" stuff depicted in Hollywood's myth-based stories.

This traveler echoed a familiar criticism of history in the cinema. Anyone taking up a discussion of Hollywood's treatment of the past is likely to encounter related complaints. Commentators often register sharp critiques of the movies' portrayals. They grumble about artistic license, manipulation of facts, and invention of dialogue and situations. Generally, they give Hollywood failing grades for its presentation of the subject.

This book challenges the familiar negative assessments and recommends a more open-minded view of cinema. It suggests that movies *can* communicate important ideas about the past, but not in the way that teachers and scholars approach the subject when they deliver lectures or write books. Comparisons with traditional methods of examining history are not fruitful. A book is vastly superior to a feature film as a source of detailed information and abstract analysis. Motion pictures cannot deliver a plethora of information or a variety of interpretive perspectives as effectively as a lengthy publication can. Nevertheless, in many important respects, the two-hour movie can arouse emotions, stir curiosity, and prompt viewers to consider significant questions.

We should acknowledge, of course, that filmmakers often take liberties in the dramas they bring to the screen. Artists leave out many details in order to make their stories simple and understandable, and sometimes they are quite cavalier in their use of historical evidence. When they push artistic liberties to irresponsible excess, criticism is justifiable. Some manipulation is inherent in all dramatizations, however—in good as well as poor Hollywood films that deal with history. Furthermore, moviemakers are not the only ones who manipulate historical evidence. In different ways, those who speak and write about history also exercise degrees of interpretive license. Teachers and scholars are selective in the way they privilege facts in their narratives, and they draw conclusions in partisan ways.

This book questions the popular view that individuals who express a passionate interest in history ought to lambaste Hollywood filmmakers for misrepresenting the past to millions of impressionable viewers. It suggests that many of the complaints we hear about cinematic history are unrealistic and irrelevant. Protests against cinematic history featured in the mass media often demonstrate little appreciation of the challenges filmmakers encounter when they attempt to bring the past to life on the screen. Critics give inadequate attention to the medium's distinctive qualities and fail to recognize the unique ways that fictional film communicates. Consequently, these debunkers lose sight of cinema's important contributions to the public's thinking about the past.

The first chapter introduces this argument by maintaining that cinematic history constitutes an important genre within the broad realm of feature films. Moviemakers rely considerably on narrative conventions that have proved successful over many years, and judgments about films are not realistic if they fail to take into account the pervasiveness and usefulness of these storytelling practices. The second chapter argues for a balanced approach in assessing cinema's treatments of the past. Through consideration of a number of feature films as test cases, I defend certain liberties taken by the filmmakers but also raise questions about troublesome excesses. The third chapter identifies outstanding examples of cinematic history, as well as some unusually poor ones. I maintain that there is no single standard for judging stellar achievements in the genre; various movies offer distinctive contributions. Four principal attributes are considered: communicating the feeling of a different time and place, interpreting an important historical situation, examining the past through a biographical perspective, and interpreting history through multiple perspectives. Chapter 4 defends filmmakers' exercise of creative license by examining the production history of a specific motion picture. The film selected for analysis aimed to render history with sophistication, and the production benefited from the input of distinguished scholars. Despite commendable efforts to portray the past authentically, however, the filmmakers took many interpretive liberties, demonstrating the role of artistic license in all history-based dramas. The fifth chapter examines connections between principal issues raised in this book and the current scholarship in cinema studies. Although I identify some useful insights in the growing professional literature on film, my analysis takes issue with a number of the film scholars' perspectives on cinematic history. Finally, chapter 6 examines familiar questions about the impact of historical dramas on their audiences. While acknowledging the difficulty of demonstrating such effects, I cite some intriguing evidence that suggests that history from Hollywood can, in fact, influence the ideas and actions of the people who view it.

A few definitions and clarifications are in order. I use the term *cinematic history* liberally. At times I employ different terms with the same intent: *docudramas* and *history-oriented movies,* for example, to refer to dramatic portrayals of the past intended for mass audiences. These include both feature films and films made for broadcast on commercial television. In some cases, the discussion also includes dramas that appeared on national public television, particularly when the narrative strategies employed in these programs relate strongly to the issues addressed in this book. There are a few references to an important foreign film as well (*Das Boot*), because that production demonstrated a specific quality of cinematic history, and Hollywood released the movie in the United States through its standard distribution system.

I give much greater attention to productions from recent years and decades than do most commentators on Hollywood's interpretations of the past. Many books and articles on this subject draw considerable attention to classic films of the early and middle twentieth century, but unfortunately, many of these productions are unfamiliar to nonspecialists. To give general readers a better opportunity to register opinions based on personal observation, I cite mostly motion pictures distributed in recent years. There are instances, of course, when discussion of an earlier film is useful. For example, no extensive commentary about cinematic history can overlook important movies of yesteryear such as *Birth of a Nation.*

I attempted to keep the narrative relatively free of the jargon and arcane vocabulary that characterizes some of the current literature on film. A good deal of that scholarship appears in language that is impenetrable to those who are uninitiated in the buzzwords of university-based cinema studies. The condition of this scholarship is ironic. Feature films communicate in powerful and exciting ways, yet much of the formal commentary about them obstructs communication. My goal is to reach both film specialists and general audiences interested in film in a manner that does not conceal opinions or interpretations.

This book also takes issue with the views of historians, film scholars, literature professionals, and others who look askance at attempts to assess Hollywood's effectiveness in portraying history on the screen. Some of these commentators view movies primarily as art, entertainment, social commentary, or business. They argue that feature films are not instruments of public education, that they do not really present history lessons. A few historians advance this argument in the extreme, advising their colleagues to disregard cinematic history (except when they wish to view film in the way they study literature). Movies, they say, belong to the realm of fiction. Some specialists in cinema studies take a different but related position. They argue that cinema can never truly represent the past. Movies do not provide accurate, authentic, truthful, or objective treatments of history, they stress; films do not offer "mirrors" of history. These observers often scorn efforts to interpret the movies' interpretations of history and recommend other approaches to studying history-oriented cinema. More fruitful, they argue, are exploration of the movies' iconography, study of the messages filmmakers communicate about the present, examination of the "higher truths" movies illuminate (despite their misrepresentations of small details), and consideration of the relativity of all historical interpretations (including those in nonfiction writing). Questions about the way movies represent history are far less important, they say, than are questions about the way movies challenge us to view history in new ways—to "revision" the past.

These objections and qualifications regarding the study of Hollywood's portrayals of the past are intriguing, but they do not make a persuasive case for turning away from discussions about Hollywood's treatment of history. As I argue in chapter 5, the tendency to dismiss historians' interest in judging cinematic history comes with a price. It segregates scholars from important discussions of the subject that are taking place beyond the academy. Outside of university campuses, media critics, politicians, and film enthusiasts are engaged in energetic debates about cinematic history's interpretations and influence. Participants in these well-publicized exchanges recognize the potential of motion pictures to affect the public's attitudes about the past. These commentators acknowledge that Hollywood productions take many liberties with the facts, but they sense that feature films sometimes manage to convey thoughtful, even insightful perspectives of history.

Academicians need to play a larger role in these public exchanges, but unfortunately, many of them keep their distance from such debates. They do not acknowledge that technology and art created new kinds of historians in the twentieth century, people who have been competing effectively with traditional historians in presenting views of the past. Some teachers and scholars are unwilling to recognize the important place cinematic historians have achieved in modern society. Others, viewing cinematic history from the perspective of postmodern scholarship, appear unable to move beyond declarations of the obvious. Stressing ad nauseam that all interpretations of history

*William Wallace (Mel Gibson, center right) leads the Scots into battle against the English in* Braveheart *(1995). In recent years, the media have featured abundant stories about the provocative and controversial portrayals of history in movies such as* Braveheart. *(Museum of Modern Art Film Archive)*

are mental constructions, not true representations, they find it difficult to address serious questions about the medium's interpretations of history. Some give little attention to the subject because they believe that history-oriented movies constitute only a small and insignificant portion of the many films released each year by Hollywood. These scholars suggest that other genres are much more popular and important in the lineup of entertainment offerings (such as action-adventure, horror, science fiction, romance, and comedy).

It is easy to respond to the claims about cinematic history's unimportant minority status. Although observers are correct in claiming that historical movies represent only a small percentage of Hollywood releases, when making claims about the genre's significance, they need to consider professional reception. Cinematic history excites inordinate public interest and critical attention. In recent years, the news media have featured abundant stories regarding the provocative historical depictions in motion pictures such as *Mississippi Burning, JFK, Braveheart, Schindler's List, Titanic,* and *The Patriot.* Journalists and television commentators have registered strong opinions about the way these films interpreted the past, and they have noted the movies' impact on audiences in the United States and the world.

History-oriented productions have also received a disproportionate share of attention from the individuals who bestow honors on American cinema. Each year, members of the Academy of Motion Picture Arts and Sciences recommend five films for Best Picture. From 1986 to 2001, one or more of the five motion pictures nominated for Best Picture featured a story set in the past. In twelve of these sixteen years, a history-oriented movie won the Oscar for Best Picture: *Platoon* (1986), *The Last Emperor* (1987), *Driving Miss Daisy* (1989), *Dances with Wolves* (1990), *Unforgiven* (1992), *Schindler's List* (1993), *Braveheart* (1995), *The English Patient* (1996), *Titanic* (1997), *Shakespeare in Love* (1998), and *Gladiator* (2000), and *A Beautiful Mind* (2001). These twelve films varied greatly in the seriousness of their treatments. In some cases, the dramas related only loosely to conditions in the past; in others, the films portrayed specific people and historical situations in considerable detail. The year that *Shakespeare in Love* won the award was an especially notable one for cinematic history. All five nominees for Best Picture of 1998 were history-oriented films (the others were *Saving Private Ryan, The Thin Red Line, Life Is Beautiful,* and *Elizabeth*). Cinematic history is, then, more than just a small blip on Hollywood's radar screen.

A broader response to all the critics who resist assessments of history from Hollywood comes from an expansive vision of the modern communications revolution. It takes a long view of cinematic history's emergence as an important source of ideas about the past. The Gutenberg press gave humankind the dominant means of presenting history for more than half a millennium. Printed interpretations reached millions of readers across the world, creating an information explosion of enormous consequence. Film, in contrast, is a relatively new medium. Its potential for communicating ideas in a dramatic format became evident only in the last hundred years. In the first quarter of the twentieth century, movies delivered stories awkwardly in silent productions supported by brief captions. Sound and Technicolor energized cinema in the second quarter of the century. By the third quarter, television was bringing numerous motion picture productions into homes, and in the last quarter, videos, cable television, DVDs, satellite transmission, the Internet, and other technologies vastly expanded citizens' opportunities to view films. Cinematic history is, then, rather new, especially as an omnipresent mode of entertainment (available not only in theaters but also in video stores and on television through the major networks, A&E, History Channel, American Movie Classics, Turner Classic Movies, HBO, and many other venues). Its power is just beginning to be recognized and understood.

Cinematic historians are more influential today than ever. Improvements in technology and art have given them prominent places as interpreters of the past. Students now reference memorable examples from cinema and television when discussing ideas about history in the classroom. Each year, new movies and television releases provoke lively exchanges in the media regarding the differences between "real" history and the reel version portrayed in docudramas. The subject of cinematic history is very much in the public arena, and from time to time, stories about a provocative or controversial example of the genre (such as *JFK* or *Schindler's List*) leap out of the entertainment pages of newspapers and appear on the news pages.

Cinematic history is too important to shove aside as simply fiction, entertainment, symbolism, or commentary about current events. The messages filmmakers communicate, directly and subtly, resonate with audiences in powerful ways, often shaping their ideas about the past's influence on the present. Cinematic history has assumed a prominent place in the public mind. As such, it deserves much more detailed and probing analysis than it has received to date.[1]

# CHAPTER ONE

# Cinematic History as Genre

When examining problems with the historical portrayals in Mel Gibson's *Braveheart* (1995), a reviewer concluded that the movie's distortions of history were hardly surprising. "What do they expect?" asked Alan Taylor in an article in the *Scotsman*. The production had been designed for the mass market. "This is Hollywood, not a BBC documentary," he observed, "and it's best to remember that everything is a sacrificial lamb [in Hollywood] to the demands of studio moguls and box office returns."[1]

This kind of cynicism toward Hollywood's handling of history is a familiar characteristic of film commentaries. Reviewers frequently point to egregious factual errors and cinematic manipulations, lambasting moviemakers for taking too many artistic liberties. Sometimes they lash out against Hollywood's storytelling in general, as did Walter Goodman, who warned in the *New York Times*, if you are looking for history, "stay away from docudramas, which are driven to distort for the sake of drama."[2] In even more biting language, he suggested that "the only good docudrama is the unproduced docudrama."[3] Jerry Kuehl, writing in the British magazine *Vision*, exhibited similar contempt for Hollywood's presentations of history. He urged filmmakers not to make historical dramas if they could produce documentaries instead. Hollywood's version of history was so flawed by misrepresentations, Kuehl argued, that movies ought to feature a disclaimer announcing, "Any resemblance between the characters portrayed in this film and any person living or dead is purely coincidental." Kuehl demanded that filmmakers be held accountable for their outrageous distortions. At stake in controversies about the movies, he asserted, "is nothing less than the old, inconclusive struggle between those who are interested in history and those who are interested in fiction."[4]

Ken Burns, the accomplished producer-director of many outstanding historical documentaries, also expressed strong suspicion of the dramatic medium. He directed strong complaints against *Glory* (1989), a much-acclaimed feature film about black soldiers who served in the Union army under a white leader during the Civil War. Burns claimed the movie suffered from several anachronisms, historical gaffes, and sins of omission. In *Glory*'s climactic battle scenes, for example, the Yankee soldiers attack Fort Wagner from the north, yet in the actual assault, the Union troops attacked from the south. Burns also made fun of the movie's characterizations. *Glory* showed nineteenth-century black leader Frederick Douglass "with his fake, glued-on beard." Furthermore, black Civil War soldiers in the film reflected a familiar variety of personality types, much like the stereotypical characters in Hollywood's World War II combat pictures. Burns also maintained that "the film missed . . . opportunities." For example, even though historians had fascinating letters at their disposal written by African Americans who had participated in the Civil War, the makers of *Glory* did not use them.[5] Burns's damning remarks about *Glory* suggested that the movie paled by comparison with his informative documentary series on a related subject, *The Civil War* (1990).[6]

Complaints such as those registered by Goodman, Kuehl, and Burns appear frequently in published reviews and in radio and television commentaries about the movies. Enthusiasts of history communicate a sense of frustration and disgust when assessing Hollywood's treatment of the past. They vigorously denounce the latest Hollywood productions, urging audiences to cast a suspicious eye on them. Often these critics affect a scolding tone when reminding audiences that veracity and authenticity are of great importance. The stakes are high, because Hollywood entertainment has become an enormously influential cultural force. Movies and television programs deliver popular perspectives of the past, stories that have considerable appeal with the youth in America and the world. Young adults obtain a good deal of their understanding about the past from dramatic films rather than nonfiction history books, critics of cinematic history point out. Students are learning history from the dramas they see on the screen, and, unfortunately, they are often subjected to a deeply flawed portrayal of the past.[7]

During the 1990s, two of Oliver Stone's movies excited particularly strident complaints about historical representation: *JFK* (1991) and *Nixon* (1995). David Armstrong argued, for example, that *JFK*'s mixture of archival and dramatic film confused young viewers. Stone presented his interpretation of John F. Kennedy's assassination as if it were the literal truth.[8] Similarly, historian Alan Brinkley warned that *JFK* delivered "what an entire generation of Americans will remember as something like the truth about the Kennedy assassination."[9] Referring to Oliver Stone's *Nixon,* Charles Colson, a former top aide to President Richard M. Nixon, warned that gullible young people "who don't know the facts" could easily be seduced by the media, "where falsehoods and distortions work their greatest harm."[10] David W. Belin, who participated in the Warren Commission's investigation of Kennedy's death, said that Stone and other Hollywood artists needed to be cognizant of their power at a time when young

Americans gained much of their knowledge about the past from movies. Belin said that filmmakers "have a moral obligation to avoid major distortion of the facts in films such as 'Nixon' and 'JFK,' which purport to tell the truth about important historical figures or events."[11]

Years ago, David Wolper, executive producer of the enormously popular TV miniseries *Roots* (1977), gave a poignant response to these familiar complaints about Hollywood's treatment of history, and other filmmakers have echoed his argument since then. When reviewers attacked *Roots* for delivering a simplistic portrayal of history, Wolper challenged them to make their own movies about slavery. He replied that if the detractors of *Roots* demanded a much more complex portrayal of history, let them incorporate all the details they desired in their own dramas about slavery, and see if anybody cared to watch. Wolper's put-down was harsh, but his challenge was an appropriate one. Those who berate filmmakers for giving primacy to entertainment values should recognize that cinematic history will never come to the screen if it cannot excite the interest of a wide range of viewers with different income levels, cultural interests, and educational achievements. These audiences will quickly turn away from cinematic history if they do not find its dramatic presentation compelling.

*Roots* was an extraordinary hit on television because it effectively employed many of the essential elements of mainstream cinematic history. David Wolper and his production team drew lessons from earlier films when fashioning their television drama. They created stories on the basis of filmmaking practices that had pleased audiences in earlier productions with historical themes. *Roots* simplified a complex historical record, focused on the experiences of just a few people, viewed issues of the past in terms of an uplifting morality tale, and populated its scenes with stark characterizations of heroes and villains. Through attention to these successful narrative devices, the creators of *Roots* drew millions of viewers to their cinematic perspectives on history.[12]

Cinema studies specialists often speak of "genre" when identifying the themes and formulas that please audiences and thus are repeated in various forms over and over in later movies. When filmmakers rely on genre, explain Harold Schecter and Jonna G. Semeiks, they are involved in a "skillful retelling of an archetypal narrative that has always exerted a powerful grip on our collective imagination." Genre has the "power to communicate stories that audiences love to be told, stories that we never grow tired of hearing."[13] Thomas Schatz, one of the most influential cinema studies professionals, has identified the principal structures of movie genres of the 1930s, 1940s, and 1950s. He notes, for instance, that westerns frequently dealt with struggles to bring civilization to a wild and untamed frontier society. Often the western hero (a man of action rather than words) was seeking revenge for violence committed against himself, his family, or his friends. Gangster movies typically followed the rise and fall of a tragic figure who emerged from a humble background and then fell into trouble with the police or with rival gangs. Horror pictures frequently showed the danger of scientific hubris, evident when inventors discovered that they could not control their creations (in a variation of this plot, an individual was reluctant to destroy a monster because of its possible value to science).[14]

Genre is never static, Schatz reminds us. It is always changing, evolving. Audiences want to see much that is familiar in a movie, but they also expect to encounter unique qualities. Viewers quickly lose interest in a story that looks and sounds like a replica of previous productions. Successful filmmakers understand this complex expectation—the mixture of story elements that are old and familiar with those that are new and intriguing—and offer moviegoers recognizable plots as well as significant elements of surprise.[15]

Societal developments can also effect changes in the genre, forcing new twists in story lines as times change. Cinematic artists often adjust traditional tales or create new plots based on recent events. In the 1950s, for example, growing fear about the impact of radiation from nuclear testing created an attractive environment for the production of horror movies about mutant insects threatening humankind, such as the huge ants in *Them* (1954). When public apprehension over nuclear testing subsided in the 1960s, these plots became less evident in sci-fi productions. Changing social conditions also affected the character of westerns. For many years, American moviegoers and television audiences loved the genre. Westerns frequently communicated upbeat tales about tough men defeating criminals or Indians and advancing the march of "civilization." That formula became less successful by the 1960s and 1970s, when the Vietnam War, racial strife, and a failing economy brought into question many of the progressive, optimistic elements of the western genre. In the late twentieth century, westerns fell out of fashion, and the few that did succeed often incorporated a good deal of parody or cynicism.[16] Also, some of the familiar western themes transformed into detective and science fiction films.

Sometimes genres run in cycles. The success of a particular blockbuster can inspire many copycat efforts in Hollywood. *The Godfather* (1972) started such a cycle, inspiring a number of new gangster movies. *Star Wars'* popularity in 1977 helped promote the development of science fiction movies. When a cycle seems to be near its end, filmmakers are likely to parody the genre. In these cases, the story outlines are so familiar that they serve as attractive targets for humor. Movies such as *The Wild Bunch* (1969), *Cat Ballou* (1974), and *Blazing Saddles* (1974) made fun of the traditional western. *Airplane!*

(1980) parodied disaster films. Historical genre has been the target of parody, too. Mel Brooks's *The History of the World, Part 1* (1981), *Monty Python and the Holy Grail* (1975), *Cheech and Chong's The Corsican Brothers* (1984), and the musical comedy *A Funny Thing Happened on the Way to the Forum* (1966) drew laughs while referencing familiar themes and characterizations from Hollywood's historical genre.

Among the most important genres are western, noir, romance, gangster, musical, horror, science fiction, woman's, thriller, detective, action-adventure, war, courtroom drama, martial arts, comedy, and disaster movies. Some movies combine genres. *Alien* (1992) was part horror, part science fiction, and part thriller. *The Silence of the Lambs* (1991) involved both the horror and the detective genres. *Guys and Dolls* (1955) combined the musical and the gangster film. *Seven Brides for Seven Brothers* (1954) mixed the western and the musical. There are also subgenres such as the "screwball comedy" (*Twentieth Century*, 1934), the "backstage musical" (*Fame*, 1980), and the Vietnam film within the war or historical genre (*Full Metal Jacket*, 1988).

Students of film remind us that genres communicate strongly through iconography. Movies from a specific genre feature familiar scenes, characters, and story structures. In terms of visual imagery, for example, classic westerns were known for their scenes of dusty towns situated on the edge of a desert. The bad guys rode dark horses, wore black clothing, and often sported beards or mustaches. Saloons, dance-hall girls, and posses were also among the familiar icons. Horror films featured gothic castles, shadowy nocturnal photography, and plenty of lightning. Gangster movies had urban settings with nightclubs, card games, and car chases; they featured tough-looking men who wore long coats and fedoras, smoked, and drank bootleg liquor.[17] Through a variety of familiar visual elements, Hollywood's genres established icons that audiences could easily recognize.

Can we identify the principal elements of historical cinema, including plots and characters as well as visual imagery? The task seems difficult, because the scope of historical film is broad. Cinematic history incorporates many different eras, geographic locations, nations, cultures, and classes. It appears quite difficult to pick out a few obvious icons. History-oriented movies may focus on Roman times or the twentieth century, on the United States or Asia, on a queen and her court or the life of an immigrant family. Cinematic history exhibits such great diversity in terms of settings, plots, and characters that it seems far less encoded than Hollywood's gangster films or horror movies are.

Yet subgenres of cinematic history do incorporate familiar conventions—popular storytelling strategies, icons, and characterizations. Movies about Roman times, for instance, often feature imposing classical buildings with huge columns and chambers. Their stories usually feature a power-hungry, egomaniacal emperor who speaks in high English and acts like an effete and sometimes sadistic aristocrat. Audience sympathy is frequently directed toward the Christians, who are victims of oppression. The heroic figure in these films usually appears in garb that contrasts sharply with the emperor's. The hero's more subdued apparel suggests a democratic attitude; he is a man of the people. Toward the end of the film, he is usually engaged in a titanic battle against powerful and dangerous enemies in a great public arena before a huge crowd.[18]

Combat movies are another subgenre of the historical film with familiar elements. These movies often focus on a platoon, introducing audiences to a small force of five to ten men. Usually there is tension between the group's leader and a feisty, rebellious soldier who at first refuses to cooperate and be a team player. The combat group is typically diverse, frequently including a guy from Brooklyn, a religiously inclined sharpshooter from the South, and a variety of other stock characters. Action in the film waxes and wanes. There are lively moments of tense firefights and calmer periods when the men talk about their girls back home and what they want to do with their lives. The conclusion of the combat movie almost always involves a superbattle that claims the lives of some of the leading characters but nevertheless produces a victory. In this lively finish, the rebellious figure in the unit usually proves his loyalty and mettle.[19]

More broadly, moviegoers can often recognize the historical genre from the texture of the film. Cinematic artists often manipulate a movie's grain and coloration, attempting to give their productions a look of period authenticity. They can adjust colors by shooting scenes through filters that provide a brownish tint. This technique creates a resemblance to the brownish orange shades of early Technicolor movies, and it also makes the film look somewhat like old color photographs stored in an attic. Not surprisingly, the History Channel features this color icon in its brownish orange logo and in the background sets in its studio. Director John Sayles took a different approach to colors in *Matewan* (1987), a movie about a coal miners' strike in West Virginia. To give his movie a historic-looking quality, Sayles washed sharp colors (such as reds and yellows) out of the scenes and emphasized the drab grays, browns, and blues.[20] Steven Spielberg operated in a related way, washing sharp colors out of *Saving Private Ryan* (1998), especially in the opening scenes depicting the D-day assault. Spielberg wanted to create the appearance of an old newsreel. He employed a different technique in *Schindler's List* (1993), in which cinematographer Janusz Kaminski used black-and-white photography throughout most of the story, giving the film a documentary-like appearance.

Audiences have also come to recognize the historical genre through the people associated with it. Just as James Cagney and Edward G. Robinson were well recognized in the 1930s as frequent actors in classic gangster movies, and John Wayne and Clint Eastwood became identified with westerns in later years, some actors become associated in the public mind with historical films. During the 1930s, Paul Muni enjoyed such recognition because of his portrayal of a number of historical figures in Hollywood biopics. More recently, Edward Hermann has been associated with cinematic history because of his roles as Franklin D. Roosevelt and Alger Hiss in televised docudramas. Sam Waterston earned the same distinction by playing President Abraham Lincoln in *Gore Vidal's Lincoln* (1988), nuclear scientist J. Robert Oppenheimer in *Oppenheimer* (1982), and *New York Times* reporter Sydney Schanberg in *The Killing Fields* (1984). In large part because of their performances in cinematic history, Hermann and Waterston have served as hosts for History Channel programs.

More specifically, how can we recognize the principal characteristics of the historical genre? Do the plots in cinematic history have a traditional structure? How do historical films characterize individuals? In what ways has the historical genre changed over the years, and why? What is the role of subgenres in cinematic history?

Questions about this important category among the major genres produced by Hollywood have received little professional attention. Despite considerable commentary about cinematic history in the mass media, including much attention to debates and controversies about the depiction of history on the screen, little has been written about the historical genre's fundamental characteristics. Robert A. Rosenstone offers some insightful commentary on generic structure in *Visions of the Past: The Challenge of Film to Our Idea of History*, but his analysis adds up to only a few pages.[21] Leger Grindon and Robert Burgoyne suggest a need for greater study of the historical genre, yet they provide little specific discussion of the broad characteristics of cinematic history in their books.[22] Other authors focus on subgenres (such as biopics and epics), describing the stories and visual achievements of such films, but they give almost no analytical treatment to the overall generic elements. Fortunately, we have a few excellent investigations of the structure of historical subgenres, such as Jeanine Basinger's informative book *The World War II Combat Film: Anatomy of a Genre*.[23]

Any attempt to identify a framework associated with this genre is, of course, subject to considerable debate. Efforts to describe a framework are inherently subjective because they call for judgments. There are no true "rules" for fabricating popular docudramas. Filmmakers do not consult a respected guidebook that lists successful strategies for the design of cinematic history. Furthermore, many other factors come into play that color the presentation of history in the movies. Individual artists stamp their personalities on their projects. Martin Scorsese, Oliver Stone, and Steven Spielberg exhibit diverse storytelling approaches and directing styles. As an auteur, each artist creates his or her own cinematic designs.

Nevertheless, we can make a cautious case for cinematic history as genre. There *are* some familiar practices in the craft. Specific films may not contain all these elements, but most Hollywood movies feature many of the basic components. Aspects of these stylistic approaches appear time after time in cinematic history because the techniques work. These approaches make the movies comprehensible and entertaining to audiences. As Schatz points out, filmmakers respond to proven "formulas"—narrative traditions or conventions that have achieved successful audience reactions in other movies.[24] Hollywood artists keep in mind common strategies that have helped make cinematic history understandable, exciting, inspiring, relevant, and intriguing to those who pay to see it.

These strategies can make risky investments in cinematic history more secure. Dramas about significant historical events or situations frequently call for expensive forms of presentation: a substantial cast of leading characters, large scenes involving crowds, panoramic perspectives, historic-looking buildings, period costumes, antique furnishings, and modes of transportation that are no longer in fashion. Historical cinema is also a risky investment because it involves a particularly challenging effort to establish an emotional "hook" that draws in the audience. Filmmakers know that it is generally more difficult to interest viewers in a story about the 1820s or the 1920s than it is to get them emotionally involved in a drama set in the present. Too many problems can easily interfere with the suspension of disbelief—a critical achievement in successful drama. The dialogue in a historical film may not ring true; actors may look silly in their dated apparel; the scenery may not appear authentic. Quite easily, the movie can communicate phoniness to the audience, drawing attention to the fact that the portrayal is staged and that the characters are only pretending that they are living in the past. James Cameron expressed this concern during the months *Titanic* (1997) was in production. The director worried that his expensive project would seem unbelievable and be one of the biggest financial disasters in the history of Hollywood. Additionally, cinematic historians confront the challenge of making historical problems and topics relevant to viewers. Audiences may be only vaguely familiar with the conditions in which the characters find themselves and the difficulties they face. Filmmakers must introduce viewers to different times and places, acquaint audiences with distinctive physical and emotional environments, and familiarize them with political and social controversies that can appear, at first glance, to have little to do with issues of the present.

Cinematic historians turn to generic strategies to make these difficult and financially risky dramas succeed at the box office and in the television ratings competition. They incorporate well-developed conventions of their craft, borrowing techniques of storytelling that have evolved over the decades.

Each of these techniques interferes in some way with the kind of interpretations that professional historians, lay history buffs, and media critics want to see on the screen. The generic strategies tend to limit the amount of specific information audiences can learn about historic situations. Employing practices of the genre, filmmakers reduce the number of characters in the stories and compress time, directing audience attention to only a few individuals and events. These familiar dramatic strategies often simplify portrayals of the past. They frame issues starkly in terms of conflicts between heroes and villains. The generic style favors highly partisan perspectives that show audiences only one side of a complex controversy. Furthermore, filmmakers draw heavily from contemporary sensibilities in framing their stories, viewing issues of the past through the lens of the present. In all these respects, the conventions of cinematic history lead to manipulations of the historical record that often trouble students of the past.

Some observers find these formulaic elements so disturbing that they dismiss cinematic history altogether. They consider their worst suspicions confirmed when they discover that filmmakers attempt to make their dramas conform to the patterns of successful entertainment. Evidence of these generic practices seems to demonstrate the pecuniary fixation of Hollywood; to critics, it confirms that filmmakers produce cinematic history to make money, not to inform or educate audiences. Detractors claim that the attention to entertainment strategies proves that filmmakers are not really interested in producing "true" pictures of the past. Instead, they employ formulas of genre and conform to the established techniques of mass entertainment. The result is Hollywood-style entertainment, but not sophisticated history.

Such a broad dismissal of cinematic history is much too extreme. It reflects a closed-minded and unsophisticated perspective. As subsequent chapters demonstrate, history-based movies *can* deliver much of value to their audiences. But assessing that value requires a recognition of the dramatic conventions that influence virtually every Hollywood filmmaker who produces pictures for mass audiences. Blaming cinematic historians for incorporating strategies of the genre is like criticizing football coaches for promoting aggressive behavior on the playing field. Judgments about coaches' effectiveness relate, most fundamentally, to their win-loss records and success in building the skills, character, and self-confidence of their players. In a related way, judgments about cinematic historians must take into account both the market appeal of their productions and their success in communicating informed, thoughtful, and provocative perspectives on the past.

How does the history-oriented movie communicate? What are some of the most familiar practices of the craft? Which narrative strategies have filmmakers repeated in a variety of ways because the techniques worked effectively in previous movies? How does Hollywood attempt to tweak genre, sometimes producing variations on familiar themes? What is the risk of deviating radically from the familiar generic practices? The following discussion identifies some of the major components of cinematic history. It serves, too, as a useful checklist for wide-eyed history enthusiasts who believe they have good ideas for historical movies. These wanna-be cinematic historians need not follow the popular formulas slavishly, but they may seriously jeopardize their projects if they disregard the established procedures wantonly.

## CINEMATIC HISTORY SIMPLIFIES HISTORICAL EVIDENCE AND EXCLUDES MANY DETAILS

When media commentators and professional historians complain that a motion picture left out too many important facts or failed to give audiences a complete picture of events, often they fail to acknowledge a fundamental structural component of cinematic history. Critics forget that a dramatic film cannot deliver a comprehensive assessment of its subject. To make history understandable and exciting, filmmakers have to narrow the scope of their portrayals. Usually they dramatize only a few events, cover a narrow space of time, and give detailed attention to the thoughts and actions of only a few key people. The subject of the movie is also rather tightly focused on one situation from the past. Memorable movies about World War II, such as *The Sands of Iwo Jima* (1949), *The Longest Day* (1962), *Tora! Tora! Tora!* (1970), and *Midway* (1976), draw attention to specific battles, not to the overall progress of the war. In this respect, Alfred Hitchcock's general observation about the movies applies very well to this genre. "Cinema is not a slice of life but a piece of cake," said the famous director.[25]

Motion pictures cannot present comprehensive, definitive studies, and filmmakers understand the foolishness of even trying to cover a topic's length and breadth. Andrian Scott, writer for the 1947 movie *Crossfire*, explained this viewpoint when he responded to critics who complained that *Crossfire* looked only at extreme forms of anti-Semitism; these reviewers wanted to see a story that dealt with the many kinds of bigotry Jews experienced in America, including the much more subtle and disguised variety. Scott acknowledged that his screenplay was "limited and confined." *Crossfire*'s story was purposefully designed to approach only one element of prejudice against Jews, he explained. His storytelling strategy was similar to the approach of theatrical writers. "To attempt to do a definitive study of anti-Semitism in one picture is a fool's errand," Scott argued. "It is proper material for pamphlets and books. But even in those media it is doubtful if definitiveness is possible. Find, if you can, a definitive one-volume analysis."[26]

Scott's defense of his film appears justified when we consider that the dialogue in a two-hour movie consumes no more than ten to twenty book-size pages (sometimes fewer). More important, that language communicates only tidbits of specific information. Words exchanged by the actors ordinarily do not present much detailed evidence about military operations, diplomatic crises, political conflicts, or important social developments. They do even less to explore ideas or to analyze and interpret the larger lessons of history. Most of the verbal exchanges in a Hollywood film deal with interpersonal relationships. The actors express love, passion, hope, frustration, humiliation, joy, and anger.

*Reds* (1982), Warren Beatty's epic drama about a radical journalist's activities during World War I and the Russian Revolution, contains little specific information about political events of the era. It offers virtually no interpretation of the causes of the Bolshevik Revolution, nor does it attempt to explain that event's significance in history. Most of the movie's dialogue relates to the tensions associated with a love affair between John Reed and Louise Bryant, two historic figures. *Saving Private Ryan* (1998) only briefly informs audiences that the movie's fighting men are part of the D-day invasion force, and the actors say virtually nothing about the issues that led America to fight against Hitler's Germany in the Second World War. *The Thin Red Line* (1998) contains only a few sentences uttered by Nick Nolte that explain why the Americans need to wrest a Pacific island from the control of Japanese soldiers. The actors in *Ride with the Devil* (1999) offer only a few brief remarks in the opening moments that suggest how disagreements between Northerners and Southerners led to the American Civil War in 1861.

Moviemakers who attempt to pack a lot of historical information into their productions incur considerable risk. Fact-laden dramas can confuse and tire audiences, and cinematic historians who lose their audiences in a labyrinth of detail and complexity may have difficulty raising funds for future projects. They can also encounter another kind of problem that is less obvious. Artists who attempt informational overload often come under fire for leaving out other essential details. By presenting a good deal of specific evidence about history, they raise the expectations of reviewers, leaving critics hungry for more.

Norman Jewison encountered these problems in his production of *The Hurricane* (1999). The movie was criticized not only because of artistic liberties taken in the script but also because Jewison invited debate over how to interpret many basic facts about Rubin "Hurricane" Carter's life. Jewison's movie introduced so many characters associated with Carter over several decades that the filmmaker gave the critics plenty of targets to attack. Similarly, Oliver Stone created abundant targets for critics in his two fact-laden political films: *JFK* and *Nixon.* Of course, Stone also invited criticism when he promoted controversial conspiracy theories in both movies.[27]

## CINEMATIC HISTORY APPEARS IN THREE ACTS FEATURING EXPOSITION, COMPLICATION, AND RESOLUTION

In ancient Greece, Aristotle described the three-act structure in dramatic presentation, and in fundamental ways, these principal components are still recognizable in today's movies. Wells Root, screenwriter for *The Prisoner of Zenda* (1952) and *Magnificent Obsession* (1954), identified a related story structure in his influential book *Writing the Script: A Practical Guide for Film and Television.*[28] In the first act of a movie, said Root, the writer introduces his characters, confronts them with a problem or crisis, introduces the antagonist, sets up difficult choices for the hero, and clarifies stakes in the crisis. In the second act, the hero's problems intensify. Finally, the writer resolves the hero's problems in the third act or ends the story tragically.[29] S. J. Perelman described this structure humorously, explaining that in the first act you put a man up in a tree, in the second act you have characters throw rocks at him, and in the third act you bring him down from the tree. Bruce Robinson, who wrote the screenplay for *The Killing Fields*, observes that "these three acts are almost inviolate in terms of the business—all producers, directors, executives always talk in terms of the three acts."[30] Robinson points out that there needs to be a problem with the relationship between the principal characters, a serious element of tension. A simple, cheerful story will not work: "A beautiful boy meets a beautiful girl, they fall madly in love, they meet each other's respective parents who adore the union, they get married, and live happily ever after—i.e., no story. But, boy meets girl, they fall in love, meet respective parents, and one is called Capulet and the other Montague and they *hate* each other, and you've got *Romeo and Juliet.*"[31]

### Act One: Exposition

In the opening minutes of a film, viewers meet some of the principal characters and learn about the social or political conditions that threaten them.

Often cinematic history sets up a rather pleasant picture of the protagonists' lives in these early minutes. Then viewers witness disturbing events that create trouble and lead to the second section of the story, the time of struggle. Early in *JFK,* for instance, Oliver Stone introduces newsreel footage showing President Kennedy presiding over a Camelot-like America. Then the assassination occurs, and the drama takes viewers through a detective-style search for the killer or killers. A similar introductory scheme figures in two of the most successful history series on television: *Roots* and *Holocaust* (1978). *Roots* opens with scenes of Africans living happily in their peaceful native villages. Then the series' first hero, Kunta Kinte, is captured by slave traders and transported to a Virginia slave market. *Holocaust* opens with a happy wedding scene in Germany. Then a few guests espouse anti-Semitism, and before long, the groom and his family suffer oppression at the hands of the Nazis.

Some docudramas change the order of this presentation and open with a shocking event, attempting to engage the audience's interest in the subject quickly. Then, in following scenes, the action slows down and the audience receives a fuller introduction to the people and the problems. Steven Spielberg took this approach in *Amistad* (1997), beginning with a provocative event as the African hero Cinque breaks from his shackles during a stormy night on a slave ship and leads his fellow slaves in a bloody mutiny. The rebels wrest control of the vessel from the captain and crew and attempt to return to Africa. This action-packed beginning is a familiar feature of many Spielberg movies. *Jaws* (1975) starts with a shark attack on a beach, one of the Indiana Jones films begins with a huge rock crashing through a cave and threatening the life of the hero, and *Jurassic Park* (1993) starts with a vicious attack by a caged dinosaur.

The artists behind cinematic history often employ this first-shock strategy. For instance, *Dances with Wolves* (1990) begins with scenes of the hero in the midst of a Civil War battle. Then the story turns more contemplative as the main character takes a lonely military assignment on the western frontier. Biographical films often start with an extraordinary event that sparks audience curiosity about the protagonist's life. Attention to this moment of crisis arouses audience interest in the individual's past, and an exploration of the background to the event follows. *Lawrence of Arabia* (1962) begins with the enigmatic figure's 1935 death in a motorcycle accident. Then the film turns back in time to show Lawrence as a young man. *Eleanor and Franklin,* a popular TV miniseries of the 1970s, begins with Eleanor Roosevelt receiving news of the death of her husband, the president of the United States. The heroine then learns that the president's secret lover, Lucy Mercer, was with him on the day of his death. As Eleanor contemplates the news, the movie shifts to the period of her youth and begins its biographical treatment.

## Act Two: Complication

The second section of the dramatic structure usually follows naturally from the disturbing events that broke the calm and happiness of the introductory setting. In this phase, the heroes begin a struggle, determined to resist the villains who have brought trouble to themselves or their communities. These tales of personal transformation often employ a story device found in Hollywood westerns: a peaceful character reluctantly chooses to fight back after witnessing injustice. These figures resemble Jimmy Stewart's character in *The Man Who Shot Liberty Valance* (1962). In that film, a peace-loving man reluctantly concludes that he must use his gun against the brutal bully, played by Lee Marvin. At this point in *Braveheart,* Scottish hero William Wallace decides that he cannot tolerate the oppressive domination of the English any longer and leads his fellow Highlanders in a fight against the evil English. In the second "act" of *Roots,* Kunta Kinte vows to escape from slavery, and in *Holocaust,* a young Jew goes into hiding, determined to join the underground resistance against the Nazis. In this segment of *Norma Rae* (1979), the spunky Norma, a textile worker, decides that she has seen too much suffering by her father in an unsafe factory, and she is fed up with management's treatment of her coworkers. The earthy rebel joins a trade union, and she boldly stands up on a factory table holding a defiant sign with the word "Strike" scratched across it.

The protagonists often experience frustration in this second phase, especially in the latter part of the film. Heroes and heroines suffer major setbacks; they fail to achieve their goals or lose ground. Toward the end of the film, they appear close to defeat. Late in "act two," for instance, the astronauts in *Apollo 13* (1995) are low on oxygen, freezing in their cabin, and losing power in the command module; they seem about to die in space. Soldiers in *Battle of the Bulge* (1965) find themselves overwhelmed by the surging German offensive, and in *U-571* (2000), the American sailors who are attempting to get back to safety in a disabled submarine look like they are about to become victims of German attackers. This familiar device of the cinematic genre—the creation of a severe crisis late in the story—works splendidly to keep the audience's emotions tied to the film.

## Act Three: Resolution

Many cinematic histories end with victory for the virtuous and heroic figures at the center of their plots. In *All the President's Men* (1976), for example, Bob Woodward and Carl Bernstein succeed in bringing down President Nixon, and captions on the screen tell the audience about other culprits in the Watergate scandal who received criminal sentences. The slaves in *Amistad* win their freedom in court, and then a British naval bombardment destroys a principal slave-trading garrison in Africa. In *The Killing Fields,* Sydney Schanberg and Dith Pran, the Asian friend Schanberg lost in the Cambodian revolution, are reunited, and in *Norma Rae,* the heroine's trade union wins an election and the right to bargain for the suffering textile workers.

History is not always so generous to the crusaders for freedom and justice, of course. Sometimes heroes and heroines lose. In a variety of ways, cinematic historians have grappled with these tragic endings, attempting to give meaning to the protagonists' struggles by suggesting some basis for hope, some means of drawing inspiration from a tragic story. Often docudramas remind audiences that slain heroes did not die in vain. At the end of Elia Kazan's *Viva Zapata!* (1952), for instance, political enemies assassinate Emiliano Zapata, but his white horse escapes to the mountains. The audience senses that public memory of the man who fought for the rights of Mexico's lowly peasants will have an impact on future generations.[32] In *Spartacus* (1960), the dying slave hero sees his infant son held up before him as a free person, and the audience senses that the hero's struggle will pave the way to freedom for many more victims of Roman oppression.[33] Late in Constantine Costa-Gavras's *Missing* (1982), Ed Horman (Jack Lemmon) realizes that his son lost his life in the violent military coup in Chile, but he vows to sue the U.S. officials who may have been implicated in the abduction. Horman's statement tells the audience that the case is not closed; critics will keep it alive (as the movie itself surely aimed to do).[34] And in James Cameron's *Titanic,* hero Jack Dawson dies on the frozen sea after the great ship sinks, but Rose DeWitt Bukater's life is changed for the better because of her brief relationship with Jack, and the memory of her young lover goes on, as Celine Dion's passionate song reminds viewers.

Some historical movies finish with half a victory for the protagonists, showing triumph but also reminding the audience that many people were not as fortunate as the survivors. *Schindler's List* effectively applies this dramatic strategy. Although Oskar Schindler was able to protect more than a hundred Jews from Nazi death camps during World War II, in a speech near the end (invented for the movie), Schindler expresses regret that he could not save more people from extermination. This scene reminds viewers of the six million European Jews whose personal stories did not end so happily. *Saving Private Ryan,* another movie directed by Spielberg, ends with triumph over the German armed forces in a fierce battle in a European village. It is a Pyrrhic victory, however, for most of the platoon members featured in the drama lay dead, including the enigmatic but lovable captain played by Tom Hanks. In a coda, an elderly Private Ryan visits the soldiers' graveyard and ponders whether he was worthy of the gift of life he received from the men who rescued him. A number of moviegoers left the theater in silence after viewing *Saving Private Ryan.*

The film's tragic ending forced them to think about the tremendous personal contributions American soldiers made in the Second World War.

## CINEMATIC HISTORY OFFERS PARTISAN VIEWS OF THE PAST, CLEARING IDENTIFYING HEROES AND VILLAINS

Critics of Hollywood dramas often demand complex portraits of the subjects being portrayed. They want to see conflicting viewpoints dramatized, demanding that the filmmaker develop two or more perspectives on historical people, events, and issues rather than just one. In this regard, they often speak glowingly about *Rashomon,* the influential 1950 motion picture by the acclaimed Japanese director Akira Kurosawa. *Rashomon* examines a murder in medieval Japan and asks What is truth? How do different individuals see it differently? Through four flashbacks, the movie exposes the audience to distinct perspectives, which stimulates thinking. Enthusiasts of Kurosawa's artistry praise his imaginative exploration of conflicting viewpoints about a specific subject. They applaud Kurosawa's creativity and encourage Hollywood filmmakers to engage in similar experiments that confront audiences with questions about perception.[35] But Hollywood's artists rarely act on these appeals. Instead of producing entertainment that gives expression to multiple outlooks, they design stories that essentially present only one viewpoint. Movies do not typically raise questions about the "truth status" of their interpretations. Through their tendency to resolve problems by the end of the story, to close the subject with dramatic resolution, they leave an impression that their interpretation is the only viable one. Filmmakers usually opt for highly opinionated, partisan interpretations of their subjects.

Why doesn't the technique applied in *Rashomon* attract many practitioners in Hollywood? Why are most filmmakers unwilling to incorporate contradictory evidence in their stories and thus expose viewers to contrasting perspectives of the past? Why do their dramatizations of history offer heavy-handed interpretations that press one conclusion on viewers?

Dramatic film is not a very good communicator of contradictions. Cinematic historians have a language reservoir of limited size to explicate contrasting views. As mentioned earlier, a script containing dialogue for a two-hour movie (free of lengthy descriptive information for the actors, director, or cinematographer) amounts to only about ten to twenty single-spaced pages. A movie's potential for communicating specific verbal information is minute in comparison to a book's capacity for delivering detailed commentary. There is no opportunity to explore multiple interpretations of events in a drama, whereas a book can attempt such an exploration in 200 or 300 pages.

Furthermore, drama forces its creators to make opinionated decisions throughout a story's development. Characters in a motion picture, whether major or minor, are never truly neutral figures. When introducing each figure to the audience, dramatists must communicate clear messages. A sinister-looking man with a mustache who is dressed in dark clothing and speaks in a surly voice suggests villainous qualities. A good-looking young man whose countenance, gestures, and attitude imply trustworthiness and sincerity can hint of heroic qualities. In setting up scenes, establishing the relationships between characters, making decisions about camera angles and lighting, composing background music for important dramatic moments, and deciding on many other visual and aural elements that go into a motion picture, cinematic historians create the building blocks for a specific thesis. Dramatic film requires them to reveal some form of partisanship in every frame. Hence, cinema's interpretations of the past almost always come to us in highly judgmental form.

Consider the partisanship of Richard Attenborough's much acclaimed movie *Gandhi,* which received the Academy Award for Best Picture in 1982. Attenborough's big-budget biographical film examined the life of the influential Indian leader Mahatma Gandhi. Many reviewers applauded the director for crafting a visually dazzling and sophisticated movie, and viewers were impressed by his characterization of Gandhi's heroism. The film gave an inspiring portrayal of Gandhi's fight against discrimination in South Africa, his efforts to break India away from British colonial rule, his commitment to nonviolent tactics, his personal dedication to maintaining a simple, ascetic life, and his courageous efforts to promote peace between Hindus and Muslims in a period of great religious conflict. But some observers drew attention to the strongly hagiographic character of Attenborough's movie, noting that the film showed the Indian leader in a highly favorable light (these observers also pointed out that the Indian government had subsidized about one-third of the cost of producing the film).

Richard Grenier presented one of the sharpest criticisms at the time. He took aim at the movie's one-sided, celebratory portrayal. Showing readers a very different perspective on the popular Indian figure, Grenier accused Attenborough of bringing "a pious fraud" to the screen. The real Mahatma Gandhi tolerated India's brutal caste system for many years and was rather late in coming around to a critique of it. Also, during Gandhi's protests in South Africa against the discrimination suffered by India-born minorities, he demonstrated little concern for the fate of South Africa's blacks. Nor was the real Gandhi always the supreme pacifist that is presented in the movie. India's famous leader enthusiastically supported England's fight in the First World War, and he

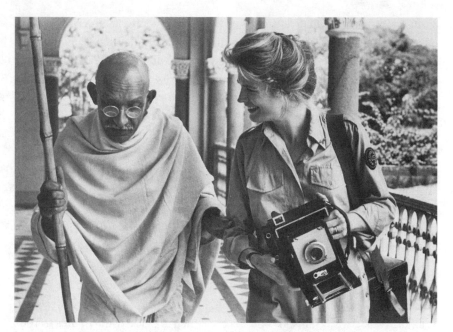

*In Richard Attenborough's* Gandhi *(1982), Ben Kingsley stars as the Indian spiritual and political leader, and Candice Bergen plays photographer Margaret Bourke-White. Like many biographical treatments from Hollywood, this movie presents its subject in a very favorable light. (Museum of Modern Art Film Archive)*

helped form the Indian Volunteer Corps. In fact, until the age of fifty, Gandhi was not ill disposed toward war at all.[36]

Fourteen years later, a playwright raised a number of related questions in a theater production called *Mahatma vs. Gandhi.* Feroz Khan's stage drama focused on the troubled relationship between Gandhi and the oldest of his four sons, Harilal. Khan's production revealed that Harilal ran afoul of the law on charges of fraud, suffered from chronic alcoholism, and engaged in sexual philandering in the red-light districts of Delhi and Bombay. The drama suggested that Gandhi had failed as a husband and a father. Khan's story maintained that the very qualities that made Mahatma Gandhi a great public leader—asceticism, self-righteousness, and single-mindedness—contributed to his obstinate behavior, didactic attitude, and unfeeling relationship with his wife and son.[37]

Could cinematic history give audiences both perspectives on Mahatma Gandhi? Was it capable of introducing audiences to a flawed figure as well as a heroic one? Hollywood's portrayal of the Indian leader, like its representation of many other historical figures, failed to offer that balance. Attenborough's portrait lacked ambiguity; it delivered a single, dominant message. The screen Gandhi came across as an earthly saint.

In many other cinematic histories as well, the fundamental interpretation is anything but subtle. Almost always, cinema sharply distinguishes between good and bad, right and wrong. In judging events and characters, there is not much gray. This convention has been evident in Hollywood-style docudramas since the early days of filmmaking. D. W. Griffith contributed significantly to the tradition of portraying heroes and villains in the extreme. His most notable film, *Birth of a Nation* (1915), favors the respected Cameron family of South Carolina and portrays villains representing northern interests, including Austin Stoneman, a powerful congressman, Silas Lynch, a power-hungry mulatto, and Gus, a renegade black soldier.

Modern-day moviemakers introduce their characters with more subtlety, but their practices only slightly obscure the fundamental partisanship. Filmmakers are less likely today to use telltale mustaches and dark clothing to distinguish villains from heroes, but they employ a variety of methods to suggest how the audience should judge the leading characters. Moviegoers understand the principal messages, learning to distinguish the good guys from the bad. In *Braveheart,* William Wallace (Mel Gibson) and his Scotsmen are clearly the figures to root for in their clash with the sinister Englishmen. In *The Patriot* (2000), Gibson is again the obvious hero in his portrayal of colonial widower Benjamin Martin. In both films, Gibson steps up to battle a group of despicable British characters.

As Attenborough did for Gandhi, screenwriters and directors often clean up the historical records of the heroic characters in their stories. Rarely do they present heroic figures with serious flaws to match their achievements. In *Spartacus,* for instance, screenwriter Dalton Trumbo and director Stanley Kubrick show the rebel leader of Roman times attempting to end slavery everywhere, when in fact, Spartacus aimed principally to get his men out of Italy. The movie characterizes the protagonist as a great humanitarian, yet the real Spartacus participated in the slaughter of hundreds of innocent Romans. *Christopher Columbus* (1985) sanitizes its explorer-hero while assigning evil (particularly enslavement of the Indians) to other Spanish members of his expedition, as well as to representatives of the Crown and the Church. Yet the real Columbus was enthusiastic about the potential for enslaving natives when he reported his discoveries to the Spanish sovereigns.

Cinematic history needs demons, too, and they are often assigned rather cavalierly. *Tucker* (1988) greatly simplifies the problems of the automobile entrepreneur who is at the center of the story, laying most of the blame for his failures on a conspiracy of powerful figures in Detroit and Washington, D.C. The movie suggests that executives from the Big Three auto companies and politicians in the nation's capital succeeded in crushing the brainchild of Preston Tucker, the visionary who tried to create a new car that featured an aerodynamic design, seat belts, disc brakes, a pop-out windshield, and fuel injection. The real Tucker failed for a variety of reasons, and many of his difficulties were self-inflicted. He rushed his new automobile into production well before significant mechanical difficulties had been resolved. He made exaggerated and misleading claims about his product to the press and raised funds for the enterprise in ways that concerned the Securities and Exchange Commission. Also, there is no evidence that leaders from Detroit's Big Three manufacturers were involved in a conspiracy against him.[38]

*Bonnie and Clyde* (1967) portrays Frank Hamer, the man who led the pursuit of Bonnie Parker and Clyde Barrow, as a nearly silent, cold-hearted lawman dressed in black. The real Hamer was a much-respected peace officer who became a folk hero in the Southwest for ending the bloody crime streak of the real Bonnie and Clyde.[39]

*The Patriot* depicts a vicious British colonel named Tavington who commits atrocities against the colonials. The characterization is based on the real-life Banastre Tarleton, who was indeed a violent military officer, but he never committed the wanton brutality seen in *The Patriot,* such as the burning of a church packed with men, women, and children.[40]

In taking these strong stands, filmmakers simplify their portrayals, glossing over the shortcomings of individuals or groups and exaggerating the sinister qualities of others. Often, they rub out the grays of history, producing portraits in white and black.

Occasionally, a filmmaker sets out to engage a controversial subject cautiously, trying not to paint a strongly partisan picture of heroes and villains. These efforts are commendable but difficult to accomplish. In such films, directors boldly challenge a basic Hollywood convention by resisting the simplistic white hat–black hat story design. By shunning the familiar partisan characterizations, however, they risk washing emotional color out of their dramas. Director Ron Maxwell experienced this difficulty with *Gettysburg* (1993). His epic film premiered briefly in movie theaters and later appeared on Ted Turner's TV network. *Gettysburg* dramatizes Michael Shaara's popular novel about the greatest battle of the American Civil War.[41] The movie characterizes both Northerners and Southerners rather favorably and features no clear villains (although, as in Shaara's book, General Robert E. Lee takes some blame for the Confederates' defeat in the famous battle). By treating both Yankees and Rebels with respect, Maxwell seemed to reflect the mood of the nation in the 1990s, a time when Americans were moving away from sectional hatreds and lost-cause polemics. *Gettysburg* presents the Civil War as a national tragedy, a costly affair in blood and treasure. Although the film blames the war on slavery, it depicts Union and Confederate officers and men with sympathy, recognizing the basic humanity of all combatants, both Southern and North-ern. This equanimity is generous, but it softens the movie's dramatic punch. Despite an impressive supporting cast of 5,000 reenactment specialists per-forming on the actual field of battle at Gettysburg in authentic uniforms, the film proved somewhat disappointing to audiences. *Gettysburg* failed to pro-duce the level of viewer interest that many Civil War history enthusiasts ex-pected. Neither the American people's fascination with the subject nor the movie's connection with Shaara's popular book could rescue it from the dra-matic weaknesses associated with a villainless story.

In contrast, *Glory* delivers a more emotionally compelling tale about the Civil War by employing the generic convention of partisanship. Edward Zwick's 1989 movie portrays the formation of African-American regiments in the Union army during the Civil War. His film clearly identifies heroes and vil-lains and directs audience sympathy to the black soldiers and their white com-manding officer, Colonel Robert Gould Shaw. *Glory* makes a prejudiced Yan-kee officer the object of scorn, although it shows him learning to respect the black soldiers after months of training them. Later in the story, various other Union officers who exploited the blacks or hampered their progress serve as the movie's heavies, and in the end, of course, Confederate soldiers represent the dangerous enemy. *Glory* portrays the Confederates only as a mass of well-armed gunmen firing on the attacking Union troops; it does not introduce them as distinct personalities. This strategy of presenting the heroes' adversar-ies impersonally reduced the likelihood of offending white southerners in the audience. Overall, *Glory*'s inspiring tale of frightened but courageous black men risking their lives for the cause of freedom succeeded in exciting viewer enthusiasm. The movie's strongly partisan picture of the war created more dramatic energy than did *Gettysburg*'s less biased approach.[42]

Dramatic film's connection with documentary film is closer in this respect than is commonly assumed. Many critics of history by Hollywood argue that documentary film is far less biased and is generally more objective in its treat-ment of historical subjects. They hold documentaries in higher regard, believ-ing that they are much less given to partisan excesses than is history delivered in the form of dramatic, commercial entertainment. These observers are wrong in their fundamental assumptions. Although documentaries often *ap-pear* to be more balanced in their treatments, they usually support a one-sided, opinionated point of view. In many respects, documentary films are as emo-tionally and politically committed in their judgments about right and wrong, good and bad, as Hollywood's dramatic productions are.

The documentary medium favors partisanship. Each decision made by a documentary maker calls for judgment, perspective, opinion. For instance, the

Gettysburg *(1993) depicts hand-to-hand combat at Little Round Top. Despite the impressive supporting cast of 5,000 reenactment specialists, the film proved somewhat disappointing to audiences.* Gettysburg *suffered, in part, from a villainless script. (Museum of Modern Art Film Archive)*

filmmaker's selection of a series of photographs depicting the Great Depression or characterizing Franklin D. Roosevelt communicates an interpretation. Similarly, the documentary maker's selection of interviewees also calls for judgment and opinion; for example, should the filmmaker pose questions to someone who was unemployed during the Great Depression, or ask questions of someone who owned a successful business throughout the 1930s? Judgment is also required when the filmmaker creates narration to describe the causes of the Great Depression or to comment on President Roosevelt's actions to combat it. Musical accompaniment, as well, can suggest a cheerful or sad perspective on the people and events under examination.

Not surprisingly, many of the best documentaries exhibit considerable partisan clout and convey strong points of view. For instance, Peter Davis's *Hearts and Minds* (1974) contains no narration, yet his juxtaposition of disturbing images and sounds adds up to a forceful indictment of U.S. intervention in the Vietnam War. Barbara Kopple's memorable *Harlan County U.S.A.* (1976) also eschews narration, yet audiences can easily recognize her message. *Harlan Country U.S.A.* presents Kentucky's striking coal miners in a favorable light and offers a critical perspective on the mining company and power company executives who oppose them. Similarly, a popular film about the experience of female workers in America's industrial plants during World War II offers a sympathetic perspective on its subject. Through interviews and pictures,

Connie Field's *The Life and Times of Rosie the Riveter* (1980) suggests that American women were treated unfairly after the war when industries forced them out of good jobs to make room for the returning GIs.

Of course, many documentary films address historical subjects with a greater sense of balance, yet these productions, too, deliver opinionated perspectives. Filmmakers cannot avoid bias, for their selection and arrangement of interviews, photos, film, narration, music, and other elements direct the presentation toward a particular outlook. Ken Burns's enormously popular television series *The Civil War* is a good example. The program received praise for its judicious treatment of a controversial subject, yet its presentation reveals an interpretive slant. Burns's documentary argues strongly that slavery was the central cause of the Civil War, and his visual and aural evidence subtly but persuasively challenges the arguments of those who maintain that the South's "peculiar institution" was less significant in stimulating the conflict than other factors were. His documentary elevates slavery and racial tensions to primary importance and suggests that disagreements over industrial and agrarian interests, tariffs, culture, and states' rights were much less important. His treatment of the Civil War also reflects the American people's post-Vietnam sensitivity about combat. Throughout the film, depictions of battles stress the tragic nature of the conflict. Whether presenting Sullivan Ballou's emotional letter to his wife, Sarah, shortly before his death at Bull Run or examining photographs of the numerous bodies of slain soldiers left on the fields at Antietam and Gettysburg, Burns's documentary concentrates on the horrible human price of war. His series resonated with Americans who were accustomed to seeing war presented on the screen in less gung-ho fashion than films produced before the Vietnam War.

Thus, both documentary films and fictional films from Hollywood tend to present partisan perspectives and accentuate clashes between heroes and villains. The medium of film provides artists with numerous opportunities to display partisanship in words, pictures, and sounds. Filmmakers recognize that they are much more likely to hook an audience's interest and emotions when their productions communicate strong points of view. They also understand that they may incur considerable financial risk if they attempt to create films with conflicting messages that communicate no particular perspective.

### CINEMATIC HISTORY PORTRAYS MORALLY UPLIFTING STORIES ABOUT STRUGGLES BETWEEN DAVIDS AND GOLIATHS

Many decades ago, Hollywood's cinematic historians were inclined to study the lives of the elite. This tendency was not just the result of the filmmakers'

*Cleopatra (Elizabeth Taylor) receives a royal reception in* Cleopatra *(1963). Like many cinematic histories produced from 1930 to 1965,* Cleopatra *focuses on the lives of the famous, rich, and powerful. (Museum of Modern Art Film Archive)*

enthusiasm for stories about the rich, famous, and powerful; movie audiences seemed particularly interested in these tales. From the 1930s to the 1950s, especially, Hollywood released abundant docudramas dealing with prominent figures from history. Some of these films looked at the ancient world, such as *Quo Vadis?* (1951), *The Robe* (1953), and *Cleopatra* (1963).[43] Others dealt with British royalty, including *The Private Life of Henry VIII* (1933), *The Private Lives of Elizabeth and Essex* (1939), and *The Virgin Queen* (1955). In Hollywood's early years, Warner Brothers developed a strong reputation for creating biopics about famous people. Warner's offerings included *Disraeli* (1929), *Alexander Hamilton* (1931), *Voltaire* (1933), *The Story of Louis Pasteur* (1936), *The Life of Emile Zola* (1937), *Juarez* (1939), and *Dr. Erlich's Magic Bullet* (1940).[44] MGM offered two biographies in 1940 about America's most famous inventor: *Young Tom Edison* and *Edison the Man*. A number of other Hollywood films examined the upper echelons of the white South in antebellum times, such as *Carolina* (1934), *So Red the Rose* (1935), and *Gone with the Wind* (1939).[45]

By the late twentieth century, however, cinematic attention to the high and mighty was less in favor. Perhaps Hollywood producers were responding to a general change in professional scholarship. In the 1960s and after, historians were increasingly approaching their subject from the bottom up rather than the top down. Their books and articles concentrated on the masses—factory workers, miners, immigrants, ethnic minorities, and other representatives of the poorer classes—rather than the privileged few who had served as emperors, kings, queens, or patriarchs and matriarchs of Southern plantations. More likely, filmmakers were responding to a broad general trend in Hollywood's pattern of storytelling. All movies about contemporary life were shifting toward a focus on the common folk. By the late twentieth century, tales about little people successfully fighting control by the rich and powerful had become a familiar staple of the popular cinema.

Frank Capra demonstrated the appeal of this formula back in the 1930s and 1940s. His films often featured noble common men doing battle with influential and wealthy politicians, bankers, and media moguls. Mr. Deeds, Jefferson Smith, John Doe, and George Bailey were humble and decent folk who struggled for good causes in *Mr. Deeds Goes to Town* (1936), *Mr. Smith Goes to Washington* (1939), *Meet John Doe* (1941), and *It's a Wonderful Life* (1946). Capra's populist heroes were often thwarted by greedy, power-hungry tycoons (frequently played by Edward Arnold). By the last reel, "David" seemed likely to fall victim to "Goliath," but Capra created a variety of contrived solutions in the final minutes of his movies to rescue the battered heroes (in the case of *Meet John Doe,* he boxed himself into a difficult storytelling corner and needed assistance from a movie viewer to devise a corny strategy for a happy ending).[46] Capra-esque tales still work well today. Most moviegoers are, after all, hardworking citizens of the lower-middle and middle classes who can easily sympathize with down-to-earth celluloid heroes. Even well-heeled movie audiences appreciate an uplifting drama depicting conflicts between the humble and the powerful.

There can be little doubt that varieties of the Capra formula continue to drive Hollywood's general entertainment in modern times. Related themes are evident in *Saturday Night Fever* (1977), which shows a clerk in a Brooklyn paint store escaping from his lowly position on weekends by competing as a dance star at the local disco. They are evident, too, in *Rocky* (1976), which tells the story of a down-and-out Philadelphia boxer stepping into the ring against a

*Attorney Ed Masry (Albert Finney) and twice-divorced high school dropout Erin Brockovich (Julia Roberts) make an unlikely team as they take on a public utility company in* Erin Brockovich *(2000). Like many modern cinematic histories from Hollywood, Steven Soderbergh's film celebrates the superior virtues of the common person. (Museum of Modern Art Film Archive)*

heavily favored champion who is supported by the sport's big-money interests. The Capra formula is also transparent in *Rainmaker,* a 1997 movie that features Matt Damon as a young, poor, struggling lawyer doing courtroom combat against a powerful law firm that represents a big insurance company.

The Capra approach is especially noticeable in historical docudramas, because the genre often contains implied messages about the supremacy of democracy over autocracy and aristocracy. It appears, for instance, in the epics about Roman times produced in the late 1950s and early 1960s. In *Ben-Hur* (1959), Judah (Charlton Heston) turns against the Romans after Emperor Tiberius oppresses the Empire's minorities, and Kirk Douglas leads a rebellion of the lowly slaves against Roman oppressors in *Spartacus*. In more recent cinematic examples, James Cameron introduces Jack Dawson, a commoner traveling in steerage who is clearly a man of greater decency and essence than Cal Hockley, the snobbish millionaire traveling in the first-class section of the luxurious *Titanic*. A similar statement about the superior virtues of the common person appears in *Erin Brockovich* (2000). Steven Soderbergh's movie features Julia Roberts as the brassy and buxom file clerk who helps win a legal challenge against the Pacific Gas and Electric Company for polluting a California desert town with toxic wastes. This story is based on the experiences of the real Brockovich, who discovered information about contamination in the 1980s.[47]

The historical genre also favors stories that place these common folk in struggles against some terrible injustice affecting them or their family or friends. Cinematic history often portrays its heroes in noble fights against oppression, exploitation, or prejudice. There is an uplifting quality in this kind of historical drama. Audiences sense early in these stories that the heroic characters are right in their beliefs, but people in positions of authority will not listen to them or respect their ideas. In *The Court Martial of Billy Mitchell* (1955), for instance, the aviator (played by Gary Cooper) warns military leaders that aircraft carriers will be essential in the next war; he predicts a future conflict with Japan and calls for a separate air force group within the U.S. military. But leaders of the armed forces find him annoying; they demote Mitchell and dismiss him as a dreamer. Similarly, *JFK* shows Jim Garrison trying to demonstrate that there was a conspiracy in the president's assassination, but few take him seriously, and even his wife thinks he may be going too far. In *Silkwood* (1983), a worker in an Oklahoma nuclear plant (Meryl Streep) attempts to prove that her fellow workers are dangerously affected by radiation, but the company denies her accusations and appears to be complicit in efforts to silence her. The reality of the early AIDS epidemic is the theme in HBO's *And the Band Played On* (1993). A researcher at the Centers for Disease Control detects the lethal new disease, but when he tries to alert the public to the danger, he confronts apathy, disbelief, and prejudice.

Two made-for-TV dramas about American involvement in recent wars defend the courage of individuals who challenge the claims of military and political authorities. *Bright Shining Lie* (1998) shows a U.S. military leader in Vietnam trying to prove that American actions in the war are losing the hearts and minds of Vietnamese villagers and harming the U.S. position. *Thanks to a*

*Ed and Beth Horman (Jack Lemmon and Sissy Spacek) search for their son after a military coup in Chile in* Missing *(1982). The movie blamed U.S. foreign policy, in part, for the Horman family's tragedy. (Museum of Modern Art Film Archive)*

*Grateful Nation* (1998) shows a U.S. Senate investigator trying to convince authorities that veterans of the Persian Gulf War are suffering from strange and related health problems. In these and many other examples of history from Hollywood, the stories arouse feelings of moral outrage among viewers. Cinematic history's protagonists face formidable obstacles in their fights for justice because of widespread public indifference or the influential resistance of powerful figures.

Modern-day cinematic history also favors stories about individuals who challenge prejudice and oppression. Spielberg's *Amistad* makes heroes of the African captives and some of the whites who attempt to defend them (particularly John Quincy Adams), and *Schindler's List* shows a hedonistic German businessman acquiring a sense of sympathy for Jewish victims of Hitler's extermination campaigns. The television movie *Judge Horton and the Scottsboro Boys* (1976) builds its tension around a struggle to free black men who were unfairly accused of raping two white women in Alabama in the early 1930s, and *Mississippi Burning* (1988) makes the catalyst for its action the brutal murder of three civil rights workers in 1964 and the struggle to find the culprits.

Sometimes the guilty party in these injustices is U.S. foreign policy, broadly speaking. Movies that focused on America's anticommunist excesses during the Cold War years were especially likely to communicate this form of outrage. In *Missing,* for instance, Jack Lemmon plays the real-life character Ed Horman, who goes to Chile to seek his missing son. As Lemmon investigates events connected to the 1973 military coup there, he discovers that U.S. officials maintained close ties with the Chilean military and may have been implicated in his son's political execution. U.S. foreign policy is also the source of human suffering in Roland Joffe's *The Killing Fields.* Joffe's film shows *New York Times* reporter Sydney Schanberg learning that secret B-52 bombings by the United States wounded many Cambodians during a time when Cambodia was a neutral nation. No director has done as much as Oliver Stone in associating U.S. policies in Vietnam with injustice and suffering. Through films such as *Platoon* (1986), *Born on the Fourth of July* (1990), and *Heaven and Earth* (1991), Stone maintained that the war brutalized Americans and created considerable hardship and pain for the Vietnamese people.[48]

Arousing a sense of moral indignation is an effective strategy for exciting the audience's interest in a historical subject. It pulls viewers into the drama, makes them care about issues addressed in the film, and attaches their sympathies to the characters that attempt to right the wrongs. It is no surprise, then, that numerous historical dramas develop stories about injustice and the struggle to correct it.

## CINEMATIC HISTORY SIMPLIFIES PLOTS BY FEATURING ONLY A FEW REPRESENTATIVE CHARACTERS

To make the plot fundamentally simple and easy to understand, cinematic historians usually focus on just a few individuals. Writers frequently "collapse" several historic figures into one or a few so that audiences can easily get acquainted with a small cast of principals. For instance, in *Bonnie and Clyde,* a young man who joins the criminals (played by Michael J. Pollard) represents several men who worked with the Barrow gang at various times, and the character's behavior in the movie combines a number of their actions and experiences. *The Hurricane* shows three white Canadians and an African American working together to help Rubin "Hurricane" Carter win release from prison, even though the real Canadian group consisted of a commune of nine to twelve members (it expanded and contracted from time to time). *The Hurricane* presents just a few composite Canadians, a strategy that helped the audience recognize these figures individually.[49]

Cinematic historians often characterize diverse groups from the past through representative stereotypes, drawing on traditions of the genre. They introduce viewers to completely fictional characters whose backgrounds and personalities reflect the diversity of people one might encounter in a historical setting. John Ford's classic western *Stagecoach* (1939) proved so effective in introducing such stereotypes that it influenced a whole generation of Hollywood westerns. Ford put a variety of stock figures on the stagecoach: a drunken doctor (Thomas Mitchell), a woman of ill repute (Claire Trevor), a handsome cowboy who was a fugitive from the law (John Wayne), a dapper and deceitful gambler (John Carradine), a comic stagecoach driver (Andy Devine), and a pompous banker (George Bancroft). These characterizations suggest a microcosm of western types. World War II movies feature a similar assemblage of stock figures whose backgrounds represent the diversity of American fighting groups. An early and particularly influential use of the formula appeared in *Bataan* (1943), and *Saving Private Ryan* borrowed heavily from the World War II combat genre, featuring a cast of familiar military characters that included a Jew, a wise guy from Brooklyn, and a deeply religious southern sharpshooter. *Glory* also reflected the pattern, focusing on a group of black soldiers that included a gung-ho intellectual, a surly rebel who learned to be a team player, an older father figure, and a stuttering former field slave.

The principal action in historical movies is generated by just one or two central figures. Cinematic historians almost always distort the historical record, giving inordinate responsibility for moving and shaking society to only a few individuals. For example, *All the President's Men* focuses on the activities of two journalists from the *Washington Post,* Bob Woodward and Carl Bernstein, and traces their investigation of the Watergate scandal. It leaves the impression that these highly motivated reporters almost single-handedly brought about the downfall of President Richard Nixon. Viewers unaware of the history of the Watergate investigations would not know from watching the film that several other individuals played significant roles, including John J. Sirica and Leon Jaworski (both judges), Senator Sam Ervin, and Nixon's own legal counsel, John Dean.[50] Another production by Robert Redford, *Quiz Show* (1995), leaves the impression that Richard Goodwin almost single-handedly exposed the television scandals of the 1950s to a shocked nation. Redford bases much of his movie's story on Goodwin's book *Remembering America: A Voice from the Sixties,* and in doing so, he overlooks the important contributions of a number of other individuals.

Occasionally, a filmmaker challenges the generic practice of focusing on the actions of one or two principal characters. John Sayles, writer and director of a number of thoughtful, low-budget movies, sometimes addresses historical subjects in this manner. Sayles's movies often feature an ensemble of principal figures rather than just one or two key personalities. He tells stories about "community," tracing the interactions of a number of people in a historic

*Carl Bernstein (Dustin Hoffman) and Bob Woodward (Robert Redford) investigate the Watergate scandal for the* Washington Post *in* All the President's Men *(1976). Alan J. Pakula's movie creates the impression that these journalists almost single-handedly forced the downfall of President Richard M. Nixon. (Museum of Modern Art Film Archive)*

setting. Examples of his attention to groups can be seen in *Matewan,* a 1987 drama about a miners' strike, and *Eight Men Out,* a 1988 film that dealt with a famous scandal in professional baseball early in the twentieth century.[51] Sayles's approach is idiosyncratic, however. When Hollywood artists and producers gamble with projects that cost much more than Sayles's low-budget productions, they are inclined to stick with the familiar storytelling formulas that have proved successful over the years.

In many respects, cinematic history promotes a "great man" or "great woman" theory of change, a perspective that has long been out of fashion in the historical profession. Movies frequently suggest that energized, aggressive, and strongly determined individuals are the primary sources of significant historical developments. Hollywood's version of history personalizes the narrative, putting dynamic people at the center of the action. Cinematic history gives little attention to the many impersonal forces that are often important factors behind major changes. It says little about broad economic developments (depressions, surges in unemployment, cycles of prosperity) and does not usually associate characters' actions with broad social trends. For example, it rarely connects a woman's rebellious behavior to the rise of the feminist movement or a labor organizer's decision to strike to national campaigns to establish the right of collective bargaining. History by Hollywood gives audiences little sense of the power of new intellectual currents or of the impact of environmental concerns on citizens' actions. Instead, it shows individuals who are rather unaffected by the changing society around them. Hollywood's heroes are rarely blown by the major winds of change. They tend to create their own personal storms, displaying admirable determination to effect large improvements in society. As self-motivated dynamos, these heroes—the "great men" and "great women" of cinematic history—transform the world around them.

Leger Grindon, a film studies specialist, criticizes this element of Hollywood storytelling in his book *Shadows on the Past*. Grindon says that this mode of interpretation runs counter to important trends in modern historical writing. He notes, for example, that writers from the Annales school had a tremendous impact on historical scholarship in the twentieth century. The French historian Fernand Braudel was one of the most influential figures leading this revolution in interpretation. Braudel urged scholars to move away from the "great man" approach to history, with its emphasis on exceptional people who acted as masters of their own fate and the fate of many others. Instead, Braudel drew attention to broad developments that occurred over vast periods of time. He examined significant economic, environmental, and institutional conditions and trends. Braudel found this big picture to be far more important and revealing than history's record of the rise and fall of kings, queens, emperors, and presidents. His wide-angle lens examined slowly moving developments rather than the specific actions of political and military leaders.[52]

Grindon praises the Italian filmmaker Roberto Rossellini for taking an impressively Braudelian approach to history in his movie *The Rise to Power of Louis XIV* (1966). Grindon observes approvingly that Rossellini's film portrayed the daily life of the French nobility, such as the etiquette at court, rather than the record of "extraordinary events" connected to Louis's politics and personal life. Rossellini's direction "cultivates detachment and contemplation in the audience," Grindon writes, and it "contemplates the necessity of confronting history without the means to completely know it." Such a movie can show that "history is not truth, but a means to knowledge, a variable method in the construction of social memory."[53] Grindon also praises the Italian director for his expression of contempt for "great man" perspectives. "What do exceptional men matter to us?" Rossellini asked. "I'm quite unmoved by the myth of the superman."[54] In view of Rossellini's skill in bringing an Annales-like perspective to the screen, Grindon judges *The Rise to Power of Louis XIV* quite superior to the rather traditional "great man" presentation in *A Man for All Seasons* (1966), which deals with a related historical setting and situation. Fred Zinneman's movie examines Sir Thomas More's troubled relationship with Henry VIII of England. More, a Catholic statesman and adviser to the king, cannot sanction Henry's divorce, and More's stand on principle leads to his execution.[55]

Grindon is certainly right in pointing out the value of Braudelian perspectives for advancing scholarship, but his observations are less relevant to cinematic history. As Grindon observes, insights from historians of the Annales school elevated research to a higher plane. That scholarship also paved the way for specialists in "social history" to challenge the traditional studies of major political and military leaders and to draw readers' attention to the lives of ordinary people. Still, a cinematic historian faces difficulties when dramatizing the perspectives of Annales scholars or the new social historians. Movies must entertain in order to secure a life in the theaters, a shelf life in video stores, and a programming life on television. Rossellini's approach (cultivating "detachment and contemplation in the audience") is not an attractive option for market-minded Hollywood executives. The format of Zinneman's film about Sir Thomas More is much closer to the familiar Hollywood pattern than the one seen in *The Rise to Power of Louis XIV.* This generic tradition is precisely what Grindon scorns—the view of a heroic personality, a driven individual who stands on principle and by doing so makes a significant impact on the world around him or her. *A Man for All Seasons* is representative of the historical genre that has emerged in Hollywood, as well as in British motion pictures that have received Hollywood's blessing in the form of wide-scale distribution. Zinneman's drama about More is in many ways a traditional biopic, a focus on the life and actions of an extraordinary individual.

In recognizing this convention of cinematic history, we need not surrender enthusiasm for the Annales perspective or deny an appreciation of social history, the field of study that illuminates the lives of ordinary people and gives less attention to the rich and famous. Sophisticated approaches to historical analysis will continue to thrive in publications, lectures, seminars, and discussions at professional meetings. These perspectives will not find much expression in Hollywood films, however. The dramatic format does not serve well as a communicator of the "big picture." Movies can easily lose audiences if they portray material that calls for statistics, abstract analysis, or attention to the condition of groups rather than individuals. Hollywood movies cannot tell us much about broad economic, social, and environmental developments. They are not attractive instruments for communicating a view of developments that take shape over hundreds of years. And in the rare moments when they focus on politics, they usually show the exploits of one or two figures rather than wide-ranging political movements involving the participation of the masses.

Still, cinematic history can perform a useful function by making the individual stand for something larger. A movie's small glimpse of life can represent a broader picture. Sir Thomas More's fight with Henry VIII can suggest the resistance to absolutism that gained strength in the Western world in later centuries. The tightly focused biographical perspective can raise important questions that have animated controversies through the ages, particularly debates about the value of standing on principle or negotiating practical compromises. *A Man for All Seasons,* limited by its tight focus on a confrontation between a few important people, can nevertheless stimulate the audience's interest in broader forms of historical inquiry. To appreciate this film's potential, though, the student of film needs to recognize the medium's conventions and limitations. History from Hollywood almost always appears in its familiar generic form, with the principal characters' encounters standing in for the experiences of hundreds, thousands, or millions.

In this respect, critics of Hollywood productions often raise irrelevant objections when they complain that a drama shows the leading characters participating in too many extraordinary developments. Critics demand a *typical* experience for the major figures when, in fact, events portrayed in the movie are designed to *represent* experiences that a much larger group of people might have. Such complaints appeared in reaction to NBC Television's popular 1978 miniseries *Holocaust.* Some critics called the story silly and unrealistic. They asked, how could a few people connect to so many important historical figures and situations? In the series, virtually all the important Holocaust-related events of the Nazi years touched the Weiss family (the principal Jewish victims in the drama). This improbable tale was too contrived, said the film's detractors.[56] Similarly, Oliver Stone's *Platoon* came under fire from some Vietnam veterans. They complained that Stone's movie gave an unrealistic portrayal of the soldiers' experiences. These veterans asserted that a typical Vietnam grunt did not come into contact with all the disturbing situations in Stone's picture, including ambushes, firefights, drug dependency, fragging (violence against American officers), and the attempted execution of Vietnamese civilians. Stone made the Vietnam experience look far worse than it actually was, the detractors charged. But of course, the intended message in a docudrama is not that the characters' experiences are typical. Cinematic history compresses many important events into the lives of leading characters to address larger historical issues.

## CINEMATIC HISTORY SPEAKS TO THE PRESENT

*The Sea Hawk,* Michael Curtiz's fast-paced 1940 movie about English privateers raiding Spanish ships in the age of Queen Elizabeth, features a frightening reference to the threat Spain's imperialism poses for all of Europe. The movie suggests that all the peoples of the continent may soon be dominated by oppressive tyrants. To confront this danger, Queen Elizabeth gives swashbuckler Geoffrey Thorpe (played by Errol Flynn and modeled after Sir Francis Drake) unofficial authority to attack the Spanish fleet. This popular film refers to conditions in its period of production as well as to conditions of the late sixteenth century. The movie's references to imperial Spain provided audiences of 1940 with thinly disguised hints about the Nazis' expanding influence over Europe.[57]

Virtually all of cinematic history references the present when interpreting the past. Filmmakers attempt to show audiences the modern-day relevance of their historical interpretations. To make cinema meaningful to audiences, artists incorporate a variety of subtle hints about their stories' connections to current issues. Indeed, in choosing their subjects, filmmakers often seek topics that relate to current fashions, attitudes, hopes, and anxieties of the viewing public.[58] Screenwriter Aeneas MacKenzie referred to this practice in an interoffice memo explaining the importance of the story he was planning about the heroism of George Armstrong Custer. At the time of production planning, the United States was moving closer to intervention in the Second World War. MacKenzie wrote, "I need not mention that this picture will be released at the moment when thousands of youths are being trained for commissions, when hundreds of new and traditionless units are being formed. If we can inspire these to some appreciation of a great officer and a great regiment in their own service, we shall have accomplished our mission."[59] *Bonnie and Clyde* also spoke to people of the times. The film dealt with criminals of the 1920s, yet aspects of the story looked familiar to audiences of the 1960s. Hollywood's Bonnie Parker and Clyde Barrow were antiestablishment, rebellious, and independent minded; they also craved celebrity. David Newman, who helped develop the original concept for this movie, promoted his project as a story about an unconventional couple that "would have been right at home in the Sixties." *Bonnie and Clyde* was not only about two historical figures, he said; it was also "about what's going on now."[60]

William Goldman, an enormously successful screenwriter, provides an intriguing example of how the creators of Hollywood movies think about the relevance of historical subjects. In his book *Adventures in the Screen Trade: A Personal View of Hollywood and Screenwriting,* Goldman writes about production planning for *The Right Stuff,* a 1983 movie (based on Tom Wolfe's bestselling book by the same title) that deals with America's struggle to send astronauts into space. He notes that current conditions in America were very much on his mind when he was developing a thesis for the movie.

When Goldman began preparing a script, the American people's confidence in their nation was at low ebb. Jimmy Carter's presidency was coming to a

*Warren Beatty and Faye Dunaway star as Clyde Barrow and Bonnie Parker, the violent gangster couple of the early 1930s. Despite its depression-era setting, Bonnie and Clyde (1967) related to the feelings of many young Americans in the 1960s. (Museum of Modern Art Film Archive)*

close. The United States had recently dealt with recession, inflation, unemployment, and a hostage crisis in Iran. America's manufactured products were shoddy, and Japan seemed ready to surpass the United States as a manufacturing giant. In reaction to this depressing state of affairs, *The Right Stuff* could send an uplifting message, Goldman argued. It could show that Americans had experienced similar anxieties back in the late 1950s and early 1960s, when they thought their country had become second-rate. The Russians had succeeded in putting a satellite in space before the United States, and then they had succeeded in sending the first animal and man into space. In contrast, American rockets were exploding on the launchpads. Then, rather slowly, the United States began to pull out of its slump, Goldman observed, and the country eventually demonstrated its technical superiority. Writing to the producers at the time of planning for *The Right Stuff,* Goldman said, "we can indicate to the audience today that we are still, in spite of our faults, a great country. Remember, this is to be a movie that, if we're lucky, sends the people home with a good feeling about America."[61] Like many members of the film community, Goldman sensed that Americans needed an uplifting, inspiring message for the 1980s, and he thought Hollywood could serve that function.

Often, new patterns of interpretation emerge over the decades as filmmakers respond to changing attitudes and changing notions of political correctness. The shifts were rather dramatic in the depiction of Native Americans. In the decades before World War II, many Hollywood films portrayed Indians as savages, showing them assaulting wagon trains and scalping their victims. A late example of this imagery appears in 1939, when Indians turn up briefly in John Ford's *Stagecoach,* standing on a cliff before descending on the surprised passengers. Ford's movie introduces the Indian group with ominous music, and the warriors look sinister. By 1942, the year *They Died with Their Boots On* appeared in theaters, Hollywood needed to exhibit more sensitivity toward Native Americans. America was at war with the Nazis, and international concern about racism had grown stronger. Raoul Walsh's movie offers a much more appealing picture of Indians than *Stagecoach* did. It portrays the Sioux warrior Crazy Horse rather favorably, while also presenting George Armstrong Custer in a positive light (the English-speaking world needed military heroes in 1942). *They Died with Their Boots On* managed to straddle this historical fence, treating the white man–red man conflict as a tragedy that did not have to happen. By 1950, Hollywood was responding to the public's heightening concern about minority rights with *Broken Arrow,* Delmer Daves's movie that encouraged sympathy for the beleaguered Apaches. John Ford later came out with a positive spin on Indians struggling to return to their homeland in Wyoming in *Cheyenne Autumn* (1964). By the early 1970s, Native Americans were the heroes of the western action movie, and whites served as the villains. *Little Big Man* (1970) and *Soldier Blue* (1970) suggest that American massacres of Indian communities resembled the U.S. soldiers' execution of Vietnamese civilians at My Lai. More recently, Hollywood has handled the complicated challenge of balancing the pressures for political correctness and dramatic complexity by distinguishing between good and bad Indians (as in *Dances with Wolves* and *The Last of the Mohicans*).[62]

As mentioned before, westerns carry different messages in different periods. For many years, their upbeat tales resonated with the public, perhaps because they related progressive stories about America's successful expansion across the frontier. Richard Slotkin noted that the heroes in traditional westerns encountered savage Indians, outlaws, power-hungry cattle barons, and other troublemakers, but the heroes usually triumphed by the conclusion of the last reel. Law and order, peace and tranquility came to the frontier community; civilization moved a step forward. This comforting narrative pattern no longer seemed appropriate in the more cynical 1960s and 1970s. Americans lost their sense of moral innocence in the Vietnam era, and economic setbacks in the 1970s left Americans feeling uncertain about the future. The progressive theme of Hollywood's traditional westerns did not resonate at a time when Americans were troubled and pessimistic. The few westerns appearing in this era depicted a decline of the cowboy, as in *The Wild Bunch* and *Butch Cassidy and the Sundance Kid* (both 1969). Hollywood also presented a dark picture of the frontier scene in *McCabe and Mrs. Miller* (1971). Robert Altman's movie focuses on an ugly town in the northwestern wilderness, where the hero keeps a lover established as a madam in a whorehouse. In the end, he dies in a snowdrift.[63]

How much contemporary meaning can we draw from the themes of cinematic history? To what degree do filmmakers reference the present in portraying the past? Grindon stretches the connections rather extensively in his analysis of *Reds,* suggesting that Warren Beatty's 1981 film contains abundant hints about modern times in its story of John Reed's activities in the early twentieth century. Grindon claims that Beatty sees John Reed as a precursor to the radical figures of the 1960s. The film's depiction of opposition to World War I resembles protests against the Vietnam War. *Reds'* attention to conflicts at the Democratic National Convention of 1916 contains messages about the divisive 1968 Democratic Party meeting in Chicago. The Emma Goldman character in *Reds* represents, in some ways, New York Congresswoman Bella Abzug, and Reed's lover Louise Bryant suggests a feminist of the 1960s and 1970s. Grindon believes that the scenes showing divisions in the radical community of Greenwich Village suggest the modern-day fights between hippies and the New Left, and the movie's portrayal of factionalism in the Bolshevik Revolution references conflicts over George McGovern's Democratic Party nomination for the presidency in 1972 and the demise of the New Left.[64]

These speculations about ties between the past and present in cinematic history are intriguing, but we should be cautious about stretching the connections too far. The search for links to current conditions can lead to a rather cynical view of Hollywood's portrayals of the past, suggesting that the stories really have very little to do with history. Film historian Pierre Sorlin falls into this trap when he says that the history employed in film is "a mere framework, serving as a basis or a counterpoint for a political thesis. History is no more than a useful choice to speak of the present time."[65] This statement expresses an extreme position on the subject. A more sophisticated view holds that history-oriented movies often reference the present, especially in their principal messages about the general lessons to be learned from their portrayals. We push the issue of relevancy too far if we suggest that filmmakers have almost nothing but the present in mind when they shape their stories. Not every event and action out of history nicely conforms to the political interests of the moviemaker. Indeed, artists who manipulate every detail for purposes of demonstrating relevancy may find that they have created agitprop or parody rather than the kind of production that audiences can accept as a representative form of cinematic history.

## CINEMATIC HISTORY FREQUENTLY INJECTS ROMANCE INTO ITS STORIES, EVEN WHEN AMOROUS AFFAIRS ARE NOT CENTRAL TO THE HISTORICAL EVENTS

Academic historians and critics in the mass media often pooh-pooh cinematic history because it gives excessive attention to the romantic activities of a movie's central characters. These critics are certainly right in observing that movies provide much more coverage of the amorous side of people's lives than mainstream academic histories do. But again, we are speaking here of reel history, a genre that, of necessity, makes love and sex prominent in dramatic entertainment. The romantic elements of a story heighten the emotional impact for most audiences; in particular, they help attract women to the theaters. Occasionally, war movies have virtually no romantic content (such as the submarine film *U-571* or the combat movie *Saving Private Ryan*), but the handsome male stars provide the attraction to female moviegoers. Most cinematic histories incorporate some portrayal of male-female mutual magnetism, and some films elevate the amorous relationship to the center of attention. Such movies usually approximate the familiar storytelling pattern: in the first act, the couple falls in love; in the second act, disagreements between them or intrusions from outside threaten their relationship; and in the final act, the lovers are reunited (or death ends their relationship tragically).

Cinematic history often focuses on the romantic aspect of life, making it one of the principal narrative themes. This attention is evident in one of the few major films to dramatize the life of Dwight David Eisenhower. This World War II hero and later president is an important figure in twentieth-century American history, but dramatists have virtually ignored his wartime and political experiences as the stuff of good drama. Filmmakers have drawn attention, however, to speculation about the possibility of a wartime romance between Eisenhower and his driver, Kay Summersby. *Ike: The War Years* (1978), an ABC television movie that features Robert Duvall and Lee Remick in the leading roles, suggests the possibility of such a love affair. Similarly, Cambridge University's famous scholar C. S. Lewis is a giant of the modern literary world, but the element of his life that made good drama concerned his late-life relationship with American Joy Davidman Gresham, a woman who adored his work. The story of Lewis's discovery of love and Gresham's death from cancer generated an emotionally powerful stage play and a touching 1993 movie (*Shadowlands*) starring Anthony Hopkins and Debra Winger.

Moviemakers often manipulate the historical record to ensure that their stories will feature a workable romantic interest. Wives and children can stand in the way of such portrayals—or certainly complicate them—so they are often erased from the story. For example, the main character in *The People versus Larry Flynt* (1996) is a single man. This plot adjustment simplifies the movie's depiction of Flynt's romantic relationship with sexually liberated Althea Leasure (Courtney Love). The real Larry Flynt (creator of *Hustler* magazine) had a wife and children during his struggles against lawsuits and censorship. Similarly, Al Capone was a married man at the time of his famous criminal exploits, but *Al Capone* (1959) shows him as a bachelor who establishes a romantic relationship with a fictional widow. Of course, many filmmakers incorporate a love relationship where none existed in the historical record. *Broken Arrow* does this in its story about Tom Jeffords, a real-life frontiersman in Arizona who tried to work out agreements between the Apaches and the U.S. military in the 1870s. The movie invents a romance and marriage between Jeffords and an Apache princess (the union brings together Jimmy Stewart and Debra Paget). In *The Private Lives of Elizabeth and Essex* (1939), Michael Curtiz creates a romance between Queen Elizabeth (Bette Davis) and Essex (Errol Flynn). The real Essex was thirty-four years Elizabeth's junior and certainly not the queen's amorous partner.[66]

The prominence of a romantic element in cinematic history does not constitute grounds for dismissing the genre's value as a perspective on the past. Romantic themes are useful for the design of successful Hollywood docudramas. They provide a vehicle for introducing history to the public in an entertaining format. The dramatic study of C. S. Lewis's relationship with Joy Davidman Gresham introduces audiences to one of the century's great men of letters. *Reds'* story of the on-again, off-again romance between John Reed and Louise Bryant exposes viewers to the life of bohemians and radical leftist revolutionaries of early-twentieth-century New York City. Romantic themes draw audiences to cinematic history, adding strong human touches to topics that may, at first glance, seem too dry for mass entertainment.

## CINEMATIC HISTORY COMMUNICATES A FEELING FOR THE PAST THROUGH ATTENTION TO DETAILS OF AN EARLIER AGE

Hollywood's directors, producers, and publicists are usually eager to advertise the authenticity of their movies, often claiming that their films pay great attention to period detail. This kind of advertising encourages audiences to believe that these movies provide a form of stimulation not available from other genres: a realistic picture of life in a distant time and place. Often filmmakers boast about conducting careful research into the historical record and sparing no effort to re-create the look of the past down to the smallest props. These claims about meticulousness are designed to give moviegoers confidence in the seriousness of the productions.

Advertising the authenticity of cinematic history is as old as the genre. D. W. Griffith, one of the first prominent cinematic historians, was emphatic in pointing to the careful research he had done during the production of *Birth of a Nation*. Griffith announced proudly that he had hired a prominent university professor in California to assist him in the interpretation of historical evidence. He also noted that veterans of the Civil War had counseled him in the design of the battles and that scenes such as the one showing Lincoln's assassination at Ford's Theater had been composed from details found in period photographs and documents.[67] A more recent example of attention to authenticity appears in the promotional efforts for *Titanic*. Publicists for James Cameron's movie emphasized that the production had used carpet woven in the fashion of the original design, created a replica of the ship's great clock at the central staircase, provided 450 authentic-looking wigs for actors and extras, and trained numerous players in the etiquette of the Edwardian era.

Historian Daniel Walkowitz points out that filmmakers do not necessarily produce great historical movies when they include plenty of authentic details in their productions. He stresses that it is not enough for Hollywood to get the shoes right or the uniform buttons correct or to feature genuine antique silverware on a dinner table. Filmmakers must also create engaging stories that raise significant historical questions, notes Walkowitz. A movie may feature numerous authentic-looking props yet still communicate poor history.[68]

Still, much of value can be achieved in motion pictures that effectively create the look and feel of a distant time and place. When movies project images of the past through myriad, often dazzling period details, they can educate audiences in a variety of subtle ways. As some historians describe the achievement, films can demonstrate the "pastness of the past," communicating a sense that conditions in historic times were, in many ways, different from those of the present. The visual elements help draw audiences into the story, encouraging them to suspend disbelief and imagine that they are witnesses to history. Bernardo Bertolucci's *The Last Emperor* (1987) established that feeling, featuring 19,000 extras (many of them soldiers from China's People's Army), 9,000 costumes, vintage cars from several decades, and extraordinary cinematography taken throughout Beijing's Forbidden City.[69] David Lean, who had a distinguished career as cinematographer before he became a director, was a master in creating the look of historical authenticity. *Lawrence of Arabia* gives audiences a memorable representation of conflicts associated with World War I in the barren and forbidding North African desert. Lean's picture includes sweeping desert vistas shot on location in Saudi Arabia. In some cases, the temperatures were so high on the set that the thermometers could not register them. Lean found the city of 'Aqaba too developed for filming, so he arranged for the construction of a duplicate of the old 'Aqaba outside of Seville, Spain. The movie's designers also created sets representing Damascus, Cairo, and Jerusalem. *Bonnie and Clyde* incorporates the music of Rudy Vallee, a film clip from the movie *Gold Diggers of 1933*, campaign posters for Franklin D. Roosevelt, and a segment from Eddie Cantor's radio program.[70] All these elements contribute to the appearance of authenticity.

Other moviemakers establish the look and feel of the past by painting on a much smaller canvas, examining historical situations in microcosm. William Wellman realized this achievement in his portrayal of the combat experience in World War II. *Battleground* (1949) presents a tightly focused picture of a small group of American soldiers fighting through a bitter winter in the Ardennes forest. German director Wolfgang Petersen also proved extraordinarily effective in establishing an authentic look in a microcosmic setting in *Das Boot* (The Boat), which received wide distribution in the United States in 1982. Petersen's movie depicts the frightening experiences of a German U-boat crew during World War II. Unlike many earlier American submarine movies, which show well-dressed sailors and generally clean submarines, *Das Boot* presents the crew as a dirty, pale, and weary bunch and reveals how cramped and cluttered U-boats could be. George Lucas also effectively communicates the "pastness of the past" in *American Graffiti* (1973). His exploration of American social history is tightly focused on a microcosmic environment, as *American Graffiti*'s entire story unfolds in a small California town on a summer night in 1962. As numerous rock and roll songs play in the background, Lucas takes audiences back to the America of hot rods, crew cuts, and girls in bobby socks.

Whereas films such as *Lawrence of Arabia* and *American Graffiti* represent superb examples of cinematic histories that successfully create the look of verisimilitude in both epic and small-story form, other history-oriented films have treated period details with much less integrity. Often these movies are low-budget, quickly made productions designed to capitalize on a popular entertainment trend. *Young Dillinger* (1965) is such an example. Its creators responded to the public enthusiasm for gangster stories that grew in the years after ABC's popular TV series *The Untouchables* (1959). Not only did *Young Dillinger*, starring Nick Adams, play loosely with facts about the gangster's exploits; the production also reflected little care for visual details associated with Dillinger's time. Except for the appearance of a few old cars, the costuming, sets, and scenery bore little resemblance to the 1920s or to the locations where

Dillinger actually engaged in crime. The gangster apparel in the movie looked like it had been tailored in the 1960s, and the scenes of police chasing criminals in cars speeding across steep mountains certainly did not suggest America's prairie, where the Dillinger gang operated.

## CINEMATIC HISTORY OFTEN COMMUNICATES AS POWERFULLY IN IMAGES AND SOUNDS AS IN WORDS

Book-oriented enthusiasts of history are accustomed to focusing on narrative when examining a movie's interpretation of the past. They give careful attention to the language employed by the actors, the captions that appear on the screen, and the major plot developments that give direction to the story. Many of these observers are more interested in the movie's communication through language than in its interpretation in images and sounds. Often, they concentrate on details in the script rather than on the visual and auditory devices employed by the director, the cinematographer, the sound engineers, and other artists and technicians who play important roles in shaping a film's presentation. Book-oriented observers of film produce useful insights on cinematic history, but they often overlook the subtle yet impressive ways that movies deliver messages.

Nonverbal techniques are not, of course, unique to cinematic history. Filmmakers use similar devices when making various kinds of commercial entertainment such as courtroom dramas, westerns, and crime pictures. Generally, specialists in cinema studies are more accustomed to analyzing visual and aural strategies than students of cinematic history are, and individuals interested in studying Hollywood's treatment of the past can sharpen their analyses by giving greater attention to the nonverbal techniques employed by moviemakers. This approach reveals that a film often communicates as powerfully with pictures and sounds as it does with words.

In *Schindler's List,* for example, Steven Spielberg presents much of his movie's essential interpretation in nonverbal form. The director introduces Oskar Schindler (Liam Neeson) in a montage of pictures that conveys a strong impression of Schindler's personal ambition. Frames showing a smart-looking suit, tie, and watch (as well as a wad of money) indicate that Schindler is an urbane man who consciously attempts to project an image of high social standing. Throughout the film, Spielberg (and cinematographer Janusz Kaminski) shoot pictures of Schindler from a low angle, presenting him as an exceedingly tall and powerful man. Spielberg introduces the story's principal antagonist, Amon Goeth (Ralph Fiennes), through visual messaging as well. Audiences first see the Nazi military officer dabbing his nose several times with a

*Oskar Schindler (Liam Neeson, right) converses with Nazi officer Amon Goeth (Ralph Fiennes, left) in* Schindler's List *(1993). Through the use of light and shadows, director Steven Spielberg and cinematographer Janusz Kaminski communicate their interpretation in nonverbal form. (Museum of Modern Art Film Archive)*

handkerchief. In another scene, the camera focuses on Goeth's nails, which are sanded and polished by a subservient woman. Spielberg and Kaminski also focus the camera on Goeth's poor posture and protruding stomach. These pictures succinctly inform viewers that the movie's villain is a self-indulgent and effete snob who is given to excess.

Visual communication in *Schindler's List* informs the audience in many other ways, as well. Sometimes images interpret the story more effectively than the words spoken by the principals. For instance, Schindler's assistant, Itzhak Stern (Ben Kingsley), a Jewish businessman, accepts Schindler's offer of an unusual manufacturing and financial relationship simply through the movements of his eyes and lips. Stern's physical response to the invitation reveals that he is suspicious about working with the German but senses that the proposed arrangement may prove useful in the Jews' difficult circumstances. Later Schindler witnesses the destruction of a Jewish ghetto. This experience, especially, moves him toward a personal commitment to help the Jews. Words do little to suggest Schindler's important inner transformation. Instead, his facial contortions inform viewers of his shock and disgust.

Spielberg and Kaminski employ numerous visual devices to arouse the viewers' sympathy for the persecuted Jews. At some points in the story, glaring lights suggest the terror of people who feel like trapped animals. In scenes showing the destruction of a Jewish community in Poland, for instance, Jews desperately attempt to conceal themselves in ghetto buildings, and German troops search for them with flashlights. Bright beams sweep across dark rooms and then fill the screen with light. Viewers have the perspective of fugitives who have suddenly been discovered. Later, when Jewish women are pushed into the concentration camp at Auschwitz, floodlights from the camp's watchtowers glare into the cameras. The powerful beams symbolize the Nazis' control over all the captives in the concentration camps; escape from the track of the searchlights seems virtually impossible. When portraying the victims' intense fear, Spielberg and Kaminski focus closely on faces. They show the Jews trembling and sweating. These pictures reveal the personal struggles of frightened people who try desperately to stay alive but recognize that their efforts are likely to fail.

*Schindler's List* also employs visual techniques to characterize the Nazis' evil. Late in the story, for example, the fate of many Jews working under Oskar Schindler depends on a decision made by a menacing-looking Nazi officer. Spielberg and Kaminski cast a dark shadow over the upper half of the Nazi's face, drawing attention to the man's ugly teeth. Lighting creates as strong an impression of the Nazi's villainy as anything he says.

Spielberg and Kaminski also employ a documentary filmmaking style to suggest that their accounting of the Holocaust aims to be realistic. Often they use a handheld camera that gives a shaky quality to the pictures. Cameramen seem to be jostled along with the rest of the Jews who are herded into city streets, forced into boxcars, and squeezed into buildings at a concentration camp. The documentary style is also evident in the camera's placement. In several instances, the audience's view of key figures is obscured by trucks and people that pass by in the foreground. Spielberg and Kaminski sometimes place the camera behind a window or a curtain, partly obscuring the view of Schindler. All these strategies, along with the use of black-and-white film, give *Schindler's List* the look of gritty actuality rather than the appearance of a slick and fictional Hollywood production.

Sound, too, contributes to the appearance of authenticity. For instance, Spielberg does not simply employ generic sounds for gunshots. He uses very different noises for rifle and revolver blasts and for close-up murders and shootings that occur at a distance. Pops, cracks, bursts, and booms punctuate the execution scenes. Sometimes the blasts are accompanied by sounds that represent exploding flesh. These distinct noises draw attention to the individual nature of each murder, making every shot horribly distinct. Spielberg accentuates the tragedy of a ghetto's destruction by providing the audience with a frightening three-dimensional auditory experience. In the scenes depicting Nazi attacks on a Jewish neighborhood, he places microphones at the center of the action. Viewers hear anguished shouts from desperate victims, screams that appear to emerge from every direction. An understated score by John Williams complements these scenes. In the course of watching an orgy of destruction and murder, the audience is hardly aware that Williams's music subtly provides emotional force to the pictures and sounds.

## DEVIL IN THE DETAILS: THE PERILS OF CONTESTING GENRE

How important is it for filmmakers to employ elements of genre when crafting a work of cinematic history? Can artists move dramatically away from the genre's conventions and still succeed broadly at the box office, in the video and DVD stores, and in the television ratings competition? Do filmmakers risk commercial failure when they dispense with many of the time-honored practices of Hollywood storytelling? Can they turn their backs on the three-act design? Can they excite strong audience response with movies that do not offer a partisan view of heroes and villains? Can cinematic historians succeed when they do not simplify plots by featuring just a few representative characters and when they do not provide morally uplifting tales about struggles between Davids and Goliaths?

Consider the problems that one very talented moviemaker faced when he created a story for the cinema that dared to break from the well-established generic standards. Ang Lee's *Ride with the Devil* (1999) was a fine movie in many respects, and it featured many fascinating and authentic-looking representations of the past. Yet the film passed almost unnoticed by the viewing public and critics in the mass media. A fundamental cause of the movie's oblivion can be traced to its unconventional story structure, which on many fronts violated Hollywood's unwritten codes that guide dramatic presentation. The director paid a price for his courage. Instead of winning accolades for creating a distinctive kind of cinematic history, he experienced the Hollywood nightmare. His film was a financial disappointment, and it disappeared into relative obscurity soon after its release. Could *Ride with the Devil* have been a commercial success if Lee and his production team had given more attention to Hollywood's storytelling practices? In view of the movie's many admirable qualities, it probably could have attracted some of the attention it deserved. *Ride with the Devil* is a good example of an intelligent cinematic treatment of history that lacks a successful narrative structure.

We can appreciate the tragedy of this film's box office failure by considering its sophistication in dealing with the past. *Ride with the Devil* delivers a remarkably sensitive and realistic-looking picture of the American Civil War in the border region of Missouri and Kansas. The story begins in the spring of 1861, when war between Union and Confederate forces is about to break out. The drama concludes at an undefined time well into the war. In subtle, often indirect ways, *Ride with the Devil* imparts a great deal of information about wartime conditions. Its most memorable portrayals relate to military actions in Missouri and Kansas, but the film also offers a plethora of interesting details about the lives of noncombatants.

Director Ang Lee's picture, based on a novel by Daniel Woodrell, presents mostly fictitious figures, but the situations these characters encounter and the behavior they exhibit are well supported in historical documents. Above all, *Ride with the Devil* demonstrates how fragile civilization in the border region became when the Civil War interrupted domestic life. The movie shows small bands of pro-Union Jayhawkers and pro-Confederate Bushwhackers raiding each other's communities at the start of the war (these attackers are following up on hostilities that had been growing since the days of "Bleeding Kansas" in the 1850s). *Ride with the Devil* presents the war from the viewpoint of the Bushwhackers. Although the slavery issue affects the Bushwhackers' attitudes, it is not a prominent factor in their belligerence. Western Missouri is home to relatively few slaves, and the Bushwhackers are much more interested in getting revenge for blood and treasure lost in raids committed by Jayhawkers and Union troops. Guerrilla warfare in the region soon escalates into brutal savagery, quite similar to the real conflicts that wrecked many homes and lives in western Missouri and eastern Kansas in the early 1860s. Taiwan-born Lee reminds Americans that these local vendettas led to senseless violence, similar to the violence that has troubled thousands in Ireland, Bosnia, and East Timor in modern times. In this manner, *Ride with the Devil* introduces movie audiences to a side of the American Civil War they did not see in *Gone with the Wind*.[71]

Lee's movie features many authentic-looking scenes portraying life in the border area during the 1860s. It shows the condition of noncombatants in exquisite detail, such as the Missouri environment of small farms and farmhouses rather than great mansions. *Ride with the Devil* also reveals that military activities in the region forced neighbors to choose sides. Confederate sympathizers became very suspicious of strangers, worrying about which side the intruders supported, yet these citizens fed and hid pro-Confederate guerrillas at great personal risk. Wartime deprivations, as the movie shows, led citizens to treasure a simple chicken dinner or a few pieces of bacon. The movie also effectively portrays the awkward nature of romantic liaisons among young people who lacked movies, television, or steamy novels to inform them about courting skills. In one of the film's best lines, Sue Lee (played by pop singer

Jewel) asks her new husband on their wedding night if he has ever made love before. "Well, I've killed fifteen men," responds Jake Roedel (Tobey Maguire).

In the film's strongest action sequences, William Quantrill (John Ales) leads his famous raid on Lawrence, Kansas, that results in the wanton murder of more than 180 male citizens. This depiction accurately portrays some of the brutal behavior recorded in the eyewitness accounts. One of the story's characters, Black John, closely resembles the psychopathic killer "Bloody" Bill Anderson, who murdered several people in the raid on Lawrence.

Another interesting character in the story is Daniel Holt (played by Jeffrey Wright), a slave who rides and fights with the Bushwhackers. Some moviegoers questioned whether an African American would have participated in the activities of Missouri's pro-Confederate guerrillas.[72] The historical records indicate that a few blacks did, in fact, play such a role. One was Henry Wilson, who lost family members in Jayhawker raids (Wilson rode with the Bushwhackers and served as a bodyguard for Quantrill). Another, John Noland, spied for the Bushwhackers.

*Ride with the Devil* is a beautifully photographed, intelligent, and informative drama about the Civil War in the borderlands. It deserved the Herodotus award it received from the History Channel for the best 1999 movie on a historical subject. Yet *Ride with the Devil* attracted only small audiences, received little attention in the mass media, and never reached the theaters in many of America's smaller communities. Lee's remarkably authentic historical portrayal failed to draw the audiences it deserved. What went wrong?

Poor marketing can hurt a new film, and evidently, *Ride with the Devil* did not receive much promotion (it lacked the sizable publicity budget needed to create a successful media blitz). It is doubtful, though, that large-scale promotion could have launched the picture as a major box office attraction. The film suffered from more than poor publicity. It so consistently evaded the principal rules of genre that it left audiences perplexed. *Ride with the Devil*'s dramatic structure, quite different from the familiar design, threw viewers off balance. Its failure provides an instructive example of the problems that can develop when a script deviates radically from Hollywood's conventions. Lee's courage in attempting to make a different kind of drama is commendable, but it is also regrettable that his clash with traditions of the genre limited the film's potential to reach many viewers who could have learned a great deal from the story.

*Ride with the Devil* lacks focus, direction, and denouement. Its dramatic structure does not closely follow the basic three-act form of most cinematic history, by which the script establishes a situation and introduces principal characters, creates problems for them, and then resolves their difficulties in the final act. The screenplay by James Schamus does not truly build toward a climax. Instead, its storytelling seems episodic, presenting a number of vignettes that lack strong connections. At some points in the drama, the audience cannot clearly distinguish which character is supposed to have the spotlight. Jake Roedel (Tobey Maguire) is the movie's principal figure, but he often fades into the background while other characters command the foreground. In the first part of the film, two Bushwhackers, Jack Bull Chiles (Skeet Ulrich) and George Clyde (Simon Baker), emerge as principals. After their deaths, other figures move to center stage. Sue Lee (Jewel), the only important female in the film, does not appear until late in the story, at which time she plays a major role. The slave (Jeffrey Wright) also emerges as a major figure late in the film after remaining rather silently in the background through much of the picture. Other characters briefly play important parts at different moments in the action, including Pit Mackeson (Jonathan Rhys Meyers in a brilliant role as a psychopathic killer), Black Jack (James Caviezel), and Willam Quantrill (John Ales). In short, Lee's movie does not focus on just a few major figures, as does most cinematic history, and its point of view shifts confusingly among several principal actors.

*Ride with the Devil* also lacks the clear-cut message evident in most cinematic history. It does not clearly identify heroes and villains. In some respects, the movie sympathizes with the Bushwhackers, especially when these pro-Confederate guerrillas become outnumbered and outgunned and have to go into hiding. Yet the movie also invites viewers to look critically at the Bushwhackers' participation in vicious slaughters (particularly the bloody massacre in Lawrence). Lee deserves praise for examining the historical events with an eye toward moral ambiguities, but the complexity he brings to this story often leaves the audience feeling bewildered rather than enlightened.

Furthermore, the film's message is obscure at the end. *Ride with the Devil* looks, in many ways, like a war picture, yet it contains no violence in its final thirty minutes. The fighting simply winds down, as Jake Roedel and his new wife, Sue Lee, attempt to build a domestic life together, as many Americans had to do in the aftermath of war. Through this soft conclusion, Lee's movie suggests a thoughtful view of the challenges Americans face when they prepare for peace. Jake Roedel's last words finish the story in a manner that accents the movie's tendency to deliver ambiguous messages. "It ain't right, and it ain't wrong. It just is," says Roedel after an encounter with two Bushwhackers who are heading off for a suicidal mission in a Yankee-controlled area.

An enthusiast of experimental drama can applaud Lee's iconoclasm in fashioning an unorthodox story structure. The director refused to conform to the familiar patterns of cinematic drama. Lee's courage is impressive, but his unique approach evidently damaged the movie's prospects for a favorable public and critical reception. Indeed, reviewers of the film were rather consistent in noting shortcomings in the dramatic presentation. These commentators praised the attention to historical detail but sensed that something was missing. Stephen Holden, writing in the *New York Times*, said the film "feels at times like an anthropological study" and observed that its view of the border wars "veers about as far from the high-romantic flourishes of 'Gone with the Wind' as a movie can go." Holden concluded that the film's "meditative quality and attention to detail" tended to "keep the story at a distance and make 'Ride with the Devil' dramatically skimpy, even though the movie stirs together themes of love, sex, death, and war."[73] Eleanor Ringel Gillespie concluded with a similar perspective in the *Atlanta Constitution*. "For some, 'Devil' will seem ultimately too scattered, too lacking in dramatic buildup and focus," wrote Gillespie. "Others may find it a sublime contemplation of the American character at a particularly revealing time in our struggle to become a nation."[74] These critics identified impressive qualities in the picture but also observed some specific difficulties in the storytelling. They did not recognize a common denominator associated with the shortcomings: *Ride with the Devil's* deviation from practices of the cinematic genre.

Would greater conformity to the conventions of Hollywood-style storytelling have seriously harmed the movie's integrity? If Lee and his writer had done less to break from traditions of the genre, could they still have produced a sophisticated commentary on history? These questions can be answered in the negative and the affirmative, respectively. As shown later in a discussion of some outstanding examples of cinematic history, filmmakers *can* borrow liberally from the traditions of dramatic presentation and also produce imaginative and intriguing cinematic perspectives on the past. Recognition of the achievements of other cinematic histories throws light on the tragedy of *Ride with the Devil's* commercial failure. Greater attention to practices of the craft could have rescued the film from obscurity and brought its many sensitive and intelligent representations of the past to a much wider audience. An understanding of this lost opportunity should serve as a valuable lesson to those who flippantly argue that cinematic historians should abandon the conventions of Hollywood storytelling. Radical departures from the familiar standards can prove artistically and financially disastrous.

# CHAPTER TWO

# Judging Cinematic History

In a sensitive review of the 1993 movie *Shadowlands,* Carlos Villa Flor identifies several of the film's manipulations of historical facts but draws greater attention to its broader achievements. Flor notes that *Shadowlands* adjusts certain details in its portrayal of a late-life romance involving the distinguished British author, theologian, and professor C. S. Lewis (played by Anthony Hopkins). At various points in the drama, the filmmakers take artistic liberties in order to design a comprehensible and entertaining story, Flor notes. They show one son instead of the two belonging to Joy Davidman Gresham (Debra Winger), the woman who eventually becomes Lewis's love interest. To give the story more action sequences, the filmmakers portray Lewis driving a car around Herefordshire (the real Lewis never mastered driving; he walked). Additionally, the movie associates Lewis with Oxford University (the most familiar symbol of English higher education, and a comfortable point of reference for moviegoers). In fact, Lewis worked at Cambridge during the years portrayed in the drama. Furthermore, *Shadowlands* places Mrs. Gresham in Lewis's home during the final days of her bout with cancer, even though she actually died in a hospital. Flor defends the artistic value of these manipulations and judges the production a success. *Shadowlands* views Lewis's life and the tragedy of Gresham's death intelligently. Its creators rearrange the historical record somewhat, yet the film holds together "as a balanced masterpiece."[1]

Flor's assessment of *Shadowlands* reveals an impressive sense of balance, a recognition that artists must shape evidence for dramatic effect and that these adjustments can sometimes serve a respectable purpose. The errors, omissions, simplifications, inventions, and manipulations in *Shadowlands* need to be identified, Flor demonstrates, but these matters do not destroy the movie's fundamental value. *Shadowlands* effectively studies the case of a talented and prominent individual who is confident of his intellectual sophistication and spiritual strength. His discovery of romance late in life and the eventual loss of his beloved wife present a stinging challenge to his Christian faith. Can Lewis maintain his confidence in the ultimate goodness of God after dealing with this tragedy? *Shadowlands,* based on an outstanding stage play, provides a

*In Glory (1989), Trip (Denzel Washington) and other soldiers of the Fifty-fourth Regiment tear up their pay vouchers rather than accept less money than the white soldiers receive. Director Ed Zwick exercised some artistic liberties in telling this story about African Americans in the Civil War, but historian James M. McPherson applauded the movie as an impressive cinematic perspective on history. (Museum of Modern Art Film Archive)*

thoughtful and ultimately uplifting view of Lewis's internal struggle. Despite its adjustments of the details in Lewis's life, the performance gives audiences plenty of attractive food for thought.

Flor's example is useful for a consideration of the challenges of assessing cinematic history. Much too often, reviewers are preoccupied with pointing out tiny factual mistakes. They focus on artistic liberties taken by filmmakers, comment cynically on Hollywood's cavalier relationship with historical evidence, and rail angrily at the cinematic artists who rearrange historical evidence in order to design compelling drama. These caustic critics can find an example of a more balanced and sophisticated analysis in Flor's insightful review.

One of the historians' favorite examples of a balanced and thoughtful approach to questions about artistic license is James M. McPherson's generous review of *Glory* (1989), which portrays the efforts of a group of African Americans fighting as Union soldiers during the Civil War. McPherson, a distinguished Civil War scholar, could easily have assumed a scolding attitude when dealing with the movie's treatment of history. As in all cinematic views of the past, *Glory*'s presentation includes manipulations of the evidence. McPherson points them out in his review but does not consider them outrageous. He

observes, for example, that the real African-American soldiers who participated in the battle of Fort Wagner attacked from south to north; *Glory* shows
them making the assault from the opposite direction. Also, *Glory* focuses on an
African-American military unit made up of former slaves, when in fact, free
blacks manned the real Massachusetts Fifty-fourth. A caption at the end of the
picture claims that the bravery of the Fifty-fourth at Fort Wagner inspired
Congress to authorize more black regiments for the Union army, but that actually occurred months before. The movie also leaves the impression that the
Fifty-fourth concluded its activities with the bloody confrontation at Fort
Wagner; in fact, the unit continued to serve through the war and participated
in several more battles and skirmishes.[2]

*Glory*'s misrepresentations do not, however, detract from its overall accomplishment, McPherson concludes. The adjustments can be defended. For example, the configuration of the Georgia beach where filmmakers shot the assault
on Fort Wagner required a southward movement. Also, notes McPherson,
most of the 188,000 black soldiers and sailors who served the Union in uniform *were slaves* until a short time before they enlisted. Furthermore, although
the bravery of the Fifty-fourth at Fort Wagner was not the only factor in
Congress's decision to authorize more black regiments, it at least helped to
transform the experiment with black soldiers into a policy of black recruit-
ment. *Glory*'s portrayal is not literally true in these and other depictions, but it
certainly contains many *symbolic* truths. Movies can teach history, McPherson
insists, as *Glory* nicely demonstrates.[3]

Our understanding of the conventions of dramatic development should
also inspire a more balanced and tolerant view of cinematic history. As we have
seen, these Hollywood traditions of storytelling often force manipulations of
evidence. Moviemakers employ successful practices of their profession, attempting to create emotionally stimulating entertainment. For instance, they
condense time and collapse several historic personalities into one or two figures. Filmmakers emphasize a biographical approach to history, treating the
experiences of a few characters as suggestive of the troubles and progress experienced by many people. Moviemakers also establish a rather simple story
structure, presenting history in the form of a three-act play that introduces situations, creates problems for the protagonists, and then resolves their difficulties or hints at a symbolic triumph in the final act. Cinematic history often delivers an uplifting conclusion, communicating a sanguine view of the potential
for human progress. It also creates a tightly focused view of the past, giving
specific attention to just a few people and events. Movies do not present the "big
picture" very effectively. They leave out much—not only details but also analysis. Cinema is certainly not comprehensive in its approach to history. Frequently

it privileges stories about war, personality conflict, romance, and tragedy. Its dramas characterize historic figures in white and black, as heroes and villains; portrayals in gray are much less evident. And of course, cinematic history often features fictional men and women, invented protagonists and antagonists whose actions and statements facilitate the filmmaker's efforts to create an entertaining tale. By employing invented characters, filmmakers can also take the action to diverse locales and give personality to specific individuals when, in fact, we know relatively little about the lives, thoughts, and emotions of these historic figures.[4]

The need for these forms of artistic license should be evident, yet critics of cinematic history continue to devote a good deal of energy to angry denunciations of Hollywood's playfulness with history. They fume against the collapsing of characters, the hero-villain depictions, the invented scenes, the simplification of plot, and other adjustments that filmmakers incorporate to produce dramatic effect. Critics also draw attention to specific factual errors, noting that *real* individuals did not speak or act in the ways depicted in the movies. They observe mistakes in presentation, too: the wrong uniform, erroneous chronology, or the placement of a leading figure where he or she could not possibly have been. By focusing on misrepresentation of details, they often miss the larger cinematic accomplishments. Preoccupied with small "lies," they fail to recognize larger "truths."

Of course, these lies can add up. They may accumulate to a disturbing level, destroying public confidence in a movie's relationship with history. Some films develop tainted reputations, and for good reason. Their manipulations of evidence take artistic license to excess. When media coverage of these problems in historical depiction becomes extensive, the negative publicity can harm a film financially and set critics against it. This condition may surprise some, because they assume that Hollywood filmmakers can distort history with impunity. But as I discuss later, some filmmakers have been called on the carpet in recent years for their failure to depict the past with integrity. They have paid a price for their manipulations in dollars and artistic reputation.

A serious and balanced look at cinematic history requires a more complex response to movies than the simplistic "thumbs up" or "thumbs down" approach of movie reviewers on television and in popular magazines. Even good cinematic history contains a great deal of fiction and manipulation of the facts, and even poor cinematic history that bends the facts to a troublesome degree can dramatize aspects of the past impressively. To state this case starkly, it is impossible to find an example of cinematic history that can be held up for unquestioned praise because it depicts the past without stretching the truth in any way. Conversely, it is difficult to find an example of cinematic history that

distorts the record so thoroughly that it should be rejected for having no redeeming value. Even problematic films frequently offer insights. In sum, we
need a sensitive effort to judge integrity and an informed view of film that bal-
ances the defense of artistic liberties with the recognition that some dramatic
flourishes can be problematic.

A comparative view of four major Hollywood films of the 1980s and 1990s
is useful in this regard, because it helps distinguish between plausible distortions and more troublesome ones. James Cameron's *Titanic* (1997) is an example of defensible exercise of artistic license. Cameron's film manages to
present an intelligent view of the past even though it contains significant manipulations of the historical record and a good deal of fictionalizing. Against
the example of *Titanic*'s achievement we can consider three motion pictures
that came under attack in the mass media for exceeding reasonable bounds of
artistic license: *Mississippi Burning* (1988), *Amistad* (1997), and *The Hurricane*
(1999). Each of these problematic films delivers some riveting drama, and
each raises important questions about racial injustice. Yet all three stretch the
truth in ways that undermine their interpretations of history. Some of the
criticisms leveled against *Mississippi Burning, Amistad,* and *The Hurricane*
were substantive, and justifiably, the public and the critics lost confidence in
the movies' integrity.

### A TITANIC ACHIEVEMENT

When James Cameron released *Titanic* late in 1997, the media gave considerable attention to his efforts to give the movie a look of historical authenticity. News stories about Cameron's re-creation of the fateful 1912 voyage made
interesting reporting, because the director had devoted a large part of his
record $200 million budget to verisimilitude. The production team created a
version of the *Titanic* on a beach in Baja California that was 90 percent the
length of the original ship. This huge set was attached in four sections so that
it could be assembled or disassembled for various scenes, with individual
parts raised or lowered into the water. Cameron's production team also built a
17 million–gallon water tank that covered eight acres, which allowed cinematographers to "sink" rooms and decks to a depth of thirty feet. The team used
smaller models of the ocean liner for staging the disaster and spent millions
on special effects that created ocean backgrounds, icebergs, and the appearance of bodies falling off decks. For the scenes depicting the leisurely days before the encounter with the iceberg, Cameron brought in carpet woven in the
designs used on the original *Titanic* and used old photographs to build the
vessel's social halls and staterooms. To give the extras an authentic appearance,

*Passengers board ship in James Cameron's blockbuster* Titanic *(1997). The production team created a replica of the liner on a beach in Baja California that was 90 percent the length of the original ship. (Museum of Modern Art Film Archive)*

he purchased 450 wigs and hundreds of hairpieces and schooled the actors in the manners and sounds of 1912 with etiquette and dialogue coaches.[5]

Despite this attention to authentic details, some critics lambasted the movie. They claimed that the syrupy love story, punctuated by a strong emphasis on class conflict, was so exaggerated and simplistic in its characterizations that it was not believable. *Titanic* "fails utterly" and is "dead in the water," declared Richard Corliss in *Time*.[6] He said that everybody in the story is a "caricature of class, designed only to illustrate a predictable prejudice: that the first-class passengers are third-class people, and vice versa." The story about Jack, Rose, and Cal "isn't half as poignant as the true ones known from books and films of the event," argued Corliss. "On this vast canvass, the problems of three little people really don't amount to a hill of beans."[7] The *Washington Post*'s Ken Ringle also reacted sarcastically to the production. *Titanic,* he wrote, is a "high-tech, low-brain, big-budget" movie. The scenes of Jack and Rose splashing around in twenty-eight-degree water with no signs of hypothermia are hardly believable, he claimed, and Cameron's depiction of lusty, good-time souls in steerage and cruel, sterile passengers in first class constitutes "kindergarten Marxism."[8] In these and other negative reviews, commentators laughed at the corny qualities of the Jack-Rose-Cal triangle and the movie's heavy-handed depictions of heroic passengers in steerage and effete snobs in first class.

*Jack (Leonardo DiCaprio) leads Rose (Kate Winslet) through the flooded first-class reception area in* Titanic *(1997). A critic complained that the movie shows Jack and Rose splashing around in twenty-eight-degree water with no signs of hypothermia. (Museum of Modern Art Film Archive)*

Critics leveled a number of other specific complaints, too. They noticed the appearance of anachronisms, such as when Rose extends her middle finger in defiance of the ship's authorities (a distinctly modern gesture). Some noticed that the story focuses on first- and third-class passengers, giving virtually no attention to the large second-class contingent on the ship. A few wondered why the filmmaker did not build the drama around real-life figures on the *Titanic* rather than the fictional characters of Jack and Rose (the elderly couple hugging each other as the boat is sinking were good candidates, for they presumably represented Isidor Straus, owner of Macy's department store, and his wife).

Others drew attention to scientific investigations of the sunken *Titanic* reported on the Discovery Channel. That program revealed that some scientists believe the ship sank so quickly because of technological flaws in its construction. The ship's builders used metal with impurities in the design of the hull, and the rivets they employed to hold the large metal pieces together popped out when the *Titanic* hit the iceberg. These difficulties, discovered through undersea exploration two and a half miles below the ocean's surface, supposedly gave a *real* explanation for the *Titanic* disaster. Fifteen hundred passengers and crew died because of shortcomings in the ship's design and materials, said enthusiasts of the television program, not because of factors advanced in the movie.[9]

These critics raise interesting questions, but not one of their complaints represents a serious assault on the integrity of Cameron's film. Even when considered in their totality rather than individually, the criticisms do not reduce the film's essential accomplishment of rendering a thoughtful and memorable perspective of the past.

The fictional Jack and Rose, objects of much derision by critics, serve a brilliant narrative purpose. Their presence facilitates Cameron's effort to study the disaster in far greater scope than would have been possible if he had focused on real figures from history. Using Jack and Rose as the protagonists allows Cameron to take the camera all over the ship—in the first-class dining hall, on the decks, alongside the captain, down in steerage, in the engine room, at the site of contact with the iceberg, and in the flooding staterooms and halls. If Cameron had used actual passengers as the key figures in the story, he would have been limited to showing them in just one section of the great vessel. Furthermore, a drama about the experiences of Mr. and Mrs. Straus would have drawn objections from detail-oriented historians who could claim that little is known about their specific thoughts and actions (and perhaps their descendants would object to depictions that were not sufficiently flattering). Cameron found a way to cover diverse events in the *Titanic* tragedy by placing his fictitious characters at the center of the most important action. Also, by focusing on the personalities of Jack and Rose, he strengthens the audience's emotional attachment to the passengers. Viewers care about the fate of the young lovers after watching their romance grow amidst their ordeals. When Jack dies on a frozen sea, viewers sense the larger tragedy. His passing symbolizes the suffering that many passengers, friends, and relatives experienced in April 1912.

Some of the specific objections to the movie can easily be dismissed. Certainly Cameron is guilty of reading the present into the past when he shows Rose making a late-twentieth-century gesture, but this is only a tiny anachronism. The complaint about Cameron's focus on first- and third-class passengers is technically correct but artistically insignificant. Simplification is inherent in docudrama, and when artists employ it, the strategy usually accents differences, so understandably, the director draws attention to the contrasts between rich and poor. A truly comprehensive movie about the tragedy would introduce us to the second-class group as well, but cinematic history cannot deliver an exhaustive treatment of all major facets.

The Discovery Channel's speculation about the effect of popping rivets and impurities in the metal is based on fascinating underwater exploration, but it hardly adds up to a stronger explanation for the tragedy than that provided in Cameron's cinematic drama. *Titanic* manages to present most of the fundamental causes of the great ship's shocking demise. The movie reveals that radio operators received several reports of icebergs ahead, but the captain and the director of the White Star Line ignored them. The ship reached the highest speed of its journey (twenty-two knots) as it approached the danger zone, and the men posted in the crow's nest lacked binoculars. The *Titanic* should have been equipped with sixty-four lifeboats, but the White Star Line had shaved that number down to sixteen to provide ample deck space for promenading guests (rules at the time did not require a full complement of lifeboats). After the rendezvous with the iceberg, the ship remained afloat only a few hours. During that brief period, the captain failed to sound a general alarm, and many crewmen were inadequately trained to handle an emergency evacuation. When the Americans and British learned about the numerous fatal errors associated with the tragedy, they screamed for reforms, and dramatic changes in regulations followed. New rules required a twenty-four-hour radio watch, adequate lifeboats for all travelers, and evacuation drills. Sea travel became much safer in subsequent decades.[10]

The fact remains that any passenger ship, even a technologically sophisticated one of the twenty-first century, could encounter difficulty if it slammed its starboard side into an iceberg at twenty-two knots, as the *Titanic* did. Cameron's movie, with its attention to the numerous human failures before and after the crash, delivers the essential explanation of why the ship lost more than 1,500 of the 2,223 people on board.

It is true, of course, that Cameron portrays the wealthy characters in the story in a consistently negative way (except for the "unsinkable" Molly Brown, who comes across as a wealthy but down-to-earth figure). Cal Hockley (who inherited a Pittsburgh steel fortune) is the most reprehensible character among the snobs who look down at Jack. One of the most memorable scenes communicating disdain for the life of the idle rich shows Rose observing the way social graces are taught to a young girl. Rose watches as a mother instructs her daughter, who is about ten years old, how to sit upright and spread her napkin in a delicate manner. This image suggests that Rose's life among such people will be boring and essentially empty.

Notions of class are fundamental in the story, and not only for purposes of entertainment. Cameron associates class distinctions with injustice. His portrayal raises some important questions: Why did a much higher percentage of first-class passengers escape on lifeboats than did passengers from steerage? Did economic and cultural prejudice affect life-and-death decisions in the moment of crisis? Statistical evidence, which the movie cannot convey, is certainly disturbing. Sixty percent of the first-class passengers escaped on lifeboats, while only 25 percent of steerage passengers did. The evidence is more dramatic for women. Virtually all the first-class women who wanted to enter the

*Lifeboats descend as the great ship goes down in* Titanic *(1997). Director James Cameron's interpretation suggests that because of class discrimination, far more first-class passengers escaped than did passengers in steerage. (Museum of Modern Art Film Archive)*

lifeboats got away on them; 94 percent of these passengers escaped. Even though a call went out to seat "women and children first," only 31 percent of third-class women escaped on the boats. Why the difference?[11] Did crewmen restrain steerage-class passengers from leaving their quarters during the first ninety minutes of the crisis when the lifeboats were filling, as the movie suggests? Were third-class passengers, who slept in the lower decks of the stern, too far away to hear warnings about the crisis? Were the poor immigrants who insisted on carrying their possessions with them slowed down in their attempt to escape? Was it because the number of passengers in third class was more than double that in first class? We cannot be certain of the answer, but Cameron makes a useful contribution to our thinking about these questions by elevating the issue of class to a prominent place in his story. He gives the subject much more attention than do the authors of major books on the *Titanic* (many of whom seem preoccupied with reports of the altruistic behavior of the rich and famous passengers). Cameron makes the class question even more central than it was in the classic 1958 movie about the event, *A Night to Remember.*

We can only speculate about the source of this concern about class. Perhaps the movie's sympathy for the poor can be attributed to the writer-director's personal experiences. Before Cameron struck gold as a filmmaker, he had completed only two years of college and worked for a while as a truck driver. He was familiar with want and struggle. We can also connect the movie's contrast between vacuous millionaires and wholesome commoners to Hollywood's formulaic approach to storytelling. As noted in the discussion about genre, American cinema often shows common people outwitting the rich and powerful. Audiences—which, after all, are mostly not so rich and famous—enjoy watching these victories. Whatever the cause, Cameron deserves applause for drawing our attention to the Edwardian society that was afloat at sea, a culture that kept the classes much more separated than in our time and that evidently favored privilege in a moment of crisis.

The movie offers another achievement, one often missed in the reviews. It speculates intelligently on the emotions demonstrated by one of the principal figures in the tragedy, Captain Edward J. Smith (Bernard Hill). Extant records of the events suggest that Captain Smith was not particularly aggressive in his initial response to the crisis. From the fragmentary evidence available, it appears that at first he was hesitant and uncertain. The movie suggests that the captain became emotionally paralyzed at a time when quick and intelligent decision making was crucial. Had he sounded the alarm to abandon ship swiftly, perhaps fewer lifeboats would have left without a full complement of passengers. In an interview on the History Channel, Cameron explained the reasoning behind this depiction. He imagined that Captain Smith was briefly in a state of shock. Once Smith learned that a rescue ship could not arrive at the *Titanic*'s location until after it sank, he knew he was a doomed man. Not only would he go down with his vessel in the tradition of a sea captain, but his reputation would be tarnished in the aftermath of the tragedy. He would be considered responsible for the deaths of hundreds of passengers and the crew in his charge. Cameron speculated that these thoughts could have affected the captain's performance in the crisis. Smith may have sensed that he was about to die ignominiously, and that realization temporarily froze him.

Through this speculation about the emotional impact of the event, Cameron exhibits one of cinematic history's greatest attributes: its potential to explore the psychological dimensions of an experience. In this respect, *Titanic* delivers an emotional punch that is frequently absent in books on the 1912 event. Cameron's *Titanic* attempts to put audiences in touch with the captain's inner feelings. His interpretation involves conjecture, to be sure, but his guesswork is informed and intelligent. *Titanic* presents a credible character that may resemble the real figure in history.

There is, of course, a broader achievement that makes *Titanic* a memorable historical film. Cameron's movie communicates a sense of what some historians call "the pastness of the past." It transports audiences to another era and, with careful attention to detail, gives them a sense that they are witnesses to the tragic journey. Cameron bombards viewers with genuine-looking images from the past—from vintage clothing to silver ashtrays of the White Star Line and 18,000 square feet of authentic-looking carpet. When Cameron produces high-tech wizardry to show the ship's demise in the final hour, his use of cinematic bells and whistles does not simply offer gratuitous entertainment (as do many other disaster stories from Hollywood). The technical tricks effectively communicate a picture of an extraordinary calamity. *New York Times* reviewer Janet Maslin summed up the achievement succinctly when she wrote, "Astonishing technological advances are at work here, but only in the service of one spectacular illusion: that the ship is afloat again, and that the audience is ultimately involved in its voyage."[12]

Thus, it is easy to become sidetracked in a consideration of *Titanic*'s treatment of history. A critic can readily bemoan the inordinate time devoted to the actions of fictitious heroes and villains such as Jack, Rose, and Cal or complain about anachronisms, groups left out of the story, or scientific discoveries that Cameron failed to mention. Such concerns deserve consideration, but even when added together, they do not detract from the film's fundamental contribution to cinematic history. *Titanic* is "true" in many important respects. It effectively identifies many of the most important factors that explain the disaster at sea. It raises significant questions about the confining role of upper-class women in Edwardian society and offers a provocative criticism of class-mindedness in that period. The film also presents its story on a marvelous set that glitters with detail. On many counts, *Titanic* delivers a thoughtful perspective on the past.

### THE REVOLT AGAINST *AMISTAD*

When do the problems with historical treatment weigh too heavily, harming a movie's credibility? How can accumulated questions about a movie's presentation of history undermine a film's reputation for delivering thoughtful perspectives? The troubled films under consideration here (*Amistad, Mississippi Burning,* and *The Hurricane*) did not become targets of attack in the mass media because the filmmakers made small mistakes with the facts. They did not lose credibility simply because the directors used the wrong dates, costumes, language, or other details. Nor did these movies come under heavy fire for failing to present the past through compelling drama. In fact, each film received considerable praise in the media for delivering powerful, emotionally riveting entertainment. The problems concerned excesses in artistic license. In these cases, the producers, directors, and writers manipulated so many elements for dramatic effect that they undermined the overall truthfulness of their historical interpretations.

Steven Spielberg's *Amistad* exemplifies a number of these difficulties. His 1997 production follows the story of fifty-three Africans who were taken from Sierra Leone in 1839 and sold to slave traders. Led by a twenty-five-year-old figure called Cinque by the Spaniards, the Africans manage to stage a revolt while their slave ship is off the coast of Cuba. The rebels order their former captors to return them to Africa, but the Spaniards deceive the Africans and manage to steer the ship toward the northwest at nighttime. Eventually the U.S. Navy takes control of the ship off Long Island Sound, and a long legal struggle to win the Africans' freedom begins. Many individuals played important roles in that effort, but Spielberg's movie gives particular attention to three historic figures: Roger Sherman Baldwin, a distinguished New Haven attorney who organized the court battles on behalf of the Africans; Lewis Tappan, a devoted abolitionist who raised money for the court appeals; and John Quincy Adams, the former president and then congressman, who presented a successful case on the Africans' behalf to the U.S. Supreme Court.

*Amistad* features some impressive dramatic moments. Most gripping are scenes of the rebellion and the slave trade. The opening sequence shows Cinque managing to break from his chains, free the other captives, and seize control of the ship. Later, in a flashback, *Amistad* shows the crew dumping some slaves into the ocean. No Hollywood film before *Amistad* displayed African mutiny or the Middle Passage more realistically. But these scenes occupy only a few minutes of a two-and-a-half-hour film. Most of the time, *Amistad* concentrates on the legal maneuverings in New England, and it came under sharp criticism for this depiction.

No single gaffe or manipulation dealt a telling blow against *Amistad*. Rather, there was an accumulation of complaints about the movie's handling of history. An abundance of small difficulties added up to a vote of no confidence from various historians and media critics, despite the film's commendable attention to an important subject from antebellum U.S. history.

Some of the criticisms pertained to minor details. Scholars pointed out, for example, that men did not wear beards and mustaches in the United States in the early 1840s; such flourishes did not become fashionable until the time of Lincoln's presidency. Historians noted, too, that there could not have been snow falling on Long Island (as the movie shows) when U.S. naval forces seized the *Amistad*. The movie's fictitious character Theodore Joadson (Morgan Freeman) secures a sailor who can help translate the Africans' Mende language; in reality, Josiah Gibbs handled that task, and he was a talented linguist, not the bumbling fool characterized in the movie. John Quincy Adams was not as committed an abolitionist as the movie suggests when he received the assignment to defend the *Amistad* captives, and his speech before the

Supreme Court ran eight hours over two days; the movie gives the appearance of a much more succinct presentation. Roger Sherman Baldwin was forty-six years old and a respected attorney when he defended the Africans, but the movie casts handsome Matthew McConaughey as Baldwin, a much younger figure. In the film, Cinque assists John Quincy Adams in creating a legal defense, a situation that never occurred. Cinque was not in Washington, D.C., at the time of the Supreme Court hearing, and only seven of nine justices were present during the Court's deliberations, not the full complement shown in the film.[13]

These and other complaints do not, even collectively, destroy the movie's value as a portrayal of history. Although the presence of beards and mustaches suggests a failure of the filmmakers to do their homework about the social customs of the era, other "errors" committed by the director and his staff can be defended. For instance, cinematic history almost always reduces long speeches to a few essential ideas, and Spielberg's decision to cast young, sexy Matthew McConaughey as Roger Sherman Baldwin is understandable in view of the actor's appeal to female audiences.

A second, more significant bombardment of criticism relates to the characterizations of specific historical personalities. Baldwin, a scholarly and distinguished Yale graduate who later became governor of Connecticut, was hardly the "dung-scrapping" real estate lawyer portrayed in *Amistad*. The movie shows him needing to be convinced to work for the Africans' freedom, but in fact, the real Baldwin was already a strong crusader for the antislavery cause. Lewis Tappan, another dedicated abolitionist, was chief fund-raiser for the legal appeals and certainly did not want the Africans to die as martyrs so that they could contribute to the antislavery cause, as the movie suggests. Tappan was head of the newly formed American Anti-Slavery Society, and he led major petition drives against slavery. He was so committed to the abolitionist cause that he did not even go home to visit his dying daughter while he was working on the *Amistad* case.[14]

Additionally, scholars criticized the appearance of the fictional African-American character Theodore Joadson. Historian Eric McKitrick pointed out that in the 1840s an African American would not have been accorded the influence and respect evident in the white characters' treatment of the fictional Joadson.[15] Another historian, Richard S. Newman, criticized the depiction differently.[16] He applauded Spielberg's effort to feature a black abolitionist in the story, but he counseled incorporation of a real-life black figure instead of an invented one. Some prominent blacks were involved in abolitionist affairs at the time, wrote Newman, including James Pennington, Robert Purvis, and James Forten.

Other historians objected to *Amistad*'s simple-minded portrayal of the abolitionist group. The movie showed the abolitionists waving crosses, looking like religious zealots, and scholars complained that this depiction suggested that the reformers were fanatics. That kind of negative assessment of antislavery activists reflects an old, conservative viewpoint that has been strongly challenged in modern scholarship. The new research, they stressed, views abolitionists of the 1840s as bold crusaders for freedom who showed the courage to challenge slavery in a political environment that was very protective of the South's interests.

Eric Foner, a prominent interpreter of nineteenth-century U.S. history, drew critical attention to the way *Amistad* was being promoted. In an influential article published in the *New York Times* op-ed section, Foner complained that publicists sent out thousands of study guides to the nation's schools recommending that students discuss the Joadson character in a study exercise. Foner questioned the value of having students study a fictional character. He also objected to the way Debbie Allen, producer of *Amistad,* enthusiastically advertised the movie's contribution to learning. In statements to the media, Allen suggested that historians had overlooked this story in their research and teaching. She claimed to have rescued the *Amistad* case from the dustbin of history. She also boldly claimed that the Africans' victory in the U.S. Supreme Court had had a tremendous impact on American society, putting the United States on the road to emancipation. Foner dismissed these claims as misleading hype. He observed that professional historians had given considerable attention to the *Amistad* case, and they certainly could not be accused of neglecting slavery. Allen was wrong, too, in arguing that the Supreme Court's decision in this case dramatically changed the status of African Americans. The *Dred Scott* decision of 1857, coming more than a decade later and involving some of the same Supreme Court justices, set back African Americans' progress substantially. The Africans from the *Amistad* won their freedom on technicalities concerning the slave trade, not on a general commitment to principles of freedom, said Foner. He concluded that *Amistad* "erases the distinction between fact and fiction" and claimed that "the film is by no means a work of history, and it is certainly not appropriate for use in the classroom."[17]

Many historians, like Foner, concluded that publicity for the movie expressed unwarranted exuberance. Scholars became suspicious of Spielberg's claim that he had enlisted accomplished historians as advisers, including Louis Henry Gates, Jr., John Hope Franklin, Howard Jones, Rebecca Scott, Clifton Johnson, and Arthur Abraham. Historians suspected that these distinguished names were being cited to help legitimize the project. Evidently, the scholars had little input in the crucial creative stages of film development, production, and promotion. Historians' suspicions seemed confirmed when two of the

*In* Amistad *(1997), lawyer Roger Baldwin (Matthew McConaughey) turns to his clients in an effort to show that the Africans were not born into slavery. A historian complained that the movie suggests that Baldwin—in real life, a middle-aged man and a committed abolitionist—was a young, "ambulance-chasing, fee-hungry attorney." (Museum of Modern Art Film Archive)*

advisers, Johnson and Abraham, objected to the movie's depictions and complained publicly that Spielberg had not taken their recommendations seriously.
Clifton Johnson, executive director emeritus of the Amistad Research Center
at Tulane University, strongly criticized the movie after its release. Contrary to
Spielberg's interpretation, said Johnson, Lewis Tappan had done more to win
the case than John Quincy Adams had. "Other characters in the story are misrepresented in the film," too, he wrote, "but none more than Lewis Tappan and
Roger Sherman Baldwin. The first is made to appear as a hypocrite and the former as an ambulance-chasing, fee-hungry attorney."[18] Arthur Abraham, former chairman of African Studies at the University of Sierra Leone, directed his
fire at the movie's depiction of African society. Abraham charged that African
culture was "badly represented in the movie" because the story "follows the
picture given by European imperialists at the end of the nineteenth century to
justify the colonial takeover."[19]

The historians' judgment of *Amistad* was not universally critical. Some acknowledged problems with the interpretation but counseled appreciation of
the movie's overall achievements. "At moments the drama is brilliant, sophisticated, and moving," wrote Bertram Wyatt-Brown, author of a number of

important books on pre–Civil War America, including a biography of abolitionist Lewis Tappan. "All in all," he said, "*Amistad* warrants praise for its attempt to make real a key moment on the road to war and eventual emancipation. No American, white or black, should miss it."[20] Howard Jones, author of a respected historical study of the slaves' case, *Mutiny on the Amistad,* also gave a generally positive assessment.[21] Jones had visited the set during the filming of the mutiny and had conferred with Spielberg. He was impressed with the director's effort to dramatize history and urged open-mindedness in judging the film's portrayal of the past. Most important, he said, *Amistad* was likely to excite the viewers' interest in learning more about history. Spielberg was reaching citizens in ways that university historians often failed to do, he argued. "Too many academics focus on satisfying fellow academics, boring the general public," said Jones. He praised Spielberg for "revealing the essential truths of a compelling story that will convince many viewers that history is interesting."[22]

How can we weigh these conflicting assessments of *Amistad*'s treatment of history? Which complaints represent powerful indictments of the movie; which pertain to defendable exercises in artistic license?

Certainly some of the moviemaker's alterations of the historical record are troublesome. The portrayal of Lewis Tappan as an abolitionist who would sacrifice the slaves as martyrs is disturbing. Also irksome are the publicists' efforts to encourage the nation's schoolteachers to lead students in discussions about *Amistad*'s fictional character Theodore Joadson.

Many other manipulations are understandable examples of artistic excess—liberties taken to advance the drama. Standing alone, the characterization of Roger Baldwin Sherman is forgivable. After all, one of the dramatic conventions of cinematic history is to show the evolution of a central figure's personality. It is much more interesting to watch Baldwin learning to appreciate the wisdom of the abolitionist cause than to see him as a fully formed antislavery crusader in his first appearance on the screen. Many cinematic histories portray the maturation of one of the protagonists. We can also understand why Debbie Allen and her publicists built up the *Amistad* case as a more important chapter of history than it actually was. When Hollywood invests millions of dollars in a production about the past, its spokespersons are likely to accentuate the significance of their subject and suggest that they alone were instrumental in bringing the story to light. The manner in which this was handled, however, badly hurt the movie's standing with history professionals. Allen's claim that scholars had overlooked the topic was wrong, unnecessarily provocative, and insulting.

Positive observations about *Amistad*'s handling of history were largely drowned out by the critical remarks. An accumulation of specific objections about historical details began to harm the movie's reputation. By the time Academy Award nominations were being collected in early 1998, the buzz in Hollywood had turned against the movie. Many people in the nation's film community were aware that Spielberg's film was the target of a good deal of complaining because of its rendition of history. As a somewhat tainted motion picture, *Amistad* did not look like a good candidate for Best Picture. The well-publicized negative feedback showed that there was a price to pay for provoking controversies about historical representation. Of course, *Titanic* swept the awards that year, and even if *Amistad* had been acclaimed by historians and media critics, it would have been up against very tough competition.

*Amistad* got into trouble because of many small distortions rather than one or two particularly outrageous ones. Standing alone, no single objection to the movie's historical depictions could have harmed its fortunes. It was the accumulation of many objections to the film's historical details that wrecked confidence in the movie's storytelling. Surveying the extensive record of protests against *Amistad*'s portrayals, one senses that the critics felt somewhat like Thomas Jefferson when he identified the colonists' reasons for revolting against the mother country. In the Declaration of Independence, the founding father wrote that no single act of British leadership created a cause for rebellion, but when many complaints added up, there seemed good reason to take action.

Why would Steven Spielberg, a respected director who had created a brilliant historical film, *Schindler's List,* just a few years before, allow *Amistad* to perform so sloppily in its treatment of history? Evidently, Spielberg was unable to give this project as much scrutiny as he would have liked. During *Amistad*'s development, he was busy inaugurating a new Hollywood studio (Dream-Works) with his two media buddies, David Geffen and Jeffrey Katzenberg. Also, by the time Spielberg was ready to edit *Amistad,* he was on location in England, filming scenes for another important history-oriented film, *Saving Private Ryan.* Under the circumstances, Spielberg could not deliver his best, and the difficulties were manifest in the production. Not only did *Amistad* fail to offer engaging entertainment in its talky presentation of the abolitionists' legal struggles; the movie also fudged the historical record to a degree that stirred a bees' nest of angry critics.

These failures are unfortunate, for there is much of value in *Amistad.* As Natalie Zemon Davis observes in her book *Slaves on Screen,* the film presents Hollywood's most memorable view of the slave trade. It surpasses many other Hollywood films in its treatment of slavery because it does not portray the Africans only as victims. *Amistad* shows the captives as agents in their own affairs; they help shape their experiences by taking bold action, risking their lives in a bloody rebellion. When he is brought to the United States, the energetic

*In Amistad (1997), Cinque (Djimon Hounsou, center) and his fellow captives are charged with piracy and murder after a rebellion on a slave ship. Steven Spielberg's movie gives sensitive attention to both the Africans' cultural distinctiveness and their diversity. (Museum of Modern Art Film Archive)*

Cinque presses his case for freedom to anyone who will listen. "Give us free!" he shouts in a memorable scene.[23] Spielberg also demonstrates greater appreciation of the Africans' cultural diversity than other filmmakers have shown. *Amistad* reminds audiences that Africans came from a variety of regions and cultures. The movie shows the captives arguing with one another, their loyalties divided along tribal lines with origins in far-off places. Spielberg also gives the film an appealing touch of authenticity by having the movie's African-born actors speak in native dialect, much as they would have sounded to real nineteenth-century abolitionists. Spielberg also manages to introduce audiences to some of the major political issues of the 1840s, such as the complexity of the slavery law and John Quincy Adams's role in raising questions about the "peculiar institution" in Congress. Also, *Amistad* features terrific acting performances, not only from well-known British veteran Anthony Hopkins (playing Adams) but also from new discovery Djimon Hounsou, a native of Benin, Africa, who was brilliant as Cinque, the captive rice farmer turned rebel.

The chorus of criticism needs to be tempered, too, by recognition that the movie's subject was difficult to tackle; it was not the kind of material that attracts the interest of most creative talent or studio executives in Hollywood. Banking the future of a new movie studio on a story about a rather obscure event from nineteenth-century American history was a bold move (*Amistad* was the first movie DreamWorks released). Historical dramas are generally risky investments. They do not represent excellent box office gambles, and they are not ideal first projects for a fledgling studio. Spielberg could have made DreamWorks' first venture resemble the other blockbusters on his resume: stories about a rabid shark, a courageous anthroplogist names Indiana Jones, a lovable extraterrestial, or a frightening group of Jurassic reptiles. A director who sometimes feels compelled to make meaningful and more risky films (such as *The Color Purple, Schindler's List,* and *Amistad*) deserves admiration.[24]

*Amistad* was not the financial success its promoters hoped it would be. The media offered much conjecture about the reasons for the movie's modest appeal. Some said that American society was too prejudiced to care about a story that focused on black heroes. Others maintained that Spielberg should have included different scenes in the movie or different characters. Numerous points of advice emerged from would-be filmmakers.

The roots of *Amistad*'s box office failure relate in large part to dramatic structure rather than to these other factors. At first glance, *Amistad* seems like a workable story for treatment on the big screen. It involves terrible oppression, a violent fight for liberation, and a tremendous courtroom struggle to secure freedom for the victims—in brief summary, a good design for successful entertainment. But a closer look at the details undermines confidence in the story's entertainment value. After the first minutes depicting the frightening mutiny, the drama must settle down and deal with treaties, laws, political negotiations, rights, speeches, and related matters. These are the elements of good historical interpretation through lecturing and writing, but they do not constitute attractive building blocks for a compelling cinematic drama. Most of the action occurs near the beginning of the film; it then turns into a largely talk-oriented story. Furthermore, *Amistad* lacks the focus of a movie such as *Schindler's List,* which fixes attention tightly on a hero (Oskar Schindler) and a villain (the Nazi Amon Goeth). *Amistad*'s script lacks a principal villain, and it features a large cast of diverse characters who play important roles in the movie's historical portrayals. There are three main protagonists—Cinque, Baldwin, and Adams—and the audience is not introduced to two of them until well into the story. In addition, there are numerous other figures that viewers need to learn something about to understand the historical developments: President Martin Van Buren; Princess Isabella II; the interpreter who communicates with the Africans; the abolitionists, including Lewis Tappan and the fictitious Theodore Joadson; and various judges. In short, *Amistad* attempts to deal with a complex historical record, and it does not conform nicely to practices of the cinematic genre. Its story is a scriptwriter's nightmare.

Like many examples of cinematic history that have come under assault for their treatments of history, *Amistad* is certainly not an unmitigated disaster. The film raises important questions about past injustices, addresses a number of complex historical issues, and, in some places, delivers powerful and memorable screen drama. Assessing its shortcomings should not be an occasion for partisan glee over Hollywood's familiar failure to set the historical record straight. Rather, such assessment ought to inspire a more reflective consideration of the movie's achievements, the opportunities it missed, and the reasons for its serious difficulties.[25]

Three conclusions are particularly salient. First, there are limits to artistic license. Manipulation of evidence and fictionalization are inherent in cinematic history, but these artistic adjustments can get filmmakers in trouble if they are exercised too liberally. In the case of *Amistad,* problems with small details added up noticeably. Second, it is not only historians who must be aware of the importance of generic practices. Filmmakers, too, need to be cognizant of the value of good dramatic structure for bringing history to the screen. In this case, an acclaimed director and his skilled screenwriter (David Franzoni) attempted to render a rather complex portrait of the past. By trying to cover too many facets of history briefly and presenting abundant characterizations superficially, they became easy targets for media critics and academic historians. Finally, the director, producer, and publicists promised too much in advertising their production. They claimed to have unearthed an important story neglected by history professionals, made unsubstantiated comments about the drama's significance, and quickly sent 18,000 copies of a companion study guide to teachers and students without vetting the publication. These provocations could have been remedied through the involvement of one or two knowing scholars from the early stages of story development through the final efforts to publicize the movie.

### FIERY REACTIONS TO *MISSISSIPPI BURNING*

*Mississippi Burning* also ran into some serious trouble regarding its depiction of history, despite notable achievements in dramatizing recent American history. The movie, directed by Alan Parker, deals with the search to find the men who murdered three young civil rights campaigners in Mississippi in 1964. The story begins with scenes of the criminal actions of Ku Klux Klan members, accompanied by a local deputy sheriff. Two FBI agents lead the hunt for the culprits: Alan Ward (Willem Dafoe), a Harvard-educated liberal who plans to follow the Bureau's law enforcement procedures, and Rupert Anderson (Gene Hackman), a Mississippian who realizes that formal approaches will not succeed in the tough Deep South environment. Anderson wants to fight the Ku Klux Klan with threats and intimidation, and Ward eventually recognizes that legal approaches will not be effective in bringing the murderers to justice. He lets Anderson shake down some redneck bullies, which helps crack the case.

Much of the action in the first half of the movie is authentic looking and dramatically powerful. The scenes at the beginning of the film showing the Klan closing in on three young men on a lonely country road demonstrate the terror that civil rights campaigners could experience in Mississippi during the tense summer of 1964. With attention to many historical details, Parker's film then follows the efforts of the U.S. government to challenge racial practices in the state and check the violent resistance to integration. Much like the actual developments during Mississippi's Freedom Summer, in the drama, President Lyndon B. Johnson sends U.S. Navy men to the area to search for the bodies, and a Choctaw Indian gives the agents information that leads to the discovery of the murder victims' car. In the same manner that real FBI agents searched for the murderers, Ward and Anderson place a bag over the head of a black youngster to conceal his identity and drive him through the streets of Philadelphia, Mississippi, hoping that he can point out suspects. The drama also reveals that television newsmen received physical threats from local citizens when they tried to cover the story for the national networks. The movie's title also reflects historical conditions. FBI agents used the code word MIBURN for their operation, short for "Mississippi burning." In these examples and in many other small details in the first half of the picture, Parker's movie offers a rather faithful depiction of historical conditions during the summer of 1964, a time when threats of violence seemed omnipresent in some areas of Mississippi.[26]

*Mississippi Burning*'s second hour veers so far from historical events, however, that it came under attack for fabricating the past and badly misleading viewers regarding the lessons to be drawn from the historical events. Most of the story in the second half is sheer fantasy, inspired by scriptwriter Chris Gerolmo's enthusiasm for the 1962 movie *The Man Who Shot Liberty Valance* (he liked the tale about a peaceful man who learns that violence is necessary in a confrontation with a violent criminal).[27] In the real events in Mississippi, FBI agents did not take their gloves off and combat KKK intimidation with their own form of physical threats. In fact, the FBI broke the case by offering $30,000 to informants. The Bureau certainly did not use an African-American agent to shake down one of the Mississippi bigots, as the movie shows. Indeed, critics complained about the movie's overall image of a determined FBI leading the fight against racial injustice in Mississippi. They pointed out that FBI

*Rupert Anderson (Gene Hackman) and Alan Ward (Willem Dafoe), a tough-minded southerner and a northern liberal, investigate the murder of three civil rights workers in* Mississippi Burning *(1988). In the first half of the movie, director Alan Parker portrays the story with sensitivity, but the second half sends a false message about the work of the FBI agents involved in the case and the role of violence in undermining racial oppression in the South during the 1960s. (Museum of Modern Art Film Archive)*

director J. Edgar Hoover was not sympathetic toward civil rights campaigns and had been harassing Martin Luther King, Jr. Nor did Hoover create opportunities for blacks to become FBI agents. Critics observed that black civil rights campaigners and their white allies who had come to the South that summer from northern universities were far more significant than the FBI in challenging Mississippi's segregationists, yet those figures got almost no coverage in the movie. *Mississippi Burning* gives the FBI agents, represented by Ward and Anderson, sole credit for the progress against racism.[28]

Critics pointed out, too, that the movie sends the wrong message about the importance of the news media in bringing change to the Deep South. *Mississippi Burning* suggests that journalism and public opinion had little influence on the events of 1964. Toward the end of the story, for instance, Anderson concludes that the FBI's efforts to find the killers had been frustrated because the search "turned into a show for the newsmen." The record of that volatile period reveals, however, that extensive media coverage of white atrocities and intimidation contributed significantly to the national political victories for racial justice in the South. The "show for the newsmen" in Mississippi and elsewhere was critical in giving the civil rights struggle leverage in Washington, D.C.

Like *Amistad, Mississippi Burning* ran into difficulty when the time came for members of the Academy of Motion Picture Arts and Sciences to select the best picture. *Mississippi Burning* received one of the five nominations, but it did not win the prize. During the period of decision making, the movie appeared to have little chance for victory, not only because of limitations in dramatic quality but also because of criticism regarding its depiction of history. *Mississippi Burning* seemed tainted. Well-publicized complaints about the film's distortions undermined its competitiveness for the top award.

Were the critics fair in lambasting the movie? Did they take into account the complications associated with portraying the past in dramatic form? Should they have been more forgiving in their assessment of the film's depiction of historical conditions and events?

In one respect, especially, the producer had a valid response to the complaints. Fred Zollo acknowledged that his movie did not draw attention to the role of southern African Americans and northern white civil rights campaigners in bringing change to the South. He argued, however, that he never intended to suggest that the FBI deserved all the credit for the fight against Klan violence in Mississippi. The movie portrayed only one aspect of the historic situation in 1964, said Zollo, and a significant one at that. After all, FBI investigators did succeed in identifying those responsible for the slayings.[29]

In the context of the generic practices of Hollywood-style filmmaking, Zollo's remarks make sense. His film could not provide a truly comprehensive view of the struggle against segregation in the Deep South. *Mississippi Burning* said little about the brave and important struggle of blacks in the campaigns, but that omission did not, in itself, suggest a racially insensitive view of events (as some critics charged). Zollo and his associates would have had an unwieldy script on their hands if they had attempted to tell the story of the black civil rights struggle, along with the story about the FBI investigation. The moviemakers needed to concentrate on one aspect of the complex story and make that element central in their drama. As Zollo maintained, the FBI tale was one story about the events, but not the only one. The appearance of this movie did not preclude production of another film that gave attention to the important work of African Americans in the fight against segregation. Other filmmakers were free to approach the events of 1964 with a different perspective.

Nevertheless, by grossly distorting the record of FBI activities and communicating broad lessons about the historical events that clashed with the lessons historians drew from them, *Mississippi Burning* deserved the flack it received from critics. The movie sends a false message about the work of FBI agents in

Mississippi, communicates a misleading interpretation of the way the agents caught the culprits, and delivers a false lesson about the role of violence in bringing change to the South in the 1960s. The second half of *Mississippi Burning* ventures so deeply into fantasy and moves so far from historical fact that the film rightly came under attack for abusing the public's trust. Artistic license found excessive expression in this production, creating serious flaws in a drama that had the potential to serve as a powerful and memorable example of cinematic history.[30]

### STORM OVER *THE HURRICANE*

*The Hurricane* represents another example of history from Hollywood that dramatizes the past in some impressive ways but has difficulty with historical interpretation. Norman Jewison's 1999 movie features a powerful performance by Denzel Washington as the imprisoned boxer Rubin "Hurricane" Carter. Jewison's engaging story seemed, at first, to be a strong candidate for major recognition at the Academy Awards ceremonies. Some thought that it might take the prize for Best Picture and also earn the Best Actor award for Washington. Then came an outburst of critical observations in the media regarding the movie's treatment of factual details from Carter's life. By the time nominations were mailed to Academy members in early 2000, the movie's reputation was too damaged to win a Best Picture nomination. Washington was nominated for Best Actor, but he lost to Kevin Spacey in that competition. Some commentators in the media speculated that controversy over the movie's truthfulness could have undermined Washington's chances, as well as the movie's prospects. Troubled by public carping over the movie's handling of facts, a frustrated Rubin Carter lashed out at the critics. When interviewed by the History Channel, he insisted that *The Hurricane* was largely true. The complainers, he protested, were obsessed with small, generally insignificant details.

Like *Amistad* and *Mississippi Burning*, *The Hurricane* has some marvelous dramatic moments. The film's most memorable scenes relate to Carter's eighteen years in prison. An especially emotion-packed example of his struggle behind bars occurs early in his incarceration. Proud and defiant, Carter refuses to follow the prison rules, and his rebelliousness earns him several days in dark, cramped, dungeon-like confinement. *The Hurricane* shows Carter at war with himself during these terrible days as he switches frequently between defiance and submission. Director Jewison and actor Washington pull off an extraordinary artistic coup in this segment. The scenes aim to enact Carter's thoughts and emotions, revealing the anger and frustration of a man confronting a tremendous test of will. Carter's emotional interior seems to become visible on

*In* The Hurricane *(1999), promising boxer Rubin "Hurricane" Carter (Denzel Washington) has his dreams destroyed when he is sentenced to serve three life terms for a murder he did not commit. Washington received an Oscar nomination for Best Actor for his impressive portrayal of Carter's long personal struggle. (Museum of Modern Art Film Archive)*

the screen. In time, the prisoner learns to live with his ordeal and projects a kind of dignity. Carter accepts few of the amenities offered to inmates, lives austerely, and claims that he enjoys a form of freedom within his imprisonment. Years pass, and Carter remains surprisingly in control of his sanity and dignity. Toward the end of the story, however, he breaks briefly in a tense scene when he is informed of delays associated with his legal defense. Carter pounds the window separating him from the prison visitors and in a cracking but angry voice demands that his supporters act swiftly. At this point in the drama, the hero appears ready to consider suicide if his struggle cannot soon be brought to a successful conclusion.[31]

*The Hurricane* offers tremendous breadth in its coverage of Rubin Carter's life. Through flashbacks, the movie traces Carter's trouble with the law. It shows him stealing clothing from a sidewalk display and reveals that he came under police investigation as a youngster when he was accused of cutting a man during a robbery. Most important, it portrays events associated with his arrest in 1967. When several white patrons are murdered in a New Jersey bar, the police pick up Carter and John Artis, a young admirer who is riding in a car with Carter. The evidence against the two is flimsy, but a racist cop manages to persuade two petty criminals to identify Carter and Artis as the culprits. At this point, Artis largely disappears from the drama, and Carter begins his lengthy stay in prison. During Carter's incarceration, various sympathizers protest publicly against the injustices he has suffered. Bob Dylan releases an album with a popular song that draws attention to Carter's tragedy. Eventually, a black teenager obtains a copy of Carter's autobiography, *The Sixteenth Round*. Excited by what he reads, the boy enlists the help of the people who have been caring for him and educating him—two men and a woman who live in a commune-style relationship. These four sympathizers meet with Carter in prison and declare their determination to help him win his freedom. They work diligently, gathering information about Carter's case and assisting his lawyers in preparing an appeal. Their efforts finally prove successful. A judge reviews evidence of serious misconduct on the part of the police and prosecutors who secured Carter's conviction many years before. The former boxer wins his freedom, and at the end the movie, the audience sees brief news footage of the real Rubin Carter in a moment of triumph.

Three articles among the many published criticisms of *The Hurricane* were especially damaging to the film's reputation. Selwyn Raab, whose investigative reporting years before had helped raise questions about the case, objected vigorously to the movie in an article published in the *New York Times*. Lewis M. Steel, one of the lawyers who had worked long and hard to win Carter's release, objected to the film's handling of facts in an essay published in the *Nation*. Also

*Denzel Washington as boxer Rubin "Hurricane" Carter in* The Hurricane *(1999). An article in* Sports Illustrated *challenged the movie's interpretation of Carter's success in the ring. (Museum of Modern Art Film Archive)*

damaging was a biting criticism of the movie's treatment of Carter's boxing experience. An article in *Sports Illustrated* clamed that *The Hurricane* lied in its portrayal of one of Rubin Carter's most important prizefights.

Raab complained that the movie gave inordinate credit to the Canadians for discovering evidence that freed Carter, overlooking the important role of several lawyers who worked diligently for a decade on the case without payment. Raab pointed out that the attorneys were much more vital in Carter's legal victory than the Canadians were. Carter's codefendant John Artis was an important figure in the case, Raab wrote, yet Artis practically vanishes from the drama once the two accused men are sentenced to prison. Raab observed that Artis was a more defensible hero than Carter was. Artis rejected offers to avoid a long prison sentence by falsely incriminating Carter, and many sympathizers were drawn to Artis's case because of his unblemished reputation and lack of a police record. Furthermore, argued Raab, *The Hurricane* makes too great an effort to portray Carter as a wronged man, failing to introduce evidence that hurt Carter's initial appeals in court. The real Rubin Carter was not a "model citizen" who easily "overcame persecution as a juvenile and remade himself as a boxer and civil rights advocate," said Raab. Carter had a long history of trouble with the law and had spent four years in prison for his involvement in three muggings before he was charged with murder. This sorry record damaged Carter's position in the murder case. *The Hurricane* also disregards troublesome facts that the police used against Carter, such as the discovery of a shotgun in his car on the night of the murders. Raab also claimed that some of the movie's depictions were simply "fairy tales." One is an invented incident showing the Canadian sleuths uncovering a secret diary kept by a police investigator. This supposedly forged document (an invention of the moviemakers) is intended to present incontestable proof that Carter's car was not the getaway vehicle. Another troublesome invention appears in a scene showing the Canadians losing control of their automobile because someone has tampered with it—a grievous example of Hollywood fabrication, Raab observed.[32]

Attorney Lewis M. Steel's article in the *Nation* covered some of the same ground as Raab's but gave particular attention to the movie's portrayal of a racist cop who is determined to haunt Carter through the years. The figure, called Vincent Della Pesca in the movie, is loosely fashioned after a real-life Italian police detective in New Jersey who was associated with the investigation. The movie's gross simplification, said Lewis, distorted and misrepresented important evidence about the way police authorities and prosecutors manufactured the legal assault against Carter. By creating just one mean-spirited villain, a rogue detective, the movie greatly exaggerates the misdeeds of a single man and minimizes the wrongs committed by numerous others.[33] Armyan Bernstein, producer of *The Hurricane,* defended the movie's portrayal as an understandable exercise of dramatic license. To keep the film down to a reasonable length, said Bernstein, the artists created a single highly prejudiced character to represent many different individuals who were involved in the injustices. Bernstein emphasized that the movie's principal message is that an innocent man received terribly unfair treatment. The critics' protests against this effort to represent a fundamental truth constituted "nitpicking," said Bernstein.[34]

An article in *Sports Illustrated* entitled "Ring of Truth" drew attention to *The Hurricane*'s portrayal of Rubin Carter's 1964 boxing match with Joey Giardello in Philadelphia's Convention Hall. *The Hurricane* shows Carter pummeling Giardello and clearly dominating him, yet the judges declare a fifteen-round victory for Giardello, appearing to favor the hometown white man. In the movie, crowds protest the obvious injustice, but the decision stands. The article in *Sports Illustrated,* however, observed that this depiction is untruthful. Press reporting on the fight supported the conclusion that Giardello won the fight impressively. *Sports Illustrated* indicated that this challenge to the movie's veracity came on top of many other objections to the movie's handling of facts about Carter's life.[35]

The ideas expressed in these articles received wide discussion in the media and contributed to the movie's vulnerability when Academy Award nominations and selections were under consideration. Did these influential complaints justifiably damage *The Hurricane*'s credibility? Were the objections serious enough to warrant a judgment that *The Hurricane* represented a deeply flawed example of cinematic history?

In this case, and in many other films of recent years that have been attacked on grounds of historical veracity, the verdict is not simply thumbs up or thumbs down. Some of the well-publicized objections are quite justified; others reflect inadequate consideration of the challenges involved in designing a compelling cinematic drama. But an overall conclusion suggests that the creators of *The Hurricane* engaged too cavalierly in controversial manipulations. They gambled excessively, cut many interpretive corners, oversimplified evidence, and invented characters and action without much attention to the possibility that their creativity could damage the movie's integrity. Their ambitious exercise of artistic license strengthened some dramatic elements in the story, but it enhanced entertainment value at the expense of the story's credibility. Eventually, the moviemakers paid a price (as did actor Denzel Washington and the subject of the film, Rubin Carter). *The Hurricane* lost ground publicly, suffering from the many controversies surrounding it.

Certainly some of the script inventions are regrettable. A stronger word may apply (stupid?), since these inventions clashed with the evidence so directly that they were sure to draw fire in the media. Creative license is necessary in good historical drama, but exercising this license in a manner that is likely to offend movie critics and moviegoers is extraordinarily risky. Although critics and audiences do not expect wholly realistic portrayals in Hollywood dramas, they do not want to be subjected to interpretations of the past that come under severe attack for their fundamental untruthfulness. *The Hurricane*'s presentation of the Carter-Giardello fight is such an example. This portrayal occurs early in the film and in black and white, giving it a newsreel-style appearance. It frames the film's central message about racism, establishing a thesis for the rest of the story. The scenes from the boxing match suggest that Carter was a victim of racial prejudice in his prizefight with a white man, and they suggest that bigotry continued to plague Carter for the rest of his life. Yet this fundamentally important depiction is problematic. The movie builds its thesis on a false foundation.

Similarly, objections to police detective Vincent Della Pesca are relevant. This detestable villain, played by Dan Hedaya, is so brutally prejudiced that he is hardly believable. The film clearly reveals that Della Pesca tries to frame the youthful Carter for crimes he did not commit. A more realistic depiction of a bigoted cop would portray a white detective who lacks the evidence he needs to positively identify Carter as the culprit but who nevertheless makes a strong assumption about his guilt based on race. *The Hurricane* never challenges audiences to imagine the complex origins of prejudice. It presents racial bigotry in the form of a vicious villain who knowingly sends an innocent man to prison. Della Pesca is so outrageously evil that he does not seem real.

A fair assessment of *The Hurricane*'s strengths and weaknesses, however, needs to take greater account of the challenges of designing cinematic drama than Selwyn Raab and Lewis M. Steel did in their stinging articles. Raab's discussion of *The Hurricane,* for example, contained many complaints about the movie's failure to introduce complex details of the murder case. Although Raab did not specifically claim that *The Hurricane* should have included all the diverse information addressed in his article, he certainly implied that a better film would have been sensitive to the many points he discussed. This leads one to ask what the film would have looked like if Jewison had attempted to incorporate all the details Raab presented in his article.[36]

This hypothetical drama would, for example, depict the brawls in pubs that Carter engaged in during his younger days, and the movie would reveal greater evidence of Carter's womanizing. It would show the two trials Carter faced in connection with the murders, each with a different racial composition, rather than the single trial featured in the movie. The Raab drama would trace the work of an investigator in the New Jersey Public Defender's Office (Fred W. Hogan) and a freelance writer (Richard Solomon), as well as the journalistic contributions of Raab himself, showing how their research helped bring new life to the appeals for a different verdict. Evidently, Raab's depiction would go into the complexities of the recantations by the two men who originally identified Carter and Artis as the men who ran from the bar. When dealing with later efforts to free Carter, Raab's drama would portray three principal defense lawyers rather than the two seen briefly in the movie, and it would show relatives and friends supporting Carter long before the Canadians came into the picture. Carter's real-life son and daughter, absent in the movie, would have roles, and the loyalty of Carter's wife's through much of his ordeal would receive greater attention than it did in the movie. Evidently, Raab's version would not end with the upbeat captions telling the audience that Carter now lives in Canada and runs an organization that seeks to correct judicial wrongs. Nor would it inform the audience (as *The Hurricane* does) that the poorly educated teenager in the story, Lesra Martin, obtained a law degree and now works in Canada. Raab would let the audience know that Carter married the female commune member after his release from prison but later ended all relations with her. Furthermore, Raab wants the audience to know that Carter eventually became disaffected with the commune members who helped him during his ordeal, complaining that they patronized him like a "trophy horse" so that he could help raise money for them and that they escorted him everywhere, censoring his words. Raab wants viewers to be aware that Lesra Martin was eventually expelled from the commune for dating a woman without the group's permission. Such realism, Raab suggests through his critique, would give the film a more honest perspective on Carter's life than the "feel-good screen afterword" offered in Jewison's production.

If studio executives were presented with these recommendations as part of a pitch for funds to support a movie production, they would probably show the presenter to the door. The executives would recognize that a script incorporating so much complex detail, so many principal characters, and such an abundance of critical evidence about the protagonist would result in a confusing and depressing story that would quickly lose its grip on the audience's emotions. Indeed, as *The Hurricane*'s producer observed, giving attention to the many complexities demanded by Raab and other critics would require a film three or four times the length of *The Hurricane*.

*Amistad, Mississippi Burning,* and *The Hurricane* are not complete failures as cinematic history. Each contains some impressive dramatic perspectives on the past, and each movie draws attention to significant historical problems associated with racial injustice. The familiar thumbs-down response to these movies' shortcomings is too simplistic, for there is much to applaud in their depictions. Yet the films' overall playfulness with historical evidence taints them sufficiently to destroy their integrity in the eyes of historians and critics in the media. The movies' weaknesses do not relate to one or two outrageous factual mistakes; rather, their problems emerge from an accumulation of troublesome interpretive liberties. These liberties led many reviewers to express distrust and made even enthusiasts of cinematic history uncomfortable. As such, these three movies are excellent models to consider in the assessment of history from Hollywood.

# CHAPTER THREE

# Awarding the Harry and the Brooks

Early in 1999, the History Channel presented its first Herodotus award (later nicknamed the "Harry") for the best movie of the previous year that dealt with the past. Timed to correspond closely with Hollywood's announcement of the Academy Award for Best Picture, the History Channel's version of the Oscar honors the Greek writer who is often referred to as the father of history. Competition in the field of cinematic history was keen that year, for all five films nominated by the Academy of Motion Picture Arts and Sciences for Best Picture of 1998 were historical in some respect. Both the History Channel and the Academy selected the same five nominees: *Shakespeare in Love, Saving Private Ryan, The Thin Red Line, Elizabeth,* and *Life Is Beautiful.* Using criteria different from those employed by members of the Academy, the History Channel's judges, led by host Sander Vanocur, chose *Saving Private Ryan* for the Herodotus (members of the Academy selected *Shakespeare in Love* for the Oscar).

Which criteria should be applied in awarding a Harry or any other prize identifying an outstanding work of cinematic history? Do the qualities that make *Saving Private Ryan* impressive apply to other strong examples of the genre? Is there a particular form of achievement that characterizes all great works of cinematic history, or do various movies offer different kinds of contributions? In contrast, what constitutes a terrible example of the genre? In which ways do some movies fail to communicate a thoughtful picture of the past? Which films mishandle history egregiously? Do many works of cinematic history qualify as unmitigated disasters, outrageously fictitious and untruthful interpretations? Might we also award a prize for terrible filmed history? With tongue in cheek, perhaps we should call this award for poor screen history the "Brooks" (recalling Mel Brooks's hilarious 1981 spoof of the historical genre, *The History of the World, Part 1*).

The discussion that follows addresses questions concerning merit by focusing on the achievements and shortcomings of specific motion pictures. It proffers ideas about ways to judge accomplishments in cinematic history through the identification of specific models of success and failure. These judgments are, of course, subjective. Scholars and film artists do not agree on specific standards for rendering history on the silver screen, and reviews of cinematic history in publications and on television reflect diverse opinions. Professional historians themselves are often sharply divided in their judgments. In the case of *Amistad* (1997), for instance, Eric Foner, a distinguished scholar of mid-nineteenth-century American history, criticized Spielberg's movie as a work of "historical fiction."[1] Another highly respected scholar of nineteenth-century American history, Bertram Wyatt-Brown, considered the movie "brilliant, sophisticated, and moving."[2] A student of historical film can find many other examples of contrasting commentaries about Hollywood's treatment of the past. Teachers, scholars, commentators in the mass media, and representatives of the public often disagree sharply about whether a film looks like a candidate for the Herodotus or the Brooks.

Recognition of the subjective quality of these judgments suggests the importance of prefacing this commentary with a caveat. The standards outlined here are personal; they do not represent universally accepted measures of approval or disapproval. Other observers may view the films under study quite differently. Still, our discussions of cinematic history are better advanced through identification of specific examples that give focus to the debates. A consideration of cinematic history is better grounded when it moves from the abstract to the specific. With this precautionary note in mind, the following assessment addresses familiar questions about impressive and regretful Hollywood productions.

## THE GROWING PROMINENCE OF "FACTION"

Many who express an interest in film and history imagine that historians have little difficulty identifying truly outrageous examples of history in the movies. Those who are highly suspicious of Hollywood's attempts to present the past as entertainment believe that numerous movies should be lambasted for grossly manipulating and misrepresenting the historical record. When a historian attempts to cite specific examples of such thoroughly wrongheaded interpretations from Hollywood, however, not many productions come to mind. Few movies qualify as comprehensive failures. Most of them, especially those produced in recent decades, contain some redeeming qualities as well as considerable shortcomings.

As illustrated in the previous chapter, cinema that comes under a good deal of public criticism for taking artistic liberties can also be praised for offering some intriguing dramatic perspectives. *Amistad* presented the slave trade in graphic form, *Mississippi Burning* (1988) gave a memorable portrayal of the dangers that civil rights campaigners faced in Mississippi in the early 1960s, and *The Hurricane* (1999) presented a gripping story of one man's struggle in the face of racial injustice. These and other flawed examples of cinematic history offer intelligent and sensitive portrayals, along with problematic doses of fiction.

The task of directing sharp attacks against Hollywood productions has become more difficult in recent years, because filmmakers have developed strategies to protect their flanks from the arrows shot by history-minded critics. Movie artists have developed narrative strategies that are less vulnerable to assault by the fact checkers. In recent years, they have produced a number of films that represent an art form that can be identified as "faction." Faction-based movies spin highly fictional tales that are loosely based on actualities. Their stories identify some real people, events, or situations from the past but blend these details into invented fables. Often the leading characters in faction are fictional people who represent a composite of several historical figures or who are largely invented to advance the drama. Drawing inspiration from myths and legends as well as traditional practices of cinematic history, the creators of faction employ history in a manner that is less subject to debate over veracity than are the biopics or historical epics of earlier years. From beginning to end, these movies send only a nebulous message about truth claims. Faction references history but does not represent it specifically.

Three popular movies of 2000 dealt with the past through faction: *Gladiator, U-571,* and *The Patriot.* Each film can be assaulted for bending the historical evidence radically in order to design an entertaining story. Yet each motion picture can also be defended as undisguised faction, a highly creative perspective on history that views the past through metaphor rather than through the portrayal of specific situations, events, and people.

*Gladiator* exhibits tremendous playfulness with the historical evidence, and it is designed as an action-adventure picture rather than a serious commentary on the past. It tells the story of a bold and talented Roman general named Maximus (Russell Crowe) who is betrayed when Emperor Marcus Aurelius (Richard Harris) dies. The new Roman leader, Commodus (Joaquim Phoenix), is jealous of Maximus's popularity and arranges to have this hero-competitor sent into slavery. Maximus trains as a gladiator in a distant Roman province and becomes the leader of a successful fighting band. Eventually, he and a few of his warrior cohorts appear in the Roman Colosseum. When Commodus discovers the identity of the mysterious star gladiator, he arranges to fight him in a public confrontation in the great arena. First, however, he commissions agents to wound Maximus. Not surprisingly (for moviegoers), the

*Maximus (Russell Crowe), a great general who is sold into slavery and trained as a gladiator, fights for his life in* Gladiator *(2000). Director Ridley Scott exercises plenty of dramatic license in this entertaining work of "faction." (Museum of Modern Art Film Archive)*

hero manages to overcome his physical handicap, and in the film's climactic fight, Maximus kills the emperor, although Maximus, too, dies in the struggle. *Gladiator* suggests that Commodus's defeat will pave the way to republican government and greater freedom in Rome.

Ridley Scott's highly entertaining movie contains some truthful elements and plenty of fiction. *Gladiator* references a number of historical actualities. Somewhat like the events depicted at the beginning of the movie, Roman legions did penetrate the southern reaches of northern Europe, confronting fierce Germanic tribes. There was, of course, an intelligent and respected Roman leader named Marcus Aurelius who died during the Danubian wars. Commodus, who took his place, was a megalomaniac and an exploitative leader, somewhat like the movie's egotistical emperor (the real figure renamed Rome Colonia Commodiana). The emperor's sister Lucilla unsuccessfully conspired with senators to bring about her brother's murder, as did the character in the movie. The historical Commodus did, indeed, enter the ring at the Roman Colosseum to do battle, and eventually, a wrestler sent by his adversaries dispatched him. Maximus is essentially a Hollywood invention, although he somewhat resembles Septimius Severus, who became emperor several months after the death of Commodus. Severus claimed to be Marcus Aurelius's son.[3]

*Gladiator* cannot be dismissed simply as cinematic mythmaking. Although it is certainly a lively, action-oriented fairy tale in most respects, the story contains enough historical details to qualify it as a work of faction. The movie's connection to the past consists of more than just occasional references to Roman names and events. *Gladiator* also raises authentic questions about life in the days of the Roman Empire. In hokey but nevertheless meaningful ways, the movie suggests that absolute power can corrupt absolutely. Its bad-emperor, good-republican morality tale sends a democratic message about the superiority of representational government over authoritarian rule.[4]

We cannot easily place *Gladiator* on a list of Hollywood's most outrageous history-oriented dramas. By delivering faction, director Ridley Scott protected his movie from serving as a convenient target for the defenders of Clio. Media critics who reviewed *Gladiator* easily recognized the film as a lively form of entertainment that often deals with history through metaphor rather than fact.

*U-571* came under greater fire for historical veracity than *Gladiator* did, because some critics thought the movie intended to send a realistic message about an important breakthrough in military intelligence during World War II. Jonathan Mostow's film tells the story of an American submarine crew charged with entering a damaged German U-boat and removing a machine used to send coded messages. Capturing this equipment could prove enormously valuable to the Allies in prosecuting the war, allowing American and British mathematicians to decipher enemy messages and learn the Nazis' attack plans. Mostow's movie shows American navy commandos seizing control of German U-boat number 571. When an enemy attack at sea then destroys the Americans' submarine, the movie's heroes have to escape on the badly damaged U-boat. The Americans eventually succeed in torpedoing enemy vessels and delivering the valuable coding device to U.S. military authorities.

During the brief time *U-571* was the top-grossing film in the United States, the media gave considerable coverage to British criticisms of the picture's treatment of history. Commentators in the British press complained that the film credited American sailors with seizing the tremendously important coding device, playing fast and loose with the historical facts. It was actually a British navy crew that carried out this mission, and it accomplished the task before the Americans formally entered World War II. In typical Hollywood fashion, said these British observers, *U-571* made the Americans look like the true and only heroes.[5]

These complaints from British critics do not amount to much, because the film was clearly marketed as a work of faction. *U-571* references history but never proposes to dramatize it specifically; its story is clearly invented. In general ways, the movie presents conditions that are essentially true. Some elements of the story relate to the experiences of various submarine crews during World War II, and, as the movie suggests, the Allies were desperate to capture the secret German equipment. Submarine warfare was highly risky, as the movie shows, and sometimes sub commanders dropped their vessels to dangerous levels to avoid depth charges, as seen in *U-571*.[6] Although Mostow's movie contains these elements of realism, it lacks the extraordinary verisimilitude of Wolfgang Petersen's brilliant movie on German submarine warfare, *Das Boot* (The Boat). *U-571* is modeled on Petersen's classic, but it lacks the gritty authenticity of his claustrophobic picture of troubled life under the sea. Furthermore, *U-571* presents its story of sub warfare in Hollywood fashion. Like the westerns that show the hero and the villain facing each other in the street of a frontier town, *U-571* portrays the Americans in combat with a single destroyer and a single German sub. The movie gives no hint of the more typical situation in World War II of surface ships of war operating in convoys and submarine wolf packs working in concert to engage several undersea vessels at once.[7]

As for the specific complaint about *U-571*'s error in giving the Americans credit for capturing the coding device, Mostow comfortably evaded the charge. A trailer at the end of the movie briefly describes three real-life incidents during World War II in which the Allies succeeded in grabbing enigma machines from German vessels. The first two efforts identified in captions pertain to successes of the British navy. The third example, coming much later than the first two, involved the U.S. Navy. By framing *U-571*'s story with this announcement, Mostow is essentially saying to the audience: "This is faction. We have told our tale from the American point of view because both U.S. and international audiences are accustomed to viewing American heroes in Hollywood films. In case you are interested, though, here are a few references to the actual incidents from history that inspired the story. No offense, Brits. As you can see, we are identifying your important contributions in this concluding announcement."

British sensitivities were aroused again a short time later when *The Patriot* made its appearance in movie theaters. Mel Gibson's inspiring tale of a tough Carolina widower, Benjamin Martin, reluctantly choosing to join the fight for American independence upset some British commentators and also drew criticism from Americans who sympathized with the British. The complainers observed correctly that *The Patriot* gives a highly biased account of the people involved in the American Revolution. It presents Benjamin Martin (Mel Gibson) and other Americans in very positive terms, and virtually all the British characters are portrayed unflatteringly. Colonel William Tavington (Jason Issacs) is a bloodthirsty killer (the characterization exaggerates the ugly deeds of the

*Lifting the flag of a new nation, Benjamin Martin (Mel Gibson) battles the British in* The Patriot *(2000). The Martin character resembles historical figures such as Francis Marion, Thomas Sumter, and Andrew Pickens, as well as familiar characters typically seen in the Hollywood war genre. (Museum of Modern Art Film Archive)*

real-life Banastre Tarleton, leader of England's Green Dragoons), and Lord General Charles Cornwallis (Tom Wilkinson) reluctantly goes along with a campaign of terror against the colonial civilian population. Captain Wilkins (Adam Baldwin), an American who serves the British as a loyalist military leader, comes across as weak and traitorous.

Like *Gladiator* and *U-571*, however, *The Patriot* is a blended work of faction, and it never hints that it presents even a semiauthentic picture of the war between the colonials and the redcoats. The movie refers to some real situations; it shows a large-scale military confrontation that resembles the American actions at Cowpens or at Guilford Courthouse, and in the end it relates the particulars of Cornwallis's defeat at Yorktown.[8] But Robert Rodat's script creates a fictitious hero in Benjamin Martin, although some of his guerrilla warfare resembles the tactics of Francis Marion, the "Swamp Fox," and his position as colonial-turned-warrior parallels, to a degree, the lives of Thomas Sumter and Andrew Pickens. For the most part, though, Rodat builds his story in the style of his earlier historical drama, *Saving Private Ryan*. *The Patriot* features many imagined characters based loosely on both the historical record and the war movie genre. Rodat's tale about a strong and once-violent figure who is loath to pick up a weapon draws inspiration, too, from the old Hollywood westerns. *The Patriot* is designed as an action-packed story about a heroic man's struggle for honor, revenge, and freedom. From beginning to end, it serves as a work of faction, a concocted story that liberally references historical figures, events, and situations.[9]

Films such as *Gladiator*, *U-571*, and *The Patriot* do not make good targets for protests against the abuses of cinematic history. These works of faction do not place real people or real events at their core. Invented characters and situations dominate the foreground; historical figures and actions appear principally in the background or at the periphery of the story. As such, these films are less vulnerable to the fact checkers than are movies that focus on specific figures from the history books, such as *Patton*, *Gandhi*, *Schindler's List*, or *Nixon*.

## IDENTIFYING CANDIDATES FOR THE BROOKS

Movies that directly characterize actual people and events from the past serve as more interesting cases for judging the problems associated with cinematic history. Films that present a number of recognizable names as major characters in a drama or that give detailed attention to specific events and situations from the past are more likely to excite attention and controversy. These stories come under greater scrutiny regarding historical representation than do films that are transparently faction oriented. When their characterizations contrast sharply with the historical record or modern-day interpretations of that record, history-minded observers often register strong protests. Critics express recognition of a filmmaker's need to exercise artistic license, but they maintain that some manipulations are unacceptably egregious. A few films test their tolerance levels to the breaking point, and such movies qualify for the unwelcome Brooks.

Gary Gallagher, an accomplished Civil War historian at the University of Virginia, has identified such a movie in a class he teaches on the war. Gallagher asks his students to evaluate the way a number of popular Hollywood films deal with the Civil War period. His students' analyses of diverse films such as *So Red the Rose*, *Horse Soldiers*, *Gettysburg*, *Shenandoah*, *Friendly Persuasion*, *Gone with the Wind*, *Glory*, *Andersonville*, and *The Undefeated* concluded that all Hollywood productions take liberties with the facts and simplify issues. Many of the films advance interpretations that are no longer popular in academic circles, but much of this cinema stimulates the public's thinking about the past in useful ways. One movie in particular, however, is so cavalier in its treatment of the facts that it serves as a good example of outrageously poor cinematic history. The Civil War movie that received the strongest criticism in Gallagher's class was *Santa Fe Trail*.[10]

Director Michael Curtiz's 1940 movie makes an interesting case study as one of the worst productions of cinematic history from Hollywood. What are the problems with *Santa Fe Trail*'s historical depictions? Are the distortions outrageous? Does the film contain redeeming qualities? How can we judge the filmmaker's exercise of artistic license?

Whatever this movie's difficulties with history, its entertainment value cannot be denied. *Santa Fe Trail* is fun to watch. Curtiz's fast-paced, action-packed flick is consistently lively, exciting, amusing, and interesting. It features an intriguing story and a notable cast, including luminaries such as Errol Flynn, Ronald Reagan, Van Heflin, and Raymond Massey.

The movie is much less impressive in its handling of history, and gross manipulations of the record appear throughout. *Santa Fe Trail* begins by showing many of the great Civil War generals graduating together in the West Point class of 1854, among them Jeb Stuart, George Armstrong Custer, Philip Sheridan, George Pickett, James Longstreet, and John Hood. Clearly this is Hollywood, not history, for the men attended the academy in widely varying years. Custer (Ronald Reagan), a principal character in the movie, was a fifteen-year-old Ohio farm boy in 1854. He entered West Point in 1857 and did not graduate until the summer of 1861, making him ineligible for many of the U.S. Army activities *Santa Fe Trail* shows him participating in. Jeb Stuart (played by Errol Flynn), the hero of the story, actually graduated in 1854.

The movie then concocts a story about some of these heroes fighting John Brown in Kansas and at Harpers Ferry, Virginia (now West Virginia). In one instance, Stuart dons civilian clothes and sneaks into a Kansas town to learn about Brown's plans to commit violence (this is a complete fabrication). Brown's men capture Stuart and take him to their secret hideout. Eventually, Stuart's military buddies free him in an assault, but Brown and some of his supporters escape (another Hollywood fairy tale). Rader, a totally fictional character from the West Point class of 1954 (played by Van Heflin), is a radical abolitionist who joins Brown's guerrillas but eventually loses enthusiasm for the cause because he does not receive the pay he had been promised. Rader turns up again as a participant in Brown's assault on the U.S. armory at Harpers Ferry. This time, he is secretly working against the guerrillas, trying to convince Brown to wait for reinforcements so that Robert E. Lee will have time to arrive with his troops. This action, too, is pure fiction. At least the movie's final scenes bear some resemblance to history; they show Lee commanding a successful assault on Brown's forces at Harpers Ferry. At the end of the story,

*In* Santa Fe Trail *(1940), U.S. military officers speak with Carl Rader, a devious character played by Van Heflin. At the center-left is Ronald Reagan as George Armstrong Custer, and at the center-right is Errol Flynn as Jeb Stuart. To the far right is Raymond Massey playing the radical abolitionist John Brown.* Santa Fe Trail, *a fast paced and entertaining film, is so replete with fabrications, misleading messages, and apologies for slavery that it mangles history. (Museum of Modern Art Film Archive)*

Brown faces death at the hangman's noose, as he did in real life, and he makes a speech using some of the language that appears in the history books.[11]

*Santa Fe Trail*'s depiction of the controversy over slavery contrasts sharply with the historical record. Some of the most ridiculous statements come from Virginian Jeb Stuart, who announces that his state has been "considering a resolution to abolish slavery for a long time." Perhaps the movie is referring to proposals for gradual emancipation that were presented in Virginia back in the early 1830s and soundly defeated. Stuart also claims that Virginians sense that the institution of slavery is morally wrong. "All they ask is time," he explains. The movie suggests that in the late 1850s, southerners, including slaveholders, were moving in the direction of complete emancipation of the slaves. It claims that white southerners intended to abolish slavery in their own time and in their own way (this was certainly not the position of the state's leading politicians). Furthermore, *Santa Fe Trail* portrays John Brown as the man who wrecked the Virginians' dream of peaceful resolution. In making this case, the movie shows no evidence of the extremes to which southern pro-slavery arguments had moved by the late 1850s, nor does it reveal that many defenders of slavery were contemplating secession well before Brown's violent actions at Osawatomie, Kansas, and at Harpers Ferry. The film simply makes Brown look like the man most responsible for the start of the Civil War.[12]

*Santa Fe Trail*'s portrayal of African-American attitudes is also outrageous. Blacks in the story seem hesitant about accepting freedom. One African American observes that providing freedom for the blacks is not enough. How are the freedmen to obtain food and shelter? he asks. In this scene, the film promotes a perspective on emancipation similar to the position of many apologists for slavery. Defenders of the institution often warned that blacks were unprepared to handle the complicated responsibilities associated with emancipation and that many of them deeply appreciated the care they received from paternalistic masters. This issue is addressed in another scene when a black woman complains about the difficulties of prospering in Kansas. "If this here's freedom, I want none of it," she declares. A black man then states his aim to achieve an easy life. He says that he hopes to go back to Texas (then a slave state) so that he can "set till kingdom come."

In sum, *Santa Fe Trail* is so replete with fabrications, misleading messages, and apologies for slavery that it mangles history. It does not use fictitious characters at the center of its drama in the manner of modern-day faction. The movie portrays specific individuals from the Civil War era in detail and shows them taking a variety of specific and important actions that never occurred. These actions represent gratuitous flourishes; they do not serve any larger interpretive purpose, nor do they symbolize important truths about the past in a metaphorical way. Instead, these distortions appear in the story simply to enhance its entertainment value. *Santa Fe Trail* looks like a good candidate for the Brooks.

Back in 1940, movie critics gave much less attention to the liberties taken in cinematic history than they do today. *Santa Fe Trail* did not come under much criticism for its historical treatment of people, events, situations, or issues. In the present, such freewheeling manipulation of details would probably create considerable controversy in the media (unless the film was so well advertised as an exercise in comedy or parody that it could easily be associated with cinematic humor). Any Hollywood production that hinted of seriousness and thoughtfulness while morphing evidence in the fashion of *Santa Fe Trail* would serve as grist for the talk-show mills on C-NBC or CNN.

*Santa Fe Trail* is a good example of Hollywood's loose relationship with history in numerous productions of the late 1930s and early 1940s. The star of *Santa Fe Trail*, Errol Flynn, was the principal actor in many of these films.

Flynn had the right persona for hero-oriented adventure stories. He was an ideal man of action, a handsome, athletic-looking figure who could stand in for American and British men of derring-do. He also exuded a comic quality. Flynn looked like he was having fun playing adventure-loving gentlemen. He appeared to relish a good sword fight or a challenge to win the heart of a beautiful and noble lady. In this respect, Flynn's appearance gave dimension and color to Hollywood's history. His involvement suggested that these tales were highly embellished, that they had been fashioned to give the famous actor the freedom to perform his familiar cinematic tricks of combat and courtship.

Other history-oriented Flynn films of the era feature similar playfulness with the historical facts. *The Charge of the Light Brigade* (1936) creates a totally fictional explanation for the suicidal actions of the British brigade. In *The Private Lives of Elizabeth and Essex* (1939), Essex (Flynn) has a romantic relationship with Queen Elizabeth, even though the real Essex was thirty-four years younger than the Virgin Queen. Another Flynn film, *The Sea Hawk* (1940), takes many liberties with historical interpretation, but the movie is less vulnerable to charges of distortion. There, Michael Curtiz features a fictional character at the center of his story. Flynn plays a dashing privateer who resembles Sir Francis Drake and other English captains who menaced the Spanish fleets in the sixteenth century.

Artistic license is exercised with particular abandon in another Flynn movie, *They Died with Their Boots On* (1942). This entertaining and humorous action-adventure picture rivals *Santa Fe Trail* in its distortions of history. Raoul Walsh's biopic about George Armstrong Custer follows the experiences of the famous general from his time as a cadet at West Point through his actions in the Civil War to his death fighting Indians at Little Big Horn. Flynn is both comic and heroic as Custer. He is an energetic and fun-loving military man who demonstrates impressive leadership skills. Custer is also moralistic. He fights alcohol consumption, struggles against corruption in the army, and attempts to protect the Indians from greedy railroad developers and gold seekers. Errol Flynn's character provided a useful cinematic icon when the United States was on the brink of war and Americans needed military heroes. *They Died with Their Boots On* offered them one from the history books.

Unfortunately, Hollywood's Custer contrasts sharply with the figure that appears in the historical records. Throughout the movie, the man and the important events in his life are grossly manipulated in the interest of entertainment and hero construction. These distortions have a cumulative effect. By the end of the film, they create a picture that seriously misrepresents the man and his times. Shortcomings in the movie's depictions are not simply related to the small details (for instance, Mrs. Custer did not meet her husband at West

*George Armstrong Custer (Errol Flynn) fires at Indians during his last stand in* They Died with Their Boots On *(1942). Raoul Walsh's characterization of Custer satisfied Americans' need for heroic military images during early U.S. involvement in World War II. (Museum of Modern Art Film Archive)*

Point, and General Custer never met the Indian leader Crazy Horse). The difficulties pertain to major distortions.[13]

Most important, George Armstrong Custer was not the great friend of American Indians suggested by the movie. *They Died with Their Boots On* shows Custer's efforts to protect the Sioux Indians of the Black Hills, trying to keep American settlers out of Sioux territory and working to prevent gold prospectors from invading the Indians' land. Custer's efforts are undermined by evil land developers who spread rumors about a gold rush. After Custer's death, his wife, Libbie, convinces General Philip Sheridan and President Ulysses S. Grant to honor her husband's request. The government must "make good its promise to Chief Crazy Horse," says Libbie. "The Indians must be protected in their right to an existence in their own country." Sheridan—the one who supposedly claimed that the only good Indian was a dead one—tells Libbie that he and President Grant will support her husband's cause. "Come my dear," says the general affirmatively. "Your soldier won his last battle after all." This cinematic lie could hardly be more glaring, for the real Custer was certainly not a crusading protector of Native Americans. He led the massacre of more than a hundred Indian men, women, and children at Washita in 1868, helped instigate the gold rush in the Sioux's sacred Black Hills, encouraged white settlers to come to the region, and marched his troops to the Little Big Horn to crush Indian resistance.[14]

The movie's effort to portray Custer as one of the Native Americans' best friends forces an extraordinary distortion of events in the film's portrayal of the battle at Little Big Horn. To make Custer look good as he leads his men into the terrible disaster, *They Died with Their Boots On* shows the hero *knowingly* facing a massacre. Custer consciously engages in a suicidal mission and tells one of the movie's villains that his soldiers will ride "to hell or to glory; it depends on your point of view." Custer's purpose is not the historic one: to pump bullets into hundreds of surprised Indians. Hollywood's hero appears to go down with his men in a blaze of glory just to make a point with the corrupt and powerful figures in Washington, D.C.

If a movie offered such a playful view of history to twenty-first-century audiences, it would probably suffer relentless attacks from critics in the press and on television talk shows. Movie reviewers in today's mass media are far less tolerant of gross distortions than their counterparts were in the early 1940s. When today's cinema places specific figures from the past at the center of a drama (such as Custer, Sheridan, or Crazy Horse), rather than fictional characters, critics often assault the portrayals. Furthermore, today's reviewers have many more venues to deliver their attacks—cable television channels, radio stations, publications, and the Internet. For Americans of 1941, however, *They Died with Their Boots On* did not excite lively disagreement over historical interpretation. It represented, instead, a delightfully entertaining and inspiring historical epic starring one of Hollywood's favorite action-adventure heroes, Errol Flynn. And like many other Flynn pictures of the era, the movie mangled history.

Filmmakers today take similar liberties with history, but they promote their stories as works of faction rather than the specific representations common in Errol Flynn's adventure pictures. Modern-day cinematic history avoids detailed portraits of noted individuals from the past and offers fewer biographies of famous figures such as the ones depicted in Flynn movies: Queen Elizabeth, Jeb Stuart, George Armstrong Custer. Today's Hollywood often privileges faction, which is less vulnerable to attack on the basis of historical accuracy. In faction, the central characters are fictional, and the actual historical figures are essentially minor or background figures in the story. Biopics continue to appear among the cinematic history entries, such as the British-made *Elizabeth* (1998), directed by Shekhar Kapur. Still, faction seems likely to remain popular as the filmmaker's safer strategy for evading the slings and arrows of media critics and historians.

If we exclude parody, it is surprisingly difficult to identify cinematic history that consistently lacks integrity in its treatment of the past. As we have observed, many Hollywood films contain abuses of fact that are worthy of objection, but these movies often feature some commendable perspectives on the past as well. There are not many movies like *Santa Fe Trail* or *They Died with Their Boots On,* which can be slammed as outrageous forays into history with real historical figures as their principal characters. And even these two films exude such a comic lightness in their treatments that harsh critics need to exercise a degree of caution. *Santa Fe Trail* and *They Died with Their Boots On* look at history with tongue in cheek, strongly suggesting that the portrayals do not represent serious examinations of the past.

Because of my duties as film commentator for the History Channel, I have become acutely aware of the difficulty of rendering a forcefully negative assessment of history from Hollywood. Each time I received an assignment to evaluate a motion picture for the channel's *Movies in Time* series, I wondered if I would get the opportunity to enjoy some good fun drubbing a film. Sooner or later, I thought, a motion picture would come up for discussion that was so egregious in its treatment of the facts that it deserved unrelenting condemnation. I thought that I could identify such a failed film as dead on arrival or, worse yet, as a "dangerous" cinematic commentary because of its gross distortions. Perhaps I could castigate the filmmakers for "brainwashing" America's youth. In every case, however, I found that the film under consideration had at least some redeeming qualities, even the highly problematic ones. Our on-camera interviews could address a movie's fabrications and failings, but I saw a need to take account of its accomplishments as well.

My review of *Jim Thorpe, All American* (1951), for example, noted that the film presents an old-fashioned, strongly positive view of the way white instructors tried to force assimilation on Indian students at schools such as the one at Carlisle. Current research has raised many questions about the way administrators and teachers tried to wash away Native American cultural traditions in such environments, I observed, and the movie's treatment of the issue would certainly draw criticism from modern-day scholars. Nevertheless, Hollywood's story about Jim Thorpe is a thoughtful consideration of the struggles and personal injustices experienced by a talented young man of minority background. The film gives more serious consideration to the problems faced by Native Americans than many other popular flicks about Indians do.[15]

Probably the worst historical film I evaluated on *Movies in Time* was *Young Dillinger* (1965). As mentioned previously, this quickly and cheaply constructed

*Kevin Costner stars as New Orleans district attorney Jim Garrison in Oliver Stone's JFK (1991). Some critics lambasted the movie for its distortion of historical evidence, but others praised it for the bold way it raised questions about recent American political history. (Museum of Modern Art Film Archive)*

production gives little attention to historical authenticity in its sets, costuming, or locales. Yet *Young Dillinger* manages to give audiences some perspectives on the notorious criminal that are basically true. It realistically portrays the life of gang members on the run, and it reveals how Dillinger's life became more constricted as law enforcement agents spread their dragnet against him.[16]

In this regard, it is appropriate to mention the Hollywood movie that often excites the most intense condemnation in conversations about Hollywood's abuses. Often, when individuals attempt to name a film that is particularly controversial in its handling of historical evidence, they point to *JFK* (1991). Oliver Stone's movie excited protest for distorting the historical record and for taking interpretive liberties. Critics note that Stone mixed actual and fictional footage in a confusing manner, leaving audiences puzzled about the distinctions between fact and fiction. They complain that many young viewers were not aware of the trickery and, after seeing the movie, concluded that there really had been a conspiracy in the Kennedy assassination. These critics are outraged that naïve moviegoers base their judgments on the false "evidence" featured in Stone's mischievous cinema.[17]

To be sure, many of the messages in *JFK* are misleading, and the preponderance of available evidence still suggests that Lee Harvey Oswald acted alone.

*Jim Garrison (Kevin Costner) at the grave of President John F. Kennedy. Oliver Stone's provocative secondary thesis in JFK (1991) is that the United States probably would not have become so involved in Vietnam's affairs if Kennedy had lived. (Museum of Modern Art Film Archive)*

Stone's thesis about a conspiracy is supported primarily by highly questionable speculation, not fact. Nevertheless, Stone's movie gives expression to many doubts about the Warren Commission's report on the assassination, questions that have motivated research by members of Congress and investigative journalists in the years since the tragic event of November 22, 1963.[18] Stone's movie dramatizes actions that conspiracy theorists imagine could have occurred, including a number of the descriptions in Jim Marrs's lengthy tome on the assassination, *Crossfire*.[19] Some historians praise Stone for his bold, experimental approach to historical investigation. Robert A. Rosenstone has been among *JFK*'s most vociferous supporters. Rosenstone argues that the movie challenges audiences to revision history. "If it is part of the burden of the historical work to make us rethink how we got to where we are and to make us question values that we and our leaders and our nation live by," writes Rosenstone, "then whatever its flaws, *JFK* has to be among the most important works of American history ever to appear on the screen."[20]

*JFK* is not indisputably wrongheaded in all its propositions. For example, Stone's important secondary thesis is that President John F. Kennedy would not have gotten America as deeply involved in the conflict in Vietnam as Lyndon B. Johnson did. Historians still debate this idea vigorously, and a number of prominent interpreters of the Kennedy years, including some who were close advisers to Kennedy, such as Arthur M. Schlesinger, Jr., and Robert S. McNamara, generally agree with Stone about Kennedy's likely actions in Vietnam, had he lived.[21] Other messages in Stone's movie, such as the director's concern about America's lost innocence in the years after Kennedy's death, address substantive matters that interest many citizens and scholars. We should note, too, that the innovative framework of Stone's movie, with its quickly paced experimental design, draws attention to itself in a unique way. Stone constantly reminds viewers that they are watching a movie, and his film frequently challenges them to question the ways they have come to "know" history.[22]

Most cinematic dramas, especially the productions of recent decades, offer something useful to the viewing public. Few modern films can simply be relegated to the trash heap. The familiar assumption that Hollywood productions often communicate nothing of value regarding history is hard to support on close examination of individual films. In view of the mixed record of productions from Hollywood, it seems that our assessments of cinematic history need to move beyond knee-jerk cynicism. We should face the imposing challenge of identifying both the successes and the failures of specific productions. By fine-tuning our critical faculties, we engage in more realistic discussions of the opportunities and limits of dramatic license.

## THE DRAMATIC DOLDRUMS

We can profit, too, from recognizing another kind of failure in cinematic history. Problems with the genre are not confined to factual errors or abuses of artistic liberties. Some films suffer from a different kind of shortcoming: they disappoint audiences or fail to attract them because they do not deliver exciting drama. This kind of misfire is unfortunate, because Hollywood addresses specific historical subjects on a very limited basis. Rarely does the U.S. motion picture industry release more than one drama in a decade that deals with a specific event or person from the past. If a production about a subject turns out to be a dud, Hollywood is unlikely to support another film on the theme for several decades (indeed, disappointing box office receipts can scare creative talent away from films on related subjects). Thus, bad cinematic history is not confined to messy treatment of the facts. Failure can also appear in the form of boring drama.

Some films drag so heavily in their dramatic development that viewers find themselves glancing at their watches or dozing off. Consider, for instance, the difficulties many viewers faced watching three movies on topics that should have served as the foundation for lively, engaging dramas: ranchers versus settlers in the American West, the making of the atomic bomb, and the struggle to convict the vicious murderer of a civil rights leader. In each case, the viewing experience proved taxing for many moviegoers.

*Heaven's Gate* (1980) traces class conflict between the powerful Stock Growers' Association in Wyoming and the humble Eastern European immigrants who tried to settle in the region. The movie references the famous Johnson County wars of 1892 and includes characters similar to "Cattle" Kate Watson and her boyfriend, two figures from western history who were hanged for cattle rustling long before the events depicted in the movie.

Director Michael Cimino spent a fortune (by 1980 standards) to give his movie an authentic look. His attention to detail is evident in the opening scenes of a graduation ceremony at Harvard University, with hundreds of extras in nineteenth-century apparel populating the campus. For other scenes, Cimino had trains rebuilt for brief appearances, covered a vast area with sod, and staged huge battles with more than a thousand extras dressed in period costumes.

Despite the attraction of western history providing background for the story and millions of dollars committed to the visual details, *Heaven's Gate* delivers terribly boring entertainment. Over the first two hours of the lengthy movie, almost nothing happens to excite viewer interest. By the time the action picks up in the final hour, the audience hardly cares about the fate of the principals. Many of the characters look like stereotypes rather than real-life figures (among them, the cattlemen's villainous leader, played by Sam Waterston). Not surprisingly, both critics and moviegoers lambasted Cimino for his costly flop. *Heaven's Gate* is now well recognized in Hollywood as one of the most embarrassing examples of directorial hubris. Evidently, Cimino was so cocky after his Best Picture award for *The Deer Hunter* (1978) that he thought he could fashion a story single-handedly and demand that the film's financial officers satisfy his every whim. Cimino's defeat was unfortunate for cinematic history as well as for Hollywood investors. An intelligently crafted drama about the Johnson County wars could have stimulated the public's thinking about life and times in the American West.[23]

*Fat Man and Little Boy* (1990) represents another failed attempt to dramatize a significant aspect of history. Roland Jaffe's movie traces the development of the secret Manhattan Project during World War II, in which scientists worked to build the first atomic bombs at Los Alamos, New Mexico, under the direction of General Leslie Groves. Paul Newman plays the general, and Dwight Schultz portrays the top scientist in the group, J. Robert Oppenheimer. *Fat Man and Little Boy* attempts to create dramatic interest in some real-life situations, such as the scientists' disagreements over whether the bomb should be dropped on Japan (it had been developed in response to the Nazis' research on the atom). It also tries to enhance the story with a fictional episode depicting a love affair between a young scientist and a nurse; eventually, the scientist becomes a victim of radiation. The production was costly (between $20 million and $25 million), and it featured a rather authentic-looking $2 million set representing the Los Alamos facilities. However, neither the expensive replica nor Newman's impressive presence in the key role could save the movie. *Fat Man and Little Boy* never developed a compelling story. It failed to create suspense, and it was a notable flop at the box office. The movie's disappointing reception is regrettable, because *Fat Man and Little Boy* could have provided a useful service, exposing audiences to some of the important debates associated with the United States' decision to use atomic bombs in World War II.[24]

*Ghosts of Mississippi* (1996) also fails to deliver exciting drama, despite its focus on a seemingly fascinating historical topic. Rob Reiner's movie, based a book by journalist Maryanne Vollers, examines the efforts of a Mississippi prosecutor to convict a white racist of the murder of civil rights leader Medgar Evers. Nearly thirty years before, the racist had escaped conviction in two trials that led to hung juries. The young prosecutor has difficulty winning the confidence of Evers's widow (Whoopi Goldberg), but he eventually convinces her that he can be trusted, and she produces a copy of the original court transcript that he has been seeking. Armed with this evidence and other information, Bobby DeLaughter (Alec Baldwin) succeeds in his courtroom efforts, sending the villain (James Woods) to prison.

*Ghosts of Mississippi* is strong in its appeal for racial justice but weak in its delivery of dramatic tension. It is a well-intended morality tale about the kind of bigotry that stained much of twentieth-century southern history.

Unfortunately, Reiner paints the movie's characters with such a heavy brush that he fails to sustain the audience's interest in them. Whoopi Goldberg is a noble, suffering saint in her role as the slain man's widow, and James Woods is almost a caricature as a snarling bigot. Alec Baldwin is transparently guilt ridden as a southern white liberal who seeks to redeem his culture from its hate-infested past; convicting the Ku Klux Klan member is a means of cleansing his conscience. These characterizations come across with such weight that the story lacks subtlety, and the individuals act in stereotypical ways. There is no mystery or suspense to the plot and very little action. After the opening scenes that lead to the assassination of Evers (an important figure whom the audience learns little about), the film turns into a dialogue-driven story featuring numerous conversations while people walk the streets of a southern town. Not surprisingly, *Ghosts of Mississippi* fared poorly at the box office.[25]

We should regret these dramatic failures rather than gloat over them. Each of the three films addresses important issues; each could have stimulated the thinking of many viewers regarding significant historical topics. The movies did not create the expected impact, however. What were the sources of the problems? Why did these films fail to arouse the interest of audiences?

Some of the answers appear obvious. In various ways, they depended too strongly on dialogue, giving inadequate attention to visual, action-oriented forms of communication. Their creators also failed to employ enough generic elements from the conventions of cinematic history. The movies' plots were too predictable, failing to surprise viewers with intriguing twists and turns in narrative development.

Enthusiasts of cinematic history can profit from an examination of the hazards associated with dramatic structure. A study of these difficulties can provide useful ideas for the critique of cinematic history. Observers of the genre need to be aware of the complex challenges filmmakers encounter when they attempt to portray the past on the screen. It is not easy to pull off successful cinematic history. A production can easily become a financial disappointment, as in the cases of *Heaven's Gate, Fat Man and Little Boy,* and *Ghosts of Mississippi.* If artists cannot manage to engage their audiences, they can quickly lose them. Filmmakers who fail to make their stories emotionally appealing are likely to find themselves experiencing artistic and financial Waterloos. It behooves critics of cinematic history to show sensitivity to the risks these artists face. An informed and realistic evaluation of their work calls for an understanding of the pressures to deliver good drama as well as good history.

Awareness of the challenges in delivering powerful drama can also prove useful when judging generally popular films that failed to live up to their potential for exciting audience interest. *Pearl Harbor* (2001) is a good example of cinematic history that falls short because of dramatic weaknesses. The movie certainly was not a complete fiasco. Its presentation of the famous Japanese air assault employs impressive graphics, and media attention to the movie helped sell many books about the history of the event that brought the United States into World War II. Nevertheless, the film came under some heavy criticism. When the production by Jerry Bruckheimer and Michael Bay failed to generate a great deal of enthusiasm among moviegoers, despite an expensive advertising blitz, some observers attributed this disappointment to the film's shallow treatment of history. They complained that *Pearl Harbor* gives the audience few intriguing details about the horrible "day of infamy." *Tora! Tora! Tora!*'s 1970 portrayal of the historic attack is much more informative and accurate, argued the critics. Bruckheimer and Bay's production does, indeed, lack the sophistication of *Tora! Tora! Tora!*'s history lesson, but that shortcoming is not the primary source of the movie's difficulties.

*Pearl Harbor* attempts to imitate the narrative and graphic strategy of James Cameron's blockbuster *Titanic* (1997), but it has few of the important dramatic elements that contributed to *Titanic*'s enormous success. Cameron's story proved intriguing from beginning to end as viewers watched the surprising twists and turns in Jack and Rose's romance, their dealings with jealous lover Cal, and their efforts to escape death. Randall Wallace, writer for *Pearl Harbor*, fashioned a story that contains few surprises. The romantic relationship between Rafe (Ben Affleck) and Evelyn (Kate Beckinsale) develops swiftly in the opening minutes of the picture. There is no dramatic tension between the two lovers until late in the story when Rafe is presumed dead and Evelyn establishes a romantic connection with Rafe's best friend, Danny (Josh Hartnett). In contrast, *Titanic* shows Jack and Rose struggling in an on-again, off-again relationship. Denouement comes late in the film when Rose gives up her seat on a lifeboat, signaling a determination to cast her fortunes with the handsome commoner.

In *Pearl Harbor*, the love story appears to be tacked on to an epic tale about the historic disaster. The romance has little connection to the extraordinary events of 1941 (critics in the mass media emphasized this problem frequently in their biting reviews). In *Titanic*, the love story is integrated into the historical presentation. Jack's low socioeconomic status and Rose's background as a representative of the eastern establishment provide a foundation for examining class distinctions throughout the drama. Furthermore, Rose's position in Cameron's story is much more integrated into the historical action than is Evelyn's position in *Pearl Harbor*. Rose interacts with the ship's officers, the crew, the wealthy travelers in first class, the immigrants in steerage, and others on the vessel. Evelyn of *Pearl Harbor* serves primarily as the pilots' love interest until late in the story when, in evidently manipulated fashion, the screenwriter shows her bravely nursing the wounded sailors.

In creating a story about two talented pilots vying for the affection of one woman, Wallace evidently borrowed a plot structure from a notable film of the 1920s. In many respects, *Pearl Harbor*'s structure resembles that of the movie that won the first Academy Award for Best Picture, William A. Wellman's *Wings* (1927). As in *Pearl Harbor,* the two male stars of *Wings* find themselves caught up in a love triangle. War resolves the conflict in *Wings,* as it does in the 2001 production. In *Wings,* only one pilot returns home alive to claim the girl. Wallace's dramatic design in *Pearl Harbor* is so transparent, however, that his plot device fails to create suspense. The audience readily understands that Ben Affleck's place in the foreground through the first half of the film strongly suggests that Evelyn will fall into his arms at the end of the story.

*Pearl Harbor* also lacks the familiar nemesis of most cinematic history—a villain whose presence symbolizes important problems faced by the protagonist. In *Titanic,* the sniveling aristocrat Cal Hockley serves this role, as does the White Star Line's J. Bruce Ismay, who insists that the ship maintain a fast course through the iceberg zone. *Pearl Harbor* provides no well-characterized cinematic villains. It does not lambaste the American military authorities who failed to prepare the island defenses adequately. The Japanese military leaders do not serve as the movie's heavies, either. *Pearl Harbor* portrays them critically but not unsympathetically. The Japanese strategists appear thoughtful and, at times, almost regretful about launching the attack. When congratulated for a brilliant war strategy, a Japanese admiral replies, "A brilliant man would find a way not to fight a war." Some of *Pearl Harbor*'s gentleness in portraying the Japanese may be attributed to the producers' marketing plans. Shortly after releasing *Pearl Harbor* in the United States, Bruckheimer and Bay distributed the movie to theaters in Asia. They promoted their film in Japan as a love story and removed the term *Jap* from some places in the dialogue.

The narrative structure created by Bay, Bruckheimer, and Wallace does not connect the audience's emotions to the fate of the victims as effectively as many other modern war stories do. In *Saving Private Ryan* (1998), for instance, viewers do not learn a great deal about the individual soldiers seen dying on the beaches of Normandy, but Steven Spielberg's cinematic strategy helps invest the audience's emotions in the fighting. Spielberg follows the attackers as they travel on the landing craft, charge into the water, struggle to secure a position on the beaches, and then attempt to mount an assault on the well-entrenched enemy. Spielberg's method helps the audience sense the soldiers' fear and pain. Viewers of *Pearl Harbor,* in contrast, see only rushed images of American servicemen falling to their deaths. Bay's approach leaves audiences feeling like spectators who are viewing an action-adventure story at a distance rather than like empathetic observers who feel a personal closeness to the tragedy.

*Pearl Harbor* was certainly not a complete financial and theatrical disaster, for it attracted enough viewers in the United States and abroad to turn a profit. The movie does, nevertheless, serve as a good example of the way a flawed dramatic structure can result in lost opportunities. A more effective storytelling design could have drawn much larger audiences to this exercise in reel history. With a more compelling presentation, the movie could have excited greater interest in the history of Japanese-American enmity and the origins of U.S. involvement in World War II. If *Pearl Harbor* had employed tools of the genre with greater sophistication and intelligence, it might have fueled even greater public interest in books about the tragedy of December 7, 1941. This $135 million movie was disappointing, not just because of its lightweight attention to historical details, but also because it failed to realize the full potential of drama as a powerful enticement to the study of history.

Thus, our answer to the familiar request to identify poor historical cinema can be multilayered but not evasive. Among the premier choices for dramas that present such a grossly distorted view of the past that they are comical in their impact are *Santa Fe Trail* and *They Died with Their Boots On*. They deserve a Brooks award. In many other cases, however, cinematic history mixes shortcomings and achievements within the same production (especially in modern-day films). We can praise Norman Jewison for the superb drama he created in *The Hurricane* and for stimulating the audience's thinking about racial injustice but regret his irresponsible exercise of artistic license, which undermined public confidence in his movie's commentary about the life of a famous figure. In a different but related way, we can applaud Rob Reiner's well-intentioned critique of southern bigotry in *Ghosts of Mississippi* but regret his failure to package the story as an exciting drama that could draw millions to his film. Jewison's movie delivers strong drama but weak treatment of the evidence. Reiner's film is less controversial in its handling of the evidence but more problematic as entertainment. *Pearl Harbor* also delivers mixed results. It presents the attack of December 7, 1941, with extraordinary technological effects, but its disconnected saga about a love triangle fails to engage audiences. In the case of *Pearl Harbor* and other examples of cinematic history, filmmakers rarely miss the history target completely. Even when their aim falls short of the bull's-eye, they often hit the perimeter enough times to excite some admiration.

When history buffs, film enthusiasts, and professional scholars attempt to identify the Hollywood movie that does the finest job portraying history, they may find their task more enlightening if they offer several examples rather than just one. After all, cinema instructs and provokes in different ways. Individual films can make strong contributions to the public's thinking about the past in one respect but be less effective in other ways. No motion picture deserves a mega-Harry because it combines all the desirable qualities of great cinematic history. Several movies do, however, serve as impressive models of specific kinds of achievement. The examples cited here represent a wide variety of cinema types, from big-budget pictures to tightly financed ones, from feature films to TV specials (including one from public television), from stories about politics to epic films about men at war, from American-made productions to a foreign-made example that Hollywood distributors adopted. The four suggested categories do not encompass all the possibilities; other forms of achievement can be identified as well. But these examples constitute some of the most important contributions good cinematic history can make to the public's thinking about the past.

## Communicating a Feeling for a Different Time and Place

We have already noted that movies are generally poor communicators of specific historical information and ideas. A student of history is likely to get a much broader understanding of the French Revolution, the American Revolution, or the Russian Revolution by devoting a few hours to reading a book about these events than by watching a movie about them. Motion pictures typically focus tightly on the lives of a few players involved in one or two major events; they do not comment broadly on great social transformations, economic changes, intellectual currents, or other wide-ranging developments. Hollywood dramas sometimes suggest viewpoints on these matters, but only peripherally, referencing them briefly in the course of telling a story. Yet in another respect, a motion picture can deliver a great deal of information to viewers. In specific scenes, a filmmaker may load up the historical stimuli, giving the audience a great deal to see and think about.

A popular war movie by German director Wolfgang Petersen demonstrated this kind of cinematic contribution. *Das Boot* (The Boat) appeared in Europe in 1981 and was an instant hit. The film went Hollywood in 1982, receiving widespread distribution in the United States and the world, and it was re-released in a longer director's cut in 1997. *Das Boot* was the eleventh highest grossing foreign film to reach the U.S. market at the end of the twentieth century. The movie's enormous success helped open Hollywood's doors to its director, and Petersen went on to make a number of action-oriented movies in the United States, including *In the Line of Fire* (1993), *Air Force One* (1997), and *The Perfect Storm* (2000).

*Das Boot* focuses on a German submarine crew during World War II that has many harrowing experiences due to the U-boats' increased vulnerability to Allied military measures. The crew eventually manages to get the damaged vessel back to port in La Rochelle, France, but the submarine is then destroyed in an air attack. The story is based roughly on the real-life experiences of Captain Heinrich Lehmann-Willenbrock, one of the top German U-boat commanders. Lehmann-Willenbrock ranked sixth in the Third Reich's navy in terms of Allied tonnage destroyed. *Das Boot* gets many of its ideas from a book by Gunther Bucheim, a sketch artist who traveled with Lehmann-Willenbrock on the U-96 during World War II.

Petersen's movie does not present a glamorous picture of good-looking, patriotic, gung-ho underwater heroes, such as the sailors seen in many earlier Hollywood movies about the U.S. Navy. *Das Boot* shows the U-boat crew living in great difficulty and danger. It offers a close-up, realistic picture of the men's cramped quarters. The claustrophobic ship is narrow and 150 feet long, and its compartments contain a maze of pipes and wires. Engine noise is almost constant. Sausages and pumpernickel hang from the pipes. The sailors look shabby; their beards grow longer as the story progresses, and they become dirty and battle-fatigued. They experience periods of boredom punctuated by frightening moments of mortal threat. *Das Boot* communicates the terror the crewmen sense when they hear the "ping-ping" sounds of an enemy's sonic searches. The submariners sweat with fear as the depth charges explode, and at times, their vessel seems about to split at the seams. Through disturbing images of danger and death, *Das Boot* delivers a powerful antiwar message and challenges the glamorous perspective of submarine warfare evident in many war movies. Petersen's drama supports the grim statistical evidence it identifies in a caption: the death toll for the men who went to sea in German U-boats during World War II was approximately 75 percent.[26]

*Das Boot*'s main contribution to historical thinking is not in the realm of providing details about the war, however. It says virtually nothing about the causes of the global conflict or the overall state of Admiral Karl Dönitz's U-boat campaign under the Third Reich. The film is memorable for a specific history lesson rather than a broad one. It packs an emotional punch because of the stimulating way it gives the audience a feeling for the submariners' experience. The information load in Petersen's movie comes not in the form of statistics or other details about the war at sea but in an abundance of evidence about specific conditions inside one vessel. *Das Boot* has a strong impact on viewers because it gives them a sense that they are being exposed to a realistic historical setting. Audiences leave the theaters feeling that they have witnessed the frightening undersea conditions of World War II combat.

One of the best American-made movies that uniquely communicates a feeling for the wartime experience is Steven Spielberg's *Saving Private Ryan*. The most memorable scenes occur near the beginning, when the movie portrays American soldiers storming the beaches of northern France on D day, 1944. Spielberg's film shows brave soldiers in action, but not in the manner of many earlier combat movies. The men are frightened as they ready themselves to charge into the hail of bullets and exploding shells. One vomits in the landing craft; another cries for his mother while under heavy fire. Several appear terribly frightened when they find themselves pinned down. There is confusion and chaos as the American soldiers are trapped on the beaches, easy prey for well-armed German units holding the high ground. The sea turns red with blood, and the noise on the beaches seems deafening. Through this horrible picture of the blind terror experienced by men in combat, Spielberg challenges the gung-ho war images from movies that made fighting seem exciting and glamorous. His employment of the handheld camera creates an impression that the viewer is present at the battlefront, witness to the making of a documentary created by cinematographers who were on the beach, exposed to bullets and mortars along with the soldiers.

Almost any movie about wartime combat produced in the new era of peace across Western Europe can be called an antiwar film. Certainly *Saving Private Ryan*'s depiction of the frightening and bloody action in the first days of American fighting in northern France makes a critical statement about World War II's impact on its participants. Yet the film suggests in subtle ways that the Americans who risked their lives in that great enterprise are worthy of praise. At the beginning, the movie shows a U.S. flag flapping in the breeze, signaling a patriotic message, and other scenes depict sacrifices made by U.S. soldiers. The portrayal of the beach invasion suggests that the soldiers are heroes, but they seem more vulnerable and hence more realistic than the one-dimensional stereotypes featured in old Hollywood war pictures. Even the soldiers who shake or cry in battle seem deserving of our salute.

After the eye-opening D-day sequences, *Saving Private Ryan* maintains audience interest by turning into a fine modern-day example of the Hollywood combat genre. Jeanine Basinger, author of the best book on Hollywood combat movies, cleverly identifies these components in a review of *Saving Private Ryan* for the American Historical Association. She observes that the combat genre often features a hero (in this case, Tom Hanks) who is forced to make

*Sergeant Horvath (Tom Sizemore), Corporal Upham (Jeremy Davies), Private Jackson (Barry Pepper), and Captain John Miller (Tom Hanks, right) are pinned down by enemy sniper fire as they try to help a terrified little girl in* Saving Private Ryan *(1998). Steven Spielberg's movie challenges the familiar gung-ho images of earlier war movies that made combat seem exciting and glamorous. (Museum of Modern Art Film Archive)*

controversial decisions. His military unit invariably includes a variety of stock characters familiar to Hollywood war films, such as a smart aleck from Brooklyn, a religious sharpshooter from the South, and a Jewish soldier. There is some form of tension within the ranks in these combat movies, as one of the tough and talented soldiers challenges the leader. But like the Private Reiben character (Edward Burns) in *Saving Private Ryan,* this rebel shapes up in the end and makes a significant contribution to the fighting. Over the course of the story, action waxes and wanes as the men experience both safety and danger (during some relaxing moments, they joke with one another and tell stories about their girls back home). The combat movie reaches a climax, notes Basinger, through a tremendous Armageddon-like confrontation with the enemy. Often the American heroes find themselves badly outnumbered and outgunned in this concluding battle, and after a difficult struggle that results in the loss of a number of characters the audience has come to respect, the Americans achieve a painful but glorious victory. As Basinger observes, *Saving Private Ryan*'s dramatic structure features all these familiar components of the genre.[27]

Despite the movie's strong conformity to Hollywood storytelling practices following the D-day scenes, *Saving Private Ryan* continues to reference history in a number of places throughout the movie and communicates a realistic impression of wartime experiences. This sense of verisimilitude is especially evident in the final battle, which shows the men trying to hold a bridge against a substantial German fighting force backed up by tanks. Working with an extraordinarily authentic-looking set representing a wrecked French town with bombed-out buildings and debris-laden streets, Spielberg draws his story to a close with another emotion-packed portrayal of the experience of combat. This segment of the film connects the audience again to the earlier messages about sacrifice and heroism. It also bases its fictional, microcosmic look at the fighting on a factual foundation from history. The Tom Hanks character resembles Major Tom Howie, a mild-mannered teacher of English literature who led his men in a costly but important firefight in the little French town of Saint-Lô a few days after the Allied landings. Howie fought with guns blazing and, like the Hanks character, died in action. A day later, with an American victory secured, soldiers draped his body with the Stars and Stripes and hoisted it on top of a pile of stones. Howie became famous among GIs as "the major of Saint-Lô."[28]

### Interpreting Major Historical Developments

We can better distinguish the second category from the first by comparing the attractions of *Saving Private Ryan* and *The Longest Day* (1962), two movies about a related theme. Each offers a perspective on D day, but in very different ways. *Ryan* looks at the situation through the eyes of a few fictitious characters and shows the experience of dangerous combat. Spielberg's movie does not present much information about the actions of major figures in the war, and it provides little detail about the Americans' overall progress during the first days of the Normandy invasion. In contrast, Darryl F. Zanuck's movie about D day delivers a great deal of historical information. It portrays the thoughts and actions of American, British, French, and German military leaders and also depicts the actions of several real-life individuals involved in the fighting. *Ryan* instructs primarily by demonstrating the emotional impact of warfare; *The Longest Day* informs through a study of the strategy of battle. *Ryan* offers almost no information about Allied military plans, the Germans' response to the attack, or the significance of the D-day invasion in the overall struggle against Hitler; *The Longest Day* delivers insights on all these subjects. Neither film is necessarily superior to the other. Each contributes in different ways to the public's thinking about the past. A comparison of the two accentuates the conclusion that good films may view the past in very different ways. There can be no single model of effective cinematic history.

*The Longest Day* is a superb epic, one of the most authentic-looking Hollywood representations of an important moment in history. Like any cinematic drama, it contains some fictional flourishes and manipulation of evidence, but the movie's overall integrity in the handling of details is highly commendable. Zanuck committed more than $10 million to the production (big bucks back in 1962) and monitored the film's treatment of historical evidence quite carefully.[29] He based many of the movie's portrayals on individuals described in Cornelius Ryan's best-selling book of 1959 by the same title, which relied on interviews with more than 1,000 participants in the engagement and sold 800,000 copies in its first year.[30] Zanuck featured some vignettes about D-day actions that seemed so incredible that critics berated him for mixing too much fiction with fact. For example, they could not believe the movie's portrayal of Lord Lovat (Peter Lawford), who exhibits colorful bravado in the film, and they challenged the authenticity of a scene showing nuns running into shellfire to aid wounded French troops. The producer confidently responded that these and other memorable depictions were well documented.

Zanuck did employ some creative license in telling his story, especially in portraying the military actions. When the facts failed to support good drama, he added touches of fiction. "Anything changed was an asset to the film," he said in defense of the adjustments. "There is nothing duller on the screen than being accurate but not dramatic." For instance, *The Longest Day* depicts efforts to seize the Pagasus bridge before the Germans could blow it up. Real Allied soldiers found no charges planted under the bridge; instead, the charges turned up in a nearby shed. The movie, however, portrays engineers bravely climbing across the bridge's girders to remove the explosives. *The Longest Day* shows American invaders blowing up a large concrete barrier and sending bulldozers and tanks through a gaping hole in the German defenses. That effort was in the invaders' original plan, but German control of the heights forced Allied soldiers to work their way behind the German defenses and attack from the rear. Zanuck opted for the more visually dramatic but fictional crashing of the barricades. Also, his movie shows the men rushing out of their landing craft, charging the beaches, and firing away at the enemy. Actually, these landings looked more like the scenes in *Saving Private Ryan*. Often the attackers dropped into the water awkwardly and had to struggle to shore behind a hail of bullets and bombs, hiding behind beach obstacles. By the time they came to rest at the base of the bluff, they were exhausted.[31]

Despite these and other adjustments of the facts, *The Longest Day* works marvelously as a three-hour epic about one of the most important military operations in world history. It gives audiences a fascinating overview of the extraordinary challenges associated with the massive operation and communicates provocative explanations for the Allies' success and the Germans' defeat in the encounters. (Fundamentally, *The Longest Day* attributes victory to the superiority of democracy over dictatorship. In one of the movie's memorable lines, a German general says, "We are disillusioned witnesses of a fact that will seem hard to believe to future historians, but it is still the truth: No one must wake up the Führer.")

*Schindler's List,* another Hollywood production set in the World War II period, also does a superb job of interpreting a major subject from history. Steven Spielberg's 1993 film examines the Holocaust but, like most cinematic history, does not attempt to cover the story comprehensively. Instead, it focuses on the experiences of one individual, a German entrepreneur named Oskar Schindler (Liam Neeson). Through his story, the audience encounters many of the significant historical developments related to the Holocaust.

At the beginning of the movie, Schindler is an urbane wheeler-dealer who courts the Nazi military authorities, hoping to gain business influence. A womanizer and a rather corrupt figure in his financial dealings, Schindler demonstrates no particular sympathy for the Jews. He takes over a confiscated enamel factory in Krakow and works out an arrangement with a talented Jewish accountant, Itzhak Stern (Ben Kingsley), to obtain the services of a large group of Jewish workers. Schindler protects these individuals from the Nazi work camps, presumably for his own economic benefit. Slowly, almost imperceptibly, Schindler acquires a strong sense of sympathy for the Jews in his charge. This personal transformation seems to come, in part, from what he witnesses of Nazi behavior. The actions of an important Nazi contact, Amon Goeth (Ralph Fiennes), are influential. Goeth is, like Schindler, a hedonist, but with a pathological mean streak. He shoots Jewish victims for sport, showing no remorse. Schindler witnesses the destruction of the Jewish ghetto in Krakow, a horrible sight that seems to affect him deeply. When Hitler's "final solution" threatens to send his Jewish workers to the death camps, Schindler manages to save them from extermination. In one of the movie's most frightening sequences, 300 women and children among Schindler's Jews are mistakenly shipped in boxcars to Auschwitz, but they are eventually returned to Schindler. The story ends with the collapse of the Third Reich and Schindler's extraordinary success in protecting the lives of the 1,100 Jews assigned to him during Hitler's campaign of annihilation. In the final minutes of the movie, Spielberg shows some of the real-life Schindler Jews in the 1990s honoring the hero at his grave site.

The success of *Schindler's List* comes not only from the gripping story but also from the effective filmmaking strategy of the director and his cinematographer, Janusz Kaminski. Except for brief sections at the beginning and end and one small flourish within the story, the movie is shot in black and white. As mentioned earlier in connection with the study of genre, this absence of color gives the film a documentary-like appearance and, as Spielberg notes, resembles the way many people first encountered the Holocaust: in newsreels. The flourish of color comes late in the story when one little girl among the many Jewish victims appears in red clothing. She is one of the youngsters attempting to escape the Nazi pursuers, but some minutes later, the audience sees her again among the dead children. Through this clever device, Spielberg and Kaminski draw the audience's attention to a single victim. Their movie points to a tragedy that destroyed 6 million European Jews, but it also attempts to personalize that extraordinary statistic by directing viewers' emotions to the experiences of one representative little girl.[32]

The movie's scenes are tremendously detailed and often quite authentic. Much of the specific action relates to behavior reported in historical research and interviews. In one scene, for instance, *Schindler's List* shows a train transporting Jews to the death camps. Along the tracks stands a little boy who draws his finger across his throat, signaling to the captives that they are heading to their deaths. In the documentary *Shoah* (1985), an elderly Polish peasant describes how he made this gesture when trains carrying Jewish victims passed through his village.

*Schindler's List* received tremendous critical acclaim around the world and won the Academy Award for Best Picture, but a minority of commentators registered some harsh criticisms. Their objections are worth considering because they illuminate some of the debates that continue to swirl around Hollywood's representations of the past, even highly sophisticated ones.

One of the most repeated charges was that Spielberg attempted to "trivialize" and "sensationalize" the Holocaust.[33] Some supported a position that Theodor W. Adorno had advanced years before: after Auschwitz, said Adorno, poetry could no longer be written. Israeli writer Tom Segev expressed this sentiment in his criticism of *Schindler's List*. "I don't think there is any need to dramatize the Holocaust," he said. "It is sufficiently dramatic in itself." Segev asserted that "every artistic treatment of the Holocaust is bound to fail."[34] One of the most vehement critics in this respect was Claude Lanzmann, creator of *Shoah,* the influential documentary about the Holocaust. Lanzmann pointed out that his film relied on the memories of witnesses and did not attempt to represent their experiences with music, archival film, or dramatizations.[35] He spoke of the "unrepresentability of Auschwitz," suggesting that Spielberg had commercialized a sacred subject.[36] "Fiction is a transgression," said Lanzmann. "I deeply believe that there are some things that cannot and should not be represented."[37]

Another criticism that appeared frequently related to the way *Schindler's List* characterizes people and groups positively or negatively. Critics complained

*Jewish plant manager Itzhak Stern (Ben Kingsley, left) speaks with his boss and protector Oskar Schindler (Liam Neeson, right) in* Schindler's List *(1993). Some critics complained that Stern, the movie's only major Jewish character, is a passive wimp. (Museum of Modern Art Film Archive)*

that the film puts Jews at the margins of the story, presenting them primarily as faceless victims. The only major Jewish character, Itzhak Stern, seems a passive wimp, they charged. Some maintained that many of the movie's minor Jewish characters are quite unappealing, coming across as money-grubbing, avaricious stereotypes. A disproportionate number of them are small in stature, large-nosed, disheveled, and unkempt, observed Sara R. Horowitz, whereas Schindler has the appearance of towering height, cleanliness, and fashionableness.[38] *Schindler's List* is not a courageous movie, critics argued, because it takes the commercial approach of presenting Jewish victims as sheep saved by a heroic Gentile. A more meaningful movie about the Holocaust would have put Jewish characters at the center of the story. Not surprisingly, representatives of other ethnic groups criticized the depictions, too. In an article published in *Foreign Affairs,* for example, Andrew Nagorski argued that the film's few images of the Polish people seem to suggest "that the only roles Poles played was to applaud Nazi terror." Nagorski also complained that *Schindler's List* leaves viewers "with no idea that the war was aimed at more than the destruction of the Jews or that there were other victims of Nazi atrocities."[39]

Others complained that the story slipped too easily into a hero-villain contrast. They objected especially to the characterization of Nazi villain Amon

Goeth. These detractors argued that Goeth's psychopathology and barbarism did not give audiences an authentic, more typical picture of a German fascist. Often, the Nazis were not monstrous products of dysfunctional families, as suggested in *Schindler's List;* many Nazis were frighteningly normal, and these brutal killers might be lawyers, corporate executives, professors, or even clergymen.

None of these criticisms fatally damages the motion picture; indeed, the appearance of these objections in the media suggests that this powerful film on a highly sensitive topic stirred the thinking of viewers, prompting them to imagine a variety of ways in which the tragedy could be depicted on the screen. Each critic projected his or her own vision of the subject. For Claude Lanzmann, the ideal film was evidently an interview-oriented documentary without dramatic representations. Sara R. Horowitz appeared to favor a story that focused on good-looking Jewish heroes and heroines, and Andrew Nagorski's picture of the tragedy would draw attention to the plight of non-Jewish victims. Each perspective would examine the Holocaust in a different manner, and each had the potential to deliver a memorable commentary about a troubling and perplexing chapter of history.

As noted in the chapter on cinematic history as genre, however, movies do not provide comprehensive portraits of a subject. They adopt points of view, focus on just one or two characters, and privilege perspectives that are likely to attract broad audience interest. For Spielberg, that opportunity appeared in the form of a drama about an unusual man who is at first indifferent to the plight of the Jews but is transformed into a heroic savior by the end of the war. Viewing the Holocaust through the perspective of Oskar Schindler's wartime actions was not the only way Spielberg could have addressed the subject, but it certainly was an attractive mechanism for drawing millions of moviegoers, an audience of mostly non-Jews, into the story.

### Probing the Past through Biography

Virtually all Hollywood perspectives on history offer biographical approaches to their subject, presenting issues and events in terms of the experiences of one or two principal figures. Movies personalize history by placing these few figures at the center of their dramas, and they trace important developments by viewing the way these individuals experienced them. By following the activities of one or two major characters, Hollywood dramas can suggest broad questions related to their experiences. Motion pictures can leave audiences wondering: Why did the hero or heroine suffer these difficulties? What lessons can be learned from the example of their struggles? By studying a few lives, movies can provoke the audience's thinking about the experiences of many others who found themselves in similar situations.

Of course, many motion pictures fail to present a sophisticated biographical treatment. They portray one-dimensional stereotypes, simplistically heroic figures who exhibit almost no shortcomings in terms of skill, motivation, or moral character. These individuals do not resemble real people; they are dramatic icons. Also, the simplistic biographical perspective often presents the protagonists as fully formed, mature individuals, giving the audience little sense of the important factors that helped shape their personalities and inform their ideas. In addition, cinematic history frequently suggests that great men and great women can change history rather easily. Hollywood productions often show strongly motivated individuals knocking over virtually every obstacle that stands between them and their goals. Such dramas fail to deliver a realistic picture of life's challenges, one that recognizes not only how individuals can influence society but also how society can have a substantial impact on individuals.

The two outstanding examples of biographical cinema under consideration here do not suffer from these familiar shortcomings. They present multidimensional personalities; their heroes and heroines are noble but also flawed. The films throw light on questions about personality formation, providing audiences with a good deal of information about the influential experiences in the characters' youth and young adulthood. The films also recognize the limitations of a single person's influence. They do not simply portray dynamic personalities dominating the people and events around them. These films introduce realistic figures, people who are shaped by history but who also manage to influence the world they live in.

These fine examples of biographical cinema are also notable for their authenticity. Although the creators exercised artistic license in the handling of evidence—as all cinematic historians do—they were generally respectful toward the historical evidence and knowledgeable about current historical interpretations. The filmmakers exhibited seriousness and sophistication in the handling of details and a determination to represent the facts about the historical figure responsibly and intelligently. Often, a fine book serves as the foundation for the portrayal, as in the two examples cited here. The filmmakers benefited from the availability of outstanding publications that dealt with the individuals and the times in a particularly sophisticated manner.

*Eleanor and Franklin* (1976), a four-hour ABC Television miniseries, bases its drama on an excellent biography of Eleanor Roosevelt by Joseph P. Lash. The author provides a great deal of personal information about the former first lady and builds his story on her letters and papers (as a friend of Mrs. Roosevelt, he was given the first opportunity to work with the documents).

Lash also interviewed many people who knew Eleanor Roosevelt, including some who had been close to the Roosevelt family when Eleanor was a child. Thanks to his privileged situation, his impressive writing skills, and his commitment to creating an honest treatment that recognized Eleanor's flaws as well as her strengths, Lash's 1971 book received an enthusiastic reception from reviewers and won the Pulitzer prize for biography.[40]

James Costigan, writer of the television series, brought additional skills to the presentation of Eleanor Roosevelt's life. Costigan composed a brilliant screenplay that effectively communicates the principal messages of the biography. His dramatic format begins by focusing on the end of the couple's relationship, depicting Eleanor's reaction to the news of Franklin's death in 1945. In the course of mourning, Eleanor recalls many of the most significant events in her life. Occasionally, these flashbacks are punctuated with brief portrayals of her days of mourning—a device that nicely provokes the viewers' thinking. The audience wonders, how did the impressive, self-confident, and admired woman of 1945 emerge from the shy and troubled child depicted in the first hour of the film?

*Eleanor and Franklin* relates a story of personal growth. It shows Eleanor suffering from low self-esteem in her early years. She senses that her mother does not love her because she lacks the beauty of the many high-society belles in the extended Roosevelt family. Eleanor cares deeply for her father, but her mother and maternal grandmother eventually treat her father like a pariah because of his bouts with alcoholism and other excesses. Later, as a shy but intelligent teenager, Eleanor attends her "coming out" dance, where she encounters her fifth cousin, Franklin, a spirited, self-confident teenager who takes a liking to her. Eventually, Eleanor goes off to a fine private school abroad and excels in her studies. At Allenswood, she quickly emerges as a leader among the young scholars and as a favorite of the woman who runs the institution. Upon returning to the United States, Eleanor meets Franklin again, and an extended period of courtship begins. The future president presses for marriage, despite his mother's insidious efforts to break up the relationship. After much delay, Eleanor and Franklin marry, and Eleanor settles into the traditional role of wife and mother. In this period, she is dominated by her husband and her mother-in-law.

Liberation comes to Eleanor in stages. The two most important developments that emancipate Eleanor from her subservient role are the discovery of Franklin's infidelity and the crisis of his battle with polio. In the first instance, Eleanor recognizes that she can no longer find personal satisfaction in wifely devotion to her husband, because he has broken her trust. In helping her husband in his struggle with polio, Eleanor asserts herself, arguing against her mother-in-law's plans to place Franklin in retirement at the family estate along the Hudson River. Eleanor encourages her husband to turn away from defeatism and depression, and she convinces him to remain active politically. She aids Franklin's political career by becoming a forceful political operator in her own right. By the end of the film, the shy and ugly duckling has transformed into a lady of great inner beauty and impressive leadership skills. A final caption recalls some of Eleanor Roosevelt's national and international achievements in the years after Franklin's death.

History is always on the periphery of *Eleanor and Franklin* rather than at the center. The TV series delivers compelling drama about personal relationships and an individual's metamorphosis; it offers only limited details about the public role of Eleanor and Franklin Roosevelt in twentieth-century American politics. Nevertheless, the biographical treatment exposes audiences to a number of important historical subjects over the course of four hours. It introduces them to the social life of the rich and famous at the turn of the century. Viewers meet President Theodore Roosevelt and learn about "reformers" in settlement houses in the early 1900s. They also learn about the political struggles between Democrats and Republicans, particularly through conversations involving the only character who manages to establish emotional closeness with both Eleanor and Franklin: FDR's adviser Louis Howe. Audiences also catch glimpses of American life in earlier times, from conditions in the rural countryside to the streets and parlors of New York City and Washington, D.C. Particularly impressive is the film's depiction of Eleanor's train trip with FDR's casket from Warm Springs, Georgia, to Washington, D.C., in 1945. It reveals a multitude of poor Americans standing along the railroad tracks, paying their last respects to the man credited with pulling their nation out of the Great Depression and leading the country toward victory in World War II. *Eleanor and Franklin* stirs curiosity about these and many other important matters associated with early-twentieth-century American history.

The film also raises significant questions about Eleanor's experiences, queries that are presented subtly rather than directly. Especially important, it exposes viewers to separate gender spheres in the upper-class social environment of turn-of-the-century America. As audiences watch Eleanor beginning her married life largely separated from her husband's professional activities, they are encouraged to ponder how women sought fulfillment under conditions inherited from Victorian times. They may ask: Which developments served to reduce divisions between men's and women's spheres of activity? Did a husband's marital infidelities or temporary removal from a professional career sometimes influence a woman's emotional emancipation, as in the case of Eleanor Roosevelt?

Above all, *Eleanor and Franklin* shows that individuals have histories, much as nations do. Character and personality are not fixed at birth; they are formed in large part from a person's interaction with the physical and social environment. In Eleanor's case, a vibrant woman learned to resist her personal demons and ultimately triumph over them. Unlike many dramas that show a fully developed figure throughout the story, *Eleanor and Franklin* explores the evolution of character and personality over time. It never suggests that it can proffer a confident explanation for all of Eleanor Roosevelt's behavior, relegating some issues to the mystery of human psychology. Yet it certainly speculates about the sources of Eleanor's notable strength and integrity, basing its guesswork on the informed observations presented in Lash's impressive biography.[41]

*The Execution of Private Slovik* (1974) is another outstanding study of an individual's place in history. Eddie D. Slovik was the only U.S. soldier to be executed for desertion in World War II. This made-for-television film about the decisions that led to his death was produced by Richard Levinson and William Link, two unusually talented and accomplished creators of prime-time programs who did a great deal to develop socially responsible entertainment. When their popular show *Mannix* came under criticism for gratuitous violence, they responded with *Columbo,* a detective show that emphasized the cerebral challenge of catching the killer rather than the physical depiction of the murder. Levinson and Link also produced a dramatic special that raised serious questions about whether television programs can influence violent behavior. Another drama by Levinson and Link dealt with the role of guns in violent crime, and still another took up the then-controversial question of tobacco's responsibility for physical illnesses. In addition to these dramatic specials on sensitive issues, Levinson and Link created popular mystery series for TV, such as *Ellery Queen* and *Murder She Wrote.*

Levinson and Link based *The Execution of Private Slovik* on a fine book by William Bradford Huie. Huie had taken an interest in Slovik's case and tracked down documents that suggested that the troubled young soldier had not been treated very sympathetically by the U.S. Army. A change in the Judge Advocate General's Office had eliminated some of the red tape blocking access to evidence in the case, and Huie studied the newly released papers and interviewed people who had known Slovick. He also talked with Slovik's wife, and she allowed him to read the many letters Slovik had written to her. The revelations in Huie's book were startling, for the Slovik execution had occurred during the last months of the war in Europe, when other war stories easily eclipsed reports about this single soldier's fate. Thus, not many people knew about the case. In fact, Slovik's wife was surprised to learn the information Huie uncovered about her husband's problems with the army.[42]

Once Huie's book was published, the Slovik case looked like a good topic for docudrama, but political controversies kept the project from reaching the screen for many years. In 1959, Frank Sinatra acquired rights to the story, and he assigned Albert Maltz, one of the Hollywood Ten, to write the screenplay. Maltz had served a one-year jail sentence for refusing to identify communists at hearings held by the House Un-American Activities Committee. Walter Winchell and Hedda Hopper brought public attention to Maltz's background, pressuring Sinatra to remove the controversial writer from the project. The American Legion lobbied for Maltz's removal, and Joseph P. Kennedy also warned Sinatra to drop Maltz. (Kennedy's son was running for president in 1960, and the elder Kennedy did not want JFK's candidacy harmed by his public association with Sinatra.) Rather quickly, Sinatra caved in to the pressure and removed Maltz's name from the film project. Sinatra also learned that it would be difficult to produce the movie as long as Dwight D. Eisenhower was alive. Eisenhower, as leader of the Allies' military campaigns in Europe, had given final authorization for Slovik's execution, and release of the film could be viewed as criticism of the famous war hero. Eventually, Sinatra gave up his efforts to produce the Eddie Slovik story, and Levinson and Link obtained the rights to it.

The television drama is extraordinarily faithful to the evidence Huie presents in his book, and it makes a commendable effort to render the details with authenticity. The script incorporates much of the language reported in the official documents, such as the comments made by military authorities during Slovik's court-martial. When the drama portrays Slovik's time in the army, it features a voice-over as Slovik (Martin Sheen) reads from letters to his wife back home. The sound track includes some of the actual music Slovik heard (particularly "Tangerine," a favorite of Slovik and his wife). The end of the movie has no artificial music, however; the audience hears only the soldiers' footsteps as they move away from the execution site. The drama follows the details of Huie's book so closely that it is difficult to find specific examples of cinematic manipulation. One of the few notable adjustments of the facts relates to the film's portrayal of the execution. The movie shows Slovik choking up and sobbing as a soldier places a hood over his head, whereas the documents indicate that Slovik was quiet and courageous. This is hardly an egregious manipulation of the evidence. Levinson and Link's embellishment only helps heighten the emotional impact of the depiction, accentuating the horror.

*The Execution of Private Slovik* makes a strong case on behalf of the victim, but it does not present the evidence in a one-sided manner. The drama shows why U.S. military leaders made a decision that seems quite wrongheaded to many who have viewed the evidence years after the fact. Levinson and Link's film portrays military authorities speaking of the Slovik case as they addressed it in 1945. Eddie Slovik refused to fight when U.S. forces were pinned down in the Hürtgen Forest and were suffering serious casualties. His case came up for court-martial at a time when American soldiers faced even greater casualties and frustration in the Battle of the Bulge. In both military engagements, a number of U.S. soldiers—including the recent, bottom-of-the-barrel draftees such as Slovik—deserted in the face of enemy fire. In the movie, various officers responsible for making decisions in the case against Slovik express concern that discipline will break down if soldiers think that they can evade military action with impunity. Slovik's case is an attractive example for these individuals, because the young deserter had a criminal record before he went into the military (Slovik was involved in only minor infractions).[43]

*The Execution of Private Slovik* also reveals that decision makers up the line in the U.S. military chose capital punishment as the sentence because the rules required it. Slovik had clearly taken responsibility for deserting and had written a note spelling out what he had done and that he would run away again if sent to the front. Some (but not all) individuals in the military passed along the recommendation for execution, expecting that such an extraordinary punishment would not actually be meted out. But when the recommendation reached the top, General Eisenhower was busy making important strategic decisions, and he let the order stand.[44]

Although the movie examines the conditions and rationales that led to Eddie Slovik's execution in front of a firing squad, it also presents a great deal of evidence that undermines the case for his execution. After focusing on Slovik's last day as a military prisoner, the movie flashes back and examines his personal background. The story characterizes Slovik much as his friends, family, and fellow soldiers remembered him—as a good-hearted but shy and troubled young man who is distrustful of institutions. As a teenager, he gets into difficulties with the law and spends a lengthy period in reform school. One of the authorities at the school takes a liking to him and urges him to find a good woman when he gets out, someone who will give him direction in his life. Slovik soon finds such a relationship, and as the counselor expected, it transforms him. Newly married and deeply in love, Slovik gets a decent job and moves into small but attractive living quarters with his wife.

This brief, happy interlude comes to an abrupt end when he receives notice to report to the military. The U.S. Army was desperate for manpower in the final, bloody year of the war and was turning to individuals such as Slovik, men with criminal records who would ordinarily be rejected. Slovik attempts to obtain deferment to care for his epileptic and chronically ill wife, but the army denies his request. Nerve-racked by the army experience, Slovik writes 376 letters to his wife in 372 days, indicating in some correspondence that he is considering desertion. He takes that action in his first combat experiences in France, running away from the firefight and turning himself in to a Canadian unit. Reporting that he was paralyzed with fear when the shelling occurred, he writes the letter to the U.S. Army that puts him on the road to the execution. In this manner, the film explains Slovik's controversial action in terms of his personal background. The biographical treatment attempts to show why this particular individual resisted the army's demands and became the test case for punishing deserters.

*The Execution of Private Slovik* presents enough heart-wrenching information to convince most viewers that Slovik should not have been shot. The drama shows that the U.S. Army needed to make an example of someone, and Slovik's case suited that purpose. Slovik already had a criminal record, and as Martin Sheen says in the film (and Slovik expressed in real life), "They are shooting me for the bread I stole when I was twelve years old." The movie never slams viewers with a heavy-handed suggestion that they must conclude in Slovik's favor, however. The preponderance of information simply weighs in most impressively on his side. Overall, then, *The Execution of Private Slovik* presents a sophisticated, fair-minded review of the principal details. It exposes the audience to both critical and supporting evidence about its subject and communicates its message with integrity and subtlety.

A ringing endorsement of the movie's softly stated point of view came out thirteen years later in a remarkable essay by one of the men who had made the military judgment regarding guilt and execution. In an article published in *American Heritage,* Benedict B. Kimmelman explained why he regretted his decision to convict Slovik. Kimmelman observed that the deliberations had not been fair; Slovik's defense counsel was not an attorney, only five witnesses spoke at the hearings, and Slovik remained mute during the court-martial. General Eisenhower did not even read Slovik's plea for mercy. Kimmelman had been taken captive by the Germans in the Battle of the Bulge, so he did not learn of Slovik's execution until after his release. The news of Slovik's death by firing squad upset him. Kimmelman had seen many U.S. soldiers demoralized, emotionally paralyzed, and unwilling to pursue combat during the brutal fighting at the Bulge. He expressed sympathy for young men like Slovik who were unable to deal with the frightening situation. Their failures deserved disciplinary action, Kimmelman acknowledged, but hardly the draconian action taken against Slovik.[45]

*Examining Controversy through Conflicting Perspectives*

*The Execution of Private Slovik* came close to presenting a balanced, two-sided perspective of the case, but the evidence associated with Slovik's personal background, the details of the military's decision making, and the distinctive nature of his punishment (as the only GI executed for desertion during the war) tended to push the film's sympathies in the direction of the victim. Do some movies succeed in creating strongly balanced portrayals of their subjects? Can cinematic history challenge audiences to make judgments by confronting them with two or more well-documented arguments? Do some dramas effectively remind audiences that interpreting history often calls for difficult decision making? Can motion pictures succeed in presenting the search for historical understanding in the fashion of a detective story, where the investigator must study evidence (in a manner, clues), weigh its significance, and decide how to employ it? Can movies encourage audiences to make personal judgments about the past and reach decisions about truth and falsehood, right and wrong, praise and criticism?

The two films under consideration are among the few that perform splendidly in suggesting that balance. Each provokes its audience, delivering a good deal of information that leads viewers in several directions as they evaluate the evidence. Each film creates a pendulum effect, swinging the audience back and forth between perspectives. During some moments in the dramas, the characterizations seem to favor one point of view, but then the sympathy shifts. Throughout the films, words and images hint of contradictory conclusions, and in the end, the stories do not bring closure to the debate. These films encourage viewers to render their own judgments.

It is tremendously difficult to fashion a drama that appears impartial, and students of these films may detect slight interpretive biases in one direction or another. Some degree of bias is likely to be evident, for no filmmaker can approach historical evidence with complete objectivity. By choosing to include specific information and to characterize individuals in a particular manner, as well as in other artistic decisions, the dramatist employs subtle but persuasive techniques that skew a film's perspective. Indeed, it is likely that key production personnel (such as the writer, producer, and director) harbor personal opinions on the subject, despite their public claims about seeking an even-handed examination of it. Still, these movies deserve acclaim for exhibiting such judiciousness in portraying controversial subjects. They are not perfect models of objectivity, but they are more effective than most films in introducing audiences to conflicting viewpoints.

One of the most familiar examples of this achievement is *Patton,* which won the Academy Award for Best Picture of 1970. *Patton*'s creators first planned to take a hagiographic stand, aiming to construct a rather one-sided, favorable perspective on a war hero, but political circumstances influenced their decision to make the characterization more complex.

Early plans to create a movie about one of America's most famous World War II generals, George S. Patton, called for a celebratory film that would honor the military figure as a hero and an inspiration for Americans. The screenplay was to praise Patton's gutsy, unconventional approach to leadership. Frank McCarthy, who had been secretary to General George C. Marshall during World War II, guided the project from the beginning and eventually became the movie's producer. He proposed the concept for the film to Darryl Zanuck of Fox and got the go-ahead to begin planning. A variety of obstacles stood in his way, however. McCarthy needed tanks, jeeps, and other equipment to give his film authenticity, but the U.S. Army would not cooperate. Patton's widow would not cooperate either. After she died, two of Patton's three children refused to work with him as well, feeling that their father had received unfair treatment from the media. George S. Patton II, a lieutenant in the army, was particularly resistant, saying that he would "shoot any SOB who makes a movie about my father." By the time McCarthy was ready to move forward with script writing and production planning (by buying rights to biographies of Patton and securing help from the Spanish army), the United States was in the thick of the Vietnam War, which created a very different condition for the movie's reception. Responding to the new political environment, McCarthy worked to create a balanced movie treatment of General Patton.[46]

From 1965 to 1969, the script went through several revisions, and U.S. military actions in Vietnam became increasingly unpopular. Public demonstrations against the war grew, young Americans protested the draft, and antiwar and antimilitary sentiments found frequent expression in the mass media. McCarthy and director Franklin Schaffner now sensed that they would have to portray their story differently and market it differently as well. They attempted to present both a positive and negative side of the general.[47]

On the one hand, the motion picture they released in 1970 gives the general a heroic characterization. Germany's military leaders praise and fear Patton. The American general expects the soldiers under him to maintain high standards of preparation and discipline. He displays a genius for war-making, yet he is also a cultured and refined figure who shows his humanity while visiting a seriously wounded soldier. Above all, the movie depicts Patton as America's most successful leader in the World War II military campaigns, a key figure in the Allies' success against the powerful German war machine. The film suggests

*George S. Patton (George C. Scott) is about to deliver a memorable speech in the first minutes of Franklin J. Schaffner's* Patton *(1970). The film presents a heroic picture of the famous general, yet it also raises serious questions about his ideas and behavior. (Museum of Modern Art Film Archive)*

that the fighting in Europe might have ended earlier if the Allied military planners had given Patton's troops the gasoline and the green light they needed to pursue the enemy deep into Germany.

On the other hand, *Patton* raises questions about the controversial military figure. It shows the general's arrogance and insensitivity (such as when he slaps a soldier who has suffered psychologically from the combat experience). The movie reveals that Patton proposed generous treatment of defeated Nazi military men at the end of the war, and it suggests that he was overly eager to engage the Russian communists in a war. Most important, the film examines

*George S. Patton (George C. Scott) prepares to land at a beachhead in* Patton
*(1970). Public agitation over the Vietnam War led the movie's producer and
director to emphasize that their film was not a simple-minded, gung-ho war
picture. (Museum of Modern Art Film Archive)*

Patton's enthusiasm for battle, his eagerness to pursue it for personal glory.
Speaking of war, Patton says, "I love it. God help me. I do love it so." In other
situations, Patton (George C. Scott) worries that the war will end before he has
a chance to direct major victories and achieve the destiny he thinks he deserves.
At one point in the film, Patton speaks of reincarnation, claiming that he had
been present on the ancient battlefields of history. The film leaves audiences
guessing: Is this man a brilliant general or a madman?

When the movie was ready for release in the spring of 1970—a volatile period of intense public controversy about America's role in Vietnam—
McCarthy and Schaffner told the media that their picture was not simply a
gung-ho, pro-war story. "This is not a war film," said McCarthy.[48] The producer

believed that viewers would find the battle scenes horrifying and recognize the movie's antiwar qualities. Schaffner maintained that Patton "was misguided and a man after a headline." He said that the general "hated peace and wanted to start trouble with the Russians."[49] In these comments to the press and in other publicity efforts, the producer and director drew attention to the two-sided nature of their characterization. Representatives of the media understood their message, interpreting the film in the way its creators suggested. "Viewing Patton: Pick Your Angle," headlined the *Wall Street Journal;* "Left, Right Hail War Picture," reported *Variety;* "Patton: Reaction Divided," stated the *Los Angeles Herald-Examiner.* The *Herald-Examiner*'s reviewer noted that *Patton* made the general look like a monster to some and a genius to others.[50]

Thus, an unpopular war helped establish the basis for an unusually balanced examination of a brilliant but highly controversial military figure from World War II. From the opening moments of the film (when Patton speaks enthusiastically to troops about the glories of combat and America's impressive military record) and throughout the picture, *Patton* challenges audiences to think, to raise questions, and to make personal judgments. More so than most Hollywood docudramas, *Patton* exposes audiences to clashing perspectives on its subject. A reviewer for the *New Yorker* succinctly identified the film's achievement when he said that the movie "appears to be deliberately planned as a Rorschach test." Patton looked like a true hero to those who believed in military values, said the writer, a "red-blooded American who loves to fight and whose crude talk is straight talk." To those who despised militarism, however, *Patton* showed "the worst kind of red-blooded American mystical maniac who *believes* in fighting." In their eyes, the general was "symbolic proof of the madness of the whole military complex."[51] In a unique and highly entertaining way, then, *Patton* manages to accomplish a rare achievement—a well-substantiated presentation of more than one perspective on a famous figure.

*Concealed Enemies* (1984) is the second outstanding example of a docudrama that brilliantly confronts viewers with conflicting evidence and challenges them to judge its significance. This made-for-TV movie produced by Peter Cook appeared on PBS Television in 1984 and won an Emmy for Best Miniseries. The WGBH-TV film presents an exceptionally balanced investigation of the confrontation between Alger Hiss and Whittaker Chambers in the 1940s. The Hiss-Chambers affair attracted public interest when Chambers, an editor at *Time* and a former Communist Party member, accused Hiss of being a fellow Communist back in the 1930s. Later, Chambers charged that Hiss had been involved in espionage and had supplied confidential documents to the Soviets. These claims were shocking, for Hiss had a distinguished reputation. He was a Harvard-educated lawyer, an important figure in the New Deal

*In the fashion of a detective story,* Concealed Enemies *(1984) reveals evidence that, at various points, appears to support the case of either Alger Hiss or Whittaker Chambers. (WGBH-TV, Boston)*

administration, and an officer in the U.S. State Department who had participated in the Yalta negotiations and the creation of the United Nations. At first, Hiss appeared to be innocent of the charges, but evidence began to mount in congressional hearings and grand jury investigations that cast doubt on Hiss's testimony. Eventually, Hiss received a sentence of five years in prison on two counts of perjury (he served forty-four months). When Hiss received his sentence, conservatives and liberals argued vehemently about his guilt or innocence. Debates over Hiss's supposed involvement with communism remained intense through the following decades.[52]

*Concealed Enemies* straddles the fence in this great debate. It presents a strong case for both Chambers and Hiss, examining much of the conflicting evidence that intrigued and confused Americans back in the 1940s. It challenges viewers with a detective-like investigation into a complex legal case, refusing to favor decisively either of the historic figures under study.

Peter Riegert (playing young Congressman Richard Nixon, who was active in the investigation) concisely states the main question that energizes the drama when he questions whether Hiss or Chambers is telling the truth. "Whoever is lying," says Nixon, "is the greatest actor America has ever produced." *Concealed Enemies* never suggests which character audiences ought to believe. Over the course of the story, the drama drops clues and reveals secrets, leading viewers to favor either Hiss or Chambers from moment to moment. When the film shows Hiss (Edward Hermann) speaking in private with his wife, lawyer, or friends, he does not act like a guilty man. He displays the indignation of a distinguished American who believes that he is innocent. Indeed, Jeff Bleckner, the director, urged his actors to play their roles in this fashion. When the actors asked him, "Am I telling the truth, or am I lying?" Bleckner responded, "You're all telling the truth, and you should play it absolutely as if you're telling the truth."[53] As the four-hour drama comes to an end, the issue of truthfulness remains in doubt. The movie's verdict remains uncertain, or at least, it is left to the viewer to judge.

Solid research and attention to historical detail enhance the quality of *Concealed Enemies*. Writer Hugh Whitmore read every book on the subject he could find and interviewed more than sixty individuals who knew the principal figures. He and actor Edward Hermann also interviewed Alger Hiss (Chambers was dead). Director Jeff Bleckner, an accomplished veteran of the TV show *Hill Street Blues*, managed to gather a number of vintage props that gave the film a feel of authenticity: 1940s automobiles filled the city streets, newsmen used old photographic equipment with huge flashbulbs of the period. Bleckner filmed the story in a slightly washed-out, brownish tint, giving his production a period look. In these and other examples of the director's attention to verisimilitude, the film strongly communicates a feeling of America in the late 1940s.

Evidence that has come to light since the release of *Concealed Enemies* tends to support the case against Alger Hiss. Documents began to emerge, especially after the end of the Cold War, that seemed to suggest that Hiss had, in fact, lied under oath. These records included files from the U.S. government's Verona Project, KGB documents, and records that had been in the hands of the Hungarian secret police. If dramatists attempted to portray Hiss's story in the twenty-first century, they might find the evidence less conflicting than it appeared to the producer, writer, and director of *Concealed Enemies* in the 1980s.[54]

*Patton* and *Concealed Enemies* represent impressive achievements, but they are bold exceptions to Hollywood's rules of genre. Usually, cinematic history does not present multiple perspectives; it does not challenge viewers with ambiguous portraits. Partisan portrayals with heroes and villains are much more common among Hollywood's productions, because they constitute safer investments. Audiences respond more readily to films that sharply distinguish good from bad, right from wrong. Cinematic history often weighs in heavily with specific judgments about people and issues. In view of the uniqueness of the balanced treatment in *Patton* and *Concealed Enemies*, the achievements of these two notable motion pictures deserve our attention.

The general thrust of the commentary on the films examined in this section has been complimentary, but the absence of strong criticism does not suggest that these films are flawless. No entry in the field of cinematic history achieves that extraordinary status. Certainly it is possible to challenge the treatment of history in each of these dramas, to draw attention to ways in which it could have probed the past with greater sensitivity and intelligence. Filmed drama can always be improved on, and our understanding of the medium's ability to both entertain and educate the public evolves as artists experiment with new techniques of presentation. The dramatic approach taken in *The Longest Day*, for instance, looks somewhat dated to the modern-day enthusiast of cinematic history. Nevertheless, all these motion pictures serve as impressive examples of the potential of film to arouse audiences' thinking about the past and connect their emotions to it. These movies and television specials are not perfect models of cinematic history, but they demonstrate some of the medium's potential to address important matters with sophistication.

# CHAPTER FOUR

# Screening History

## *A Test Case*

In September 1980, a movie crew took possession of several blocks in downtown Charleston, South Carolina, to film a story set in the year 1822. When shooting a busy market scene that was designed to look like a typical shopping situation in early-nineteenth-century Charleston, the set designers gave close attention to historical details. They filled the city's open-air market with vegetables, placed a number of goats and chickens near the stalls, and situated scores of people in and around the facility. These extras were exquisitely dressed in fashions of the 1820s. The set designers also covered Charleston's asphalt streets with dirt, and they arranged for drivers in horse-drawn carriages to ride around the periphery of the market area. All these efforts helped establish a proper background for the movie's depiction of a typical 1820s morning in the port city. At the precise moment when all the props and people were in place, two elderly ladies who were visiting Charleston for the first time came around a corner and set their eyes on the marvelous scene. One turned to the other and exclaimed, "My goodness, they really do historic restoration right in Charleston!" Her comment offered amusing testimony to the filmmakers' careful efforts to give a few blocks of the city an authentic-looking appearance.[1]

The made-for-television movie that resulted from these efforts, *Denmark Vesey's Rebellion* (1982), offered more than just elaborate visual details. Professional historians were involved in planning the project from the earliest stages of its development. Far more than in most cases of cinematic history, skilled academicians played important roles in designing the film's story. They contributed to conceptualizing the screenplay, scrutinized early drafts of the script, and identified information in the historical archives that provided factual foundations for the drama. These scholars discussed their recommendations personally with the writer and the producers, who incorporated many of their suggestions in the film. The production of *Denmark Vesey's Rebellion* involved a partnership between scholars and filmmakers who cooperated in an effort to create a sophisticated cinematic interpretation of the past.

Despite these commendable attempts to deal responsibly with history, the makers of *Denmark Vesey's Rebellion* exercised a good deal of creative license in making their movie. They employed a number of generic conventions in the design of their story; they simplified complex information, collapsed several historical figures into a few, and compressed the presentation of events. They also mimicked the familiar three-act docudrama format, shaping their story in terms of exposition, complication, and resolution. The writer, director, and producers created dialogues between historic figures, even though there was no specific evidence that such conversations ever took place. On a number of occasions, the filmmakers speculated boldly about the motivations of important historic figures, and they showed these individuals taking actions that may or may not have actually occurred. In a variety of ways, the film's creators massaged facts, manipulated details, and manufactured evidence in an effort to present understandable and entertaining television drama.

An inside look at the making of *Denmark Vesey's Rebellion* can illuminate the complexity of bringing history to the screen. It reveals that filmmakers must exercise artistic license when producing historical drama. Even when these artists intend to honor the historical record, as the makers of *Denmark Vesey's Rebellion* hoped to do, they are often compelled to fictionalize. This example of significant compromising in a serious attempt to produce cinematic history provides a useful lesson for the cynical critics of docudrama who insist that filmmakers should present only accurate and authentic depictions of history. This case shows that dramatizing the past *requires* invention, that the practice of cinematic history is *inherently* creative. The case reveals, too, that even when filmmakers sincerely try to create a production that is educational and instructive, they must pay close attention to the traditions of the cinematic genre.

The following discussion of *Denmark Vesey's Rebellion* is much more personal than other analyses that appear in this book, because I was closely connected to this production. From 1976 until the film's national broadcast on PBS Television in 1982, I worked as a principal creator of the film project, participating in everything from the original conception and planning, fund-raising, and development to shooting on the set, postproduction work, and public promotion. Thus, my commentaries on this project spring from personal experience rather than formal study.

The opportunity to work on a film came unexpectedly in 1976, when I received a call from an individual working with the PBS station in Miami, Florida. WPBT, the local PBS affiliate, had received a planning grant from the National Endowment for the Humanities (NEH), and producers at the station were seeking ideas for television shows. The grant allowed the station to communicate with humanists around the United States, and as an academic who had published some books and articles about slavery, my name turned up on the list of invitees. A representative of the station, himself a historian, asked that I write a few pages identifying concepts for programming. The invitation intrigued me, not only because it came with an honorarium (in those days, humanities scholars were not in the habit of receiving paychecks for consultation activities), but also because the opportunity to imagine a TV series that dealt with history sounded very exciting. I quickly tapped out ten pages of description calling for dramas about slavery in the United States. My proposal stressed that in recent years, much of the most important and controversial research in American history had dealt with the "peculiar institution." This subject interested the public, I said, principally because of the recent successes of the civil rights movement. Americans wanted to learn more about the origins of racial injustice and the historic struggle against it. The time was ripe, I argued, for a series of dramatic films that traced the experiences of real people whose lives had been affected by slavery. Each drama could serve as a window, providing audiences a view of a different issue from the history of slavery in America.

My connections with the world of television and film expanded quickly in that period. Shortly after I sent the ten-page proposal, producers at WPBT invited me down to Miami to discuss the idea in person. They soon gave me the title of project director, a term used by the NEH to identify the individual who guides one of its funded film projects through the various stages of development. A project director also serves as the principal liaison in dealing with the NEH. Beyond that, nothing was certain about my responsibilities; the job description was vague, and it had different meanings in the various production organizations that received grants. As I discovered over several years of association with NEH-supported projects, the scope of a project director's responsibilities depended on the individual's determination to stick his or her nose into the filmmaking activities and on the production people's tolerance for working with an academic. I was fortunate in teaming up with two talented and cooperative executives who gave me considerable latitude, especially in the early stages of the project: R. Shepherd Morgan, the executive producer, and Yanna Kroyt Brandt, the producer. Working with Morgan and Brandt, I named the subjects for study, developed treatments for the programs (story outlines with descriptions of scenes and characters), wrote the bulk of the grant applications (particularly the historical and dramatic narratives), and worked closely with professional screenwriters in creating the scripts. I also assembled a team of scholar-advisers that included historians at the height of scholarship on slavery and race relations at the time: Ira Berlin,

David Brion Davis, Eric Foner, Eugene D. Genovese, Herbert Gutman, Nathan Huggins, Benjamin Quarles, Armstead Robinson, Willie Lee Rose, William Shack, Kenneth M. Stampp, and Peter Wood.

Raising money for these productions constituted an enormous challenge. In view of the limited funds received annually by the NEH, my production associates and I had to seek financial support for each production as if it were an individual project. In each case, the application process essentially started anew, as we defended a film concept all over again to a new team of NEH judges. Furthermore, each film required two major grants—one for scripting, and a second for production. A production grant from the NEH was never sufficient to allow shooting to begin; it merely provided seed money, which then had to be supplemented by financial support from corporate underwriters. The producers and I remained busy for several years seeking approximately $1 million in funding for each film. Throughout this process, we had to justify the programming not only in terms of its scholarly appeal but also with a view toward its attractiveness as entertainment. The NEH program officers, corporate underwriters, and PBS officials kept an eye on production values, not just the educational potential and cultural worth of the programs.

Over a period of several years, our production team received funding to complete three films. Two years after *Denmark Vesey's Rebellion* appeared, PBS broadcast *Solomon Northup's Odyssey*. The Northup story dealt with a free black man who had been kidnapped into slavery. Northup spent twelve years in bondage in Louisiana before a sympathetic white man communicated information about his condition to friends in the North and succeeded in getting him released. *Charlotte Forten's Mission* (1985) related the story of an African-American woman who went to the South to help freedmen during the Civil War. The Northup and Forten films later appeared on the Disney Channel as well. WPBT also received NEH funding for the planning and scripting of additional films about John Punch, a runaway slave in early colonial America, and Moncure Conway, a white antislavery Virginian.[2] Unfortunately, we could not obtain sufficient corporate funding to support production of these scripts.

An important distinction between interpreting history for the reading audience and interpreting it for film and TV viewers struck me forcefully when I arranged the first meetings of our production team. These sessions brought together the executive producer, the producer, a couple of prospective writers, and the group of academic advisers. After much discussion, the scholars recommended production of a program that swept across broad social, economic, and racial issues but lacked a central focus on the experiences of one or two specific individuals from history. The scholars selected a topic I had identified in the NEH application as one of the most intriguing and well-documented stories about slavery to emerge in recent scholarship. The subject was the Port Royal Experiment, which consisted of efforts by federal officials to bring freedom, economic progress, landownership, and education to slaves of the South Carolina and Georgia sea islands that came under Union control during the Civil War.

I tried to press the scholars for ideas about how we could create a compelling and manageable drama out of such a huge, amorphous history. This subject was tremendously important, I confessed, and it had been splendidly interpreted in a respected book by one of our advisers, Willie Lee Rose.[3] But how could we find the foundations for a drama within Rose's vast and complex analysis? Several advisers suggested that our dramatists could surely come up with a way to shape a workable story. They argued that we should not miss the opportunity to bring Rose's groundbreaking interpretation to the screen. Her book threw important light on the emancipation experience, they argued, and television audiences could learn a great deal from a presentation of the issues.

After that meeting, one of the writers and I devoted an enormous amount of time to researching subjects related to Rose's book. We tried to create a workable structure for a script, but our efforts proved frustrating. The numerous people and events covered by our study constituted an ordinary amount of material for a book but were an extraordinary scope for a ninety-minute television drama. We soon began to flounder. A basic outline for the script did not emerge comfortably from the evidence, and when we tried to impose a form on the information, we engaged in heavy fictionalization, imagining "typical" behavior for a number of invented characters or historical figures about whom we knew very little. Seeking to jump-start this stalling project, I conferred with the producers, and we decided that travel might prove helpful. We arranged for our writer to meet for two days with Willie Lee Rose and then to travel to the sea islands of South Carolina so that he could gain some personal exposure to the region and work with local documents. This strategy failed to produce an impressive screenplay. Our story about the Port Royal Experiment continued to be unwieldy and unfocused.

By this time, I had become convinced that we were on the wrong track. The story of the Port Royal Experiment—a great topic for a book—was too broad for a filmed docudrama. I sensed that we could achieve greater progress looking at the activities of one individual who had participated in the "rehearsal for Reconstruction." That effort, however, would take more research and much more time. I eventually identified Charlotte Forten as the subject for such a film. Forten, the daughter of a distinguished African American in Philadelphia, had gone to the sea islands during the Civil War to teach the freedmen and left a diary tracing her experiences. By the time we settled on the interesting

Forten story, our first two docudramas on African-American figures from the nineteenth century were already well in development.

While we were still struggling with the Port Royal story, a more manageable topic was already on the table: the film project dealing with Denmark Vesey's slave conspiracy. I became increasingly excited about that subject's potential, because the essential elements of compelling drama appeared to be present. Vesey had been a slave but eventually won his freedom, yet Vesey's children continued to live in bondage. Rather late in life, around the age of sixty, Vesey became the leader of a plan to conduct a massive slave revolt centered in Charleston, South Carolina, with the goal of freeing the region's slaves. At the eleventh hour, however, some blacks revealed the plot, and Charleston authorities arrested Vesey and many of his associates. They convicted a number of the conspirators, sending some of them, including Vesey, to the gallows and banishing others from the United States.

By focusing particularly on the exploits of Denmark Vesey, we had the components of fascinating drama. Vesey's bold plot had a tremendous impact on white Southerners. It struck fear in their hearts, provoking efforts to tighten controls over slavery in the South. These efforts, in turn, antagonized Northerners and led to growing criticism of the oppressive institution. Our dramatization could show audiences how problems with slavery led to significant sectional confrontations in the antebellum period. Also, an examination of Vesey's experiences could teach audiences about the day-to-day lives of slaves and explore the complexity of the master-slave relationship. In the course of portraying Vesey's life, our film could reveal how blacks struggled for individual dignity in the difficult, race-conscious society of the slave South. Our program could also suggest the difficulties slaves faced when they resorted to violence to protest their condition.

Devising a conspiracy of my own, I scheduled the next meeting of producers, writers, and scholars in Charleston, South Carolina. My goal was to excite their interest in the Vesey drama by placing them at the site of the insurrectionist leader's activities. I hoped that they would sense the story's potential as they walked the streets of the historic city. The tactic was only partially effective, however. It worked with the producers and writers, but not as well with the scholars. A majority of the historians agreed to support further research and development of a treatment about Vesey, but they still chose the Port Royal Experiment as the first project to receive full script preparation. Several months later, the failings of the Port Royal screenplay had not been resolved, and I begged again for support of the Vesey script. After several more communications with the advisers, I finally won approval to make the Vesey story the first order of business.

Recalling the agony of that early experience in script creation, I do not see the advisers' commitment to the Port Royal story as a narrow-minded failure to understand the nature of filmed drama. I was perhaps more responsible than anyone for putting the production team in a morass, since the program about Port Royal had been my idea in the first place. When applying for scripting grants, I found that it was easy to extol the value of a TV program that examined the efforts to help African Americans move from slavery to freedom in the sea islands. The Port Royal Experiment represented a microcosm of the South's struggles with Reconstruction after the Civil War, I argued. It gave us a fascinating window into an important chapter in American history. My description sounded wonderful in a grant application, but it certainly did not provide a useful blueprint for designing cinematic history. When my colleagues and I tried to turn that description into a working script, we discovered that our plan was much too vague.

The struggle over the Port Royal story provided a valuable lesson for all the academics associated with the project, myself included. In order to turn academic history into cinematic history, we needed to learn how to communicate through film. At first, we did not truly appreciate the distinction between nonfiction and drama. We turned to our familiar narrative devices: citing vast amounts of data, relating stories about numerous historical characters, interpreting many important events that occurred over a long span of time. Working in that mode, we thought that Willie Lee Rose's book about the "rehearsal for Reconstruction" looked like a suitable subject for television. But, as we discovered, it was not easily translatable into television drama. We were facing a different kind of interpretive challenge in this case, one that was not as pressing when we wrote articles and books about history. Our film project required not only that we raise important questions about history but also that we try to imagine the answers in the form of an understandable and entertaining story for the screen.

Could we educate and entertain at the same time? Were these two principal goals mutually supporting, or were they in conflict with each other? Did progress toward one goal necessarily undermine advancement toward the other? Our filmmaking experience suggested some answers.

At first glance, the Vesey story looks like an easy one for dramatization. There are abundant records in the historical archives related to the conspiracy, including testimony from a number of slaves implicated in the insurrection plot and an official report on the trial proceedings. We also found published interpretations of the events by the governor of South Carolina and the mayor of Charleston, newspaper articles, personal letters, and a variety of other primary sources. The documentary record of the Vesey conspiracy is certainly one of the strongest among the cases of slave rebellion in American history. This wealth of available evidence helped us create dialogues that nicely reflected the historical record. When we needed to put words in the mouths of actors, we could often draw directly from extant papers of 1822. In the film, Denmark Vesey (Yaphet Kotto) sometimes speaks in the same language that appears in the records. His fellow insurrectionists take an oath of allegiance using words reported in the testimonies, and a judge announces Vesey's sentence in language drawn directly from the lengthier 1822 version. A publicist advertising our film for prospective television audiences could cite this documentation and claim that the movie gave an authentic picture of history. "Based on the facts!" a promotion blurb could exclaim. "Actors speak the very words of the historic figures!"

Yet even these heavily documented archival records provide just a few pieces of a complex puzzle. The record does not show what blacks or whites said to one another unofficially behind closed doors. Virtually all the private conversations in the drama had to be imagined. Also, we do not know much about Denmark Vesey's personal motivation in leading a slave rebellion. The papers contain only a few words suggesting that he was angry because, despite winning his own freedom in an 1800 lottery, his children remained in slavery. We know that Vesey found inspiration for revolt in Bible passages and that he was aroused by what he read in some published documents containing congressional debates on slavery. Still, these reports constitute only tiny bits of information that hint at motivation. A dramatist must surmise why a man who enjoyed the comforts of freedom would risk his life and those of many friends in such a dangerous plot.

Despite hundreds of pages of extant documents on the case, the most important details of Vesey's personal background are essentially limited to a lengthy footnote appended to the official report of the conspirators' trial. That brief commentary begins with these words: "As Denmark Vesey has occupied so large a place in the conspiracy, a brief notice of him will, perhaps, not be devoid of interest." Not be devoid of interest, indeed! Numerous books and articles have been published on the 1822 plot that interpret and inform at length about the possible meaning of the nineteen sentences in this one-paragraph footnote. Much like the authors of those publications, those of us who worked on the film speculated about the meaning of those words. In two flashbacks, our film traces Captain Joseph Vesey's (Donald Moffat) discovery of a fourteen-year-old slave (James Bond III) in the Caribbean, a lad whom the captain finds unique in his "beauty, alertness, and intelligence." We guessed about the conditions that could have led Captain Vesey to favor the youngster and make him a "pet" on his ship, then sell him into slavery and sometime later take him back on

*Denmark Vesey (Yaphet Kotto) is a successful free black man in 1822 Charleston, South Carolina, in* Denmark Vesey's Rebellion *(1982). Much has been written about Vesey, but specific details about his personality, ideas, and plans are limited. As often happens in the making of a docudrama, the filmmakers had to engage in a good deal of speculation to present the character on the screen. (Robert Brent Toplin)*

a return voyage. We had to imagine a situation in which Denmark Vesey approached the captain (his owner) many years later and sought to buy his freedom with money won in a Charleston lottery. How would a slave approach his master with such a request? And, like the authors of scholarly books about the subject, we had to interpret the single paragraph's characterization of Vesey as a man whose "temper was impetuous and domineering in the extreme."[4]

When I met with the scholars and production personnel to discuss these questions about the portrayal of Vesey, the exchanges turned quickly to controversy. Participants in the meeting disagreed about the goals of the conspirators. Documents from 1822, compiled by whites in South Carolina, portrayed the plot's leader in highly critical terms—as a vicious rebel motivated by blood lust. In contrast, late-twentieth-century historians had written many sympathetic words about the black freedman, pointing to Vesey's intelligence and courage. Even in failure, said these scholars, Vesey's plot showed southern whites that the blacks were not as happy in bondage as the slave owners were inclined to believe. Members of our advisory board clearly favored the second interpretation, but they were divided in the conclusions they drew from specific evidence in the archives. To some, the historic Vesey was a great hero, a freedom fighter much like the Founding Fathers of the American Revolution or the modern-day leaders of the civil rights movement. Others agreed that Vesey's struggle against slavery was noble, but they wondered whether the real historic figure could have resembled the hate-filled rebel described in the documents. These historians observed that some reports from 1822 described a vicious man who aimed to destroy Charleston in an orgy of rape, pillage, arson, and mass murder. Perhaps, said one scholar, the historic Vesey was a madman like Charles Manson. Or perhaps we could conclude that Vesey's reasons for rebelling were good, but his intended actions were likely to harm many innocent people.

The scholars also disagreed on the goals of the conspirators. Some were inclined to believe reports from 1822 indicating that the rebels aimed to seize control of the ships in Charleston harbor and escape en masse to Haiti, which had abolished slavery in 1804. That interpretation cast a favorable light on the plot. But other historians wondered whether there was some validity to reports that suggested a more frightening outcome. They pointed to comments in the historic documents indicating that the conspirators wanted to create a terrible slaughter. This evidence raised the same questions as the interpretation of Vesey's intentions did, they noted. Although the modern-day observer cannot help but be sympathetic to the slaves' fight against oppression, a student of the subject has to acknowledge the disturbing information and decide how to deal with it. They pointed to papers from 1822 showing that a number of people believed that the rebels intended to murder hundreds of white Charlestonians and set fire to the city. The citizens of Charleston who described these plans also believed that the insurrectionists planned to direct their sexual passions at the city's white women. How should we deal with these conflicting observations? Our decision was significant, for it could lead to a depiction of events that cast the insurrectionists' enterprise either favorably or unfavorably.

When designing the script, we privileged the sympathetic view of Vesey's personality, actions, and goals, but we also gave voice to some of the conflicting perspectives. Our fundamental characterization of the rebel leader is complimentary. We show Denmark Vesey to be strongly motivated by a desire to free his family from bondage, and we suggest that he had developed a principled notion about freedom from his reading of the Bible and antislavery documents. Justifying our emphasis on positive qualities was not difficult. We recognized that fearful whites had written the principal documents about the case, and they had probably described the blacks' motivation in very critical terms. Their references to rape, for instance, echo a fear that consistently appears in nineteenth-century claims about slaves' intentions toward southern white women. Perhaps white South Carolinians gave so much attention to assertions about lust, violence, and brutality because they did not want to give expression to a different motivation—the drive to achieve emancipation from oppression. Nevertheless, we felt an obligation to show that other visions of the revolt appeared in the documents. In the film, some of the slaves express an eagerness for murder and revenge, particularly Peter Poyas (Samm-Art Williams), one of the individuals who was especially associated with violent intentions in the slave testimonies.

Our portrayal of Denmark Vesey, however, conforms to the favored practices of cinematic history. It clears him of petty hatred or the desire for gratuitous violence. The film presents Vesey in heroic terms. He comes across essentially as a fighter for justice. Violence is not his goal; rather, violence represents a means to accomplish his dream of emancipation for South Carolina's slaves. *Denmark Vesey's Rebellion* does not portray its central figure as a saint, but it certainly does not present him as a deeply flawed leader. The film attributes to other participants in the plot some of the thirst for violence and revenge that commentators mentioned in the documents.

William Freehling, a historian of the antebellum South, raised some objections to these portrayals in an article published shortly after our film's appearance on national television. Freehling observed that there was plenty of evidence in the archives suggesting that the Vesey revolt would have been a bloody affair if it had not been crushed by the authorities. The slave conspirators did not intend to be gentle with their oppressors, he pointed out. Freehling

*The author discusses plans for the portrayal of Denmark Vesey with actor Yaphet Kotto on the set of* Denmark Vesey's Rebellion *(1982). (Robert Brent Toplin)*

complained that *Denmark Vesey's Rebellion* presents the slave leader and many of his followers flatteringly, minimizing a commitment to violence that was surely on their minds. In this fashion, television perpetuates myths. Unpleasant, antisocial behavior by blacks is eliminated from the story, said Freehling. Denmark Vesey the bigamist, terrorist, and militant revolutionary of history is not evident in the drama. *Denmark Vesey's Rebellion* gives audiences black history in the manner they like it. It makes them comfortable by portraying an attractive hero, Freehling argued.[5]

Freehling is quite right in analyzing these issues from the perspective of academic history, but his observations are not particularly relevant to the fashioning of reel history. When writing books about this subject, Freehling can digress about the many possible motivations of the rebels and speculate on how the violent revolt might have played out. In the course of creating a drama, however, the opportunities for entertaining diverse interpretations are limited. Especially in the presentation of the central figure, an attempt to show him throughout the film as a representative of two poles in characterization—freedom fighter and mass murderer—would have been difficult. Drama forces the artist to choose a position and support it in the form of the actor's dress, facial appearance, voice inflection, and many other message-sending elements. Conforming to the favored practices of most cinematic history, we chose to characterize the protagonist in a favorable light.

By thinking only in terms of academic history rather than with a view toward the structure of reel history, Freehling had difficulty recognizing some of the notable achievements of the film. *Denmark Vesey's Rebellion* gives much more expression to alternative views of the past than do most docudramas. In fashioning the script, the writer and I tried to make the dialogue reflect conflicting viewpoints about important people and events. The characters' words communicate many of the opposing ideas exchanged in the advisory board's discussions. Late in the drama, for instance, a slave asks Rolla (the governor's servant, played by Cleavon Little) whether Rolla could slay his own master, and he answers quickly in the affirmative. Later, Rolla tells Peter Poyas that he cannot believe what he said. Rolla observes that his master has been good to him, and he does not want to kill. He confesses that he is in the plot for his wife and children, "not for Denmark Vesey." Poyas then announces that he will be happy to murder the governor for Rolla. Poyas insists that Denmark Vesey is a great hero, and he challenges Rolla's commitment to the plot. "Maybe he's a madman; did you ever think of that?" Rolla responds. Through this dialogue and in other exchanges between leading characters, we communicate a variety of viewpoints discussed by the scholars and suggested by some of the diverse opinions expressed in the archival materials.

If Denmark Vesey serves as the film's hero, who is the villain? We avoided the stereotypical portrayals of whites that were fashionable in television docudrama at the time. The film's slave owners and spokesmen for slavery are not simply exploitative, insensitive, or sadistic types who demonstrate no consideration for the blacks. Instead, we drew on the research of Eugene D. Genovese (a board member) and other authors, attempting to give dimension to the characterization of South Carolina's whites. The approach we took in this interpretation is articulated in a letter I sent to the director, Stan Lathan, during the formative stages of the production. At the time, I was responding to the excitement about *Roots* (1977), the tremendously successful miniseries about slavery. Some members of the production team worried that our film would seem redundant if it appeared just a few years after the release of ABC's smash hit. I responded as follows:

> Since the appearance of *Roots,* other shows have attempted to touch the same audience nerve (*A Woman Called Moses* and *Freedom Road,* for example) but they have all failed to come even close to *Roots'* success. The problem was not just one of production quality; it was a matter of subject. There can be only one *Roots* . . . at least for a few decades. If someone is going to educate TV audiences further on the subject, and interest them further, they are going to have to offer something new. And that brings us to a fundamental

question about our pilot program. What new information can we present to our audience? What new messages will stir their thinking about the history of slavery and its meaning for our lives today?

Perhaps it is time to go beyond the characters of *Roots*. We can stun audiences (and give them a more sophisticated understanding of slavery at the same time) by showing that the real problem was not simply one of good blacks exploited by bad whites. The real tragedy in this history concerns the way all people can become victims of a system. As we see in the script, a message about human relationships emerges which transcends the familiar black-white or North-South perspective. The story suggests that sometimes blacks and whites genuinely cared for each other as people, as in the cases of the Bennett-Rolla and Hammett-Bacchus relationships. Slavery was the institutional wedge driven between them. The system made them reluctant antagonists. This is a major message of our program—that by building inequality into a social structure we kill the potential of people to be decent, caring and good to each other. Some (though certainly not all) of the masters were basically decent people, but the system made them "bad."

As audiences begin to see the complexity of personalities and their relationships, I hope the insights will jolt them out of their chairs. When they realize that each actor is not fulfilling the expected stereotypical role, hopefully their minds will begin to spin as they ask themselves: How did these people get into this fix? How will they get out? Who or what is to blame? In short, they will find themselves drawn into a historical detective story. A plot unfolds, clues are introduced to help them fit pieces of the puzzle together. But at the end of the story there is still enough complexity to make the effort to draw conclusions difficult. No doubt, they will see Denmark Vesey as an authentic hero, yet they will also find themselves relating with empathy to some of the white Charlestonians such as Governor Bennett.[6]

Our film does have one truly nasty villain, Captain Dove, drawn right out of the archival records. The Dove of history displayed much more doubt about the blacks' original claims of innocence than Governor Bennett did, and he urged the authorities to treat rumors of a conspiracy with greater seriousness. When another black came forward with reports of a slave plot, Dove felt vindicated, and he proved a particularly aggressive leader of the effort to apprehend Vesey and his supporters.

A more complex villain in the film is Benjamin Hammett (Ned Beatty), a Charleston businessman who owns one of the story's principal slave figures, Bacchus. Hammett represents a good example of the contradictions in slavery that I addressed in the letter to the director. He demonstrates concern for the well-being of Bacchus (Bernie Casey), yet he works actively to control the activities of Charleston's slaves and, especially, the city's free blacks. Our drama portrays a deep sense of attachment between Hammett and Bacchus. One of the emotional high points in the film occurs when Hammett visits Bacchus while the slave awaits his execution. Hammett asks how he "went wrong" with Bacchus, expressing disbelief that his loyal slave plotted to kill him. Bacchus articulates the idea of an "institutional wedge" that I identified in the letter, asserting that his principal goal was to be free, not to kill. He acknowledges that Hammett was good to him but claims that the master never saw him as a person, only as a good horse or a very smart dog. Bacchus then chases his master away, proclaiming that death is not so horrible, for he had pretty much been asleep until Denmark Vesey awakened him with questions about his slave condition. The film shows Hammett leaving the prison in disbelief. Not recognizing Bacchus's fundamental humanity, the master remains confused and frustrated.

Our portrayals of two other whites in the story are also designed to suggest the complexity of relationships in slavery and the notion of an institutional wedge. We show Captain Joseph Vesey to be a kindly man who demonstrates a sincere liking for his intelligent and handsome young slave. But the captain also commands absolute power in the relationship and uses that authority with devastating effect when he summarily expels young Denmark from his ship. Governor Bennett (William Windom) is portrayed much like he appears in the records, a generous man who is slow to recognize that a genuine slave conspiracy is afoot and that it involves a few of his trusted servants. Toward the end of the film, Bennett finally recognizes the danger and proclaims that he will become a tougher master in his household. Bennett also applies these lessons to public affairs, saying that state and local authorities need to maintain much active vigilance over the slave population. In these comments, Bennett stands in for many southerners of the 1820s and 1830s who turned away from their "liberal" attitudes toward slavery and increasingly sanctioned strong controls over the blacks' activities, including the lives of freedmen.

Every new entry in a genre needs to offer something surprising—narrative developments that are different from the familiar fare—and it is in these characterizations of both blacks and whites that I believe *Denmark Vesey's Rebellion* makes its most important contribution. Our film features heroes and villains—familiar characterizations in historical drama—but it also introduces a number of characters that represent flawed heroes and partially redeemed villains. In this manner, the film provokes audiences, challenging them to think about the terrible injustices that could turn blacks and whites into mortal enemies.

As discussed in the chapter on genre, dramatic film does not allow much room for hedging. In portraying characters, depicting events, and interpreting behavior, the medium favors partisanship, commitment, strong opinions. Our preparation of the script called for a firm judgment concerning a fundamental question about the film's subject. We had to decide whether the slave conspiracy in Charleston truly existed.

In 1964, University of Chicago historian Richard Wade published an influential article in which he maintained that the Vesey plot was largely a figment of the imagination of nervous white Charlestonians. Writing in the *Journal of Southern History,* Wade claimed that evidence for a large-scale, well-planned slave insurrection was lacking. Charleston and South Carolina officials believed the wildest rumors, said Wade. Reacting in the hysterical manner of the Salem witch hunters, they pointed a finger at many people who may have been innocent.[7] Many years later (in 2001), Michael P. Johnson continued and expanded this debate by arguing that Vesey and his associates had been victimized by a conspiracy involving coerced black witnesses, white supporters, and the courts.[8]

Our advisory board's first reaction to Wade's challenge was to circle the wagon trains. Citing the evidence of many other historical studies (including the writings of William Freehling) and reflecting on their own readings of the primary documents, the scholars maintained that there was substantial support for the conclusion that a major slave conspiracy existed in Charleston in 1822. Through the course of this discussion, however, we agreed to keep an open mind and investigate the issue further. The research I conducted as a result of the exchanges led to some intriguing conclusions. Evidence suggested that although the plot had been real, Wade raised some relevant questions. Above all, he seemed correct in suggesting that the number of slaves associated with the plot had been grossly inflated in some official reports. Figures as high as 9,000 conspirators had been mentioned by the authorities, and this large estimate of the number of participants found its way into many modern-day history books. My research suggested that the slaves used exaggerated figures as a means of dealing with potential recruits who doubted their chance of success. The conspirators hoped to inspire confidence by claiming that they had the backing of thousands of slaves. Nervous whites later repeated these extraordinary numbers to drum up support for restrictive measures against black slaves and freedmen. Although it is difficult to identify a specific figure, evidently about fifty or sixty slaves were reasonably well-informed of the plot. Once the recruiters communicated information to others, they assumed an enormous risk of betrayal.

As in the case of other controversies about historical interpretation, we tried to give viewers an appreciation of this debate through the dialogue in the screenplay. At various points in the story, individual actors express their hopes and frustrations regarding the attempt to recruit insurrectionists. Their comments show varying degrees of confidence or pessimism about achieving a mass uprising (just as we found conflicting evidence in the documents). Ironically, then, we owe a debt to Richard Wade. Although we could not agree with his conclusions, his questions helped us probe more deeply into an important debate about the size of the conspiracy.

When I worked on the treatment and script for *Denmark Vesey's Rebellion,* I was unaware of the conventions of cinematic history, the traditional storytelling practices, yet I turned quite naturally to these familiar elements in fashioning a drama for the screen. There were, for example, far too many principal characters in the historic documents for a comprehensible story. Television audiences would easily become confused by the plethora of both black and white individuals involved in the events around Charleston. To deal with this problem, I recommended the collapsing of multiple figures into one. For instance, when I found that two of Governor Bennett's key servants, Ned and Rolla, had been deeply involved in the plot, I combined the individuals. Finding that Rolla's activities were somewhat more interesting and better reported, I let him serve as the composite figure. Documents also indicated that Denmark Vesey had many wives; one report spoke of seven. Scriptwriter William Hauptman and I settled on two, giving each character significant roles in the story. We also compressed events into a limited space of time, leaving the impression that the conspiracy and its discovery occurred in a much briefer period than was actually the case.

One of the most striking manipulations in the film appears at the end. Both the producers and the advisers were troubled by the difficulty of dealing with the sad conclusion. Denmark Vesey loses his struggle for the cause of freedom, and he dies with the hangman's noose around his neck. Some worried that the drama would prove depressing rather than inspiring and that audiences would reject the film because of its gloomy ending. Eventually, I discovered a way out of this narrative dead end. Reading some old documents, I learned that Vesey's son had been a special guest of honor at ceremonies held in Charleston near the end of the Civil War, marking the city's liberation from Confederate control. Vesey had had a number of sons, I acknowledged, but we could imagine that the one identified in the documents was the very Sandy Vesey who had been involved in the conspiracy and banished from the United States by South Carolina authorities. In other words, our story could show that one of the principal rebels lived to see the day of freedom from slavery.

My suggestion inspired a completely invented conclusion to the drama. Our film shows Sandy Vesey (David Harris) arranging an escape from Charleston. But before leaving the region, he visits the grave site of his father, and there he encounters his mother, Beck (Mary Alice). Sandy takes a step forward, looking very sad. "He won't be forgotten," proclaims Sandy.

"Forgotten?" responds his mother. "Why they can't mourn him in Charleston. That's how much they're scared of him, even though he's dead. Your father will never be forgot. He let the truth out. They can't pretend we're happy in slavery any more." As Sandy sets off on his journey, hoping to reach Philadelphia, Beck calls out, "Tell them who he was. Just tell them who he was."

This portrayal is a product of our imagination rather than a reflection of the historical record and represents a bold exercise in artistic license. Nothing like the mother-son encounter ever happened, at least to our knowledge. Yet the scene helps give the movie an inspiring, uplifting finish, and it addresses some larger truths. Authorities in Charleston did, in fact, try to expunge evidence of Denmark Vesey's activities, and they refused to publish anything he said in his lengthy speech delivered in court. South Carolina's leaders were afraid of his legacy. Vesey's actions helped communicate the slaves' discontent, and on many occasions in the years leading up to the Civil War, abolitionists cited his example. Furthermore, by the late twentieth century, Charlestonians, including many of the city's white citizens, were giving greater recognition to Vesey's place in history. As Beck hoped in the film, people eventually learned "who he was." Indeed, our drama aimed to make a larger audience aware of him.

I took many lessons away from the experience of working on the Vesey production and other historical films, but two stand out in particular. The first relates to how I came to look at cinematic history, thinking increasingly about the production history and production personnel behind each film. The second concerns the fundamental tension over questions about truth and fiction. As a result of my experience in filmmaking, I am convinced that all cinematic history calls for considerable artistic creativity, even serious productions that receive academic stamps of approval.

All students of dramatic film should be exposed to the production experience, for familiarity with the various stages of film development can be invaluable for the study of cinematic history. Students can learn a great deal from script writing, production planning, working on the set, editing, and participating in various postproduction activities. Presence on the set is especially useful, because it changes forever one's perspective on dramatic motion pictures. After witnessing the busy activities of the production team, one is unlikely to sit back in a theater passively watching a movie. The suspension of disbelief becomes more difficult once one is aware of the many artistic decisions that go into cinematic history. Seeing the way cinematographers, gaffers (electricians), grips (laborers who handle a multitude of jobs on the set), property managers (responsible for props), script supervisors (who keep track of scene-to-scene details), and others go about their business leads one to look for signs of these artists' handiwork in the finished product. The experience makes one look carefully at camera angles, observe how a director places actors in relation to one another in a scene, consider which point of view the camera is taking, notice the choice of lighting, pay close attention to costuming and makeup, listen carefully for sounds and music, and observe numerous other elements that communicate messages to the audience.

In one respect, the experience tends to spoil future movie entertainment. After seeing work on a set, the student of film cannot simply thrill to the exploits of a movie's heroes. When watching Mel Gibson in *The Patriot,* for example, the experienced individual will analyze the production, thinking about the ideas that director Roland Emmerich wished to convey when he set up a shot. The student will view Mel Gibson as an actor working hard at his job rather than as Ben Martin, the fictional character fighting the British in America's Revolutionary War. Suspension of disbelief becomes difficult once the viewer thinks of cinema as a production rather than as just an entertaining story. At another level, however, exposure to the production process provides a fascinating education. It reveals film in much greater complexity, sharpens one's sensitivity to the diverse methods by which the medium communicates, and makes one aware of the many subtle ways that images and sounds affect viewers' emotions.

Firsthand experience in the filmmaking process also encourages the observer to think about the medium as a production rather than as simply the finished product. Much of published film commentary relates to the completed work, to the words, sounds, and images that appear in a motion picture. Generally, less attention is directed to the activities of the many people who play important roles in crafting the production. After cooperating with writers, producers, directors, and numerous other artists associated with preproduction, filming on the set, and postproduction, the student of film is inclined to raise different questions when analyzing a movie: Who initiated the project? Which people guided the script's development? Which people or organizations funded the film, and why did they invest in it? To which audiences were they directing their movie? Were they influenced by the successes of related films? How did traditions of the genre impact their planning? Did key production personnel disagree on the film's interpretations of history? If so, how and why? In what ways did current events affect the choice of historical subject and the decisions about interpretation? What were the politics of the people who were most influential in shaping the story? Did their political ideas influence the film's perspectives? How did the movie's creators and publicists market the production? To which interests and attitudes did they appeal? What did the promoters expect the audience's demographics to be? In what ways did the movie provoke controversy over its historical interpretations, and how did its creators respond to those criticisms?

My experience working on *Denmark Vesey's Rebellion* and other films suggests that the study of cinematic history needs greater attention to these behind-the-scenes issues. Historians, especially, can profit in their investigations by applying to film the perspective that they apply in their general research on the past. They can view movies historically, tracing the process of film development. Their discussions of cinematic history need not be limited to the words, sounds, and images in the movie's finished version. Much can be learned about a film's relationship to history by studying the cinematic historians behind the production and their experiences in researching, developing, and marketing their story.

Another lesson I learned concerns the familiar debate about filmmakers' manipulation of history. When I faced the challenge of designing dramas for television that portrayed the past responsibly, I discovered that some distortion of the evidence is inevitable. No matter how deeply committed I was to rendering a story that told the truth about the past, I often found it necessary to fictionalize. There were too many gaping holes in the evidence for me to claim that the film was genuinely representational. I had to imagine how events and interactions took place, proffering educated guesses about a history that remained substantially concealed from the modern investigator. Indeed, most of what my production associates and I dramatized constituted informed speculation, for no historian knows exactly how Vesey and other historic figures dressed, walked, talked, or thought. Also, the documents available from 1822 offered conflicting evidence, for Vesey's contemporaries often disagreed when they described the rebellion and the people behind it. We, the filmmakers, had to make numerous judgments about the validity of these conflicting claims. We needed to privilege some of the evidence, shaping our vision of the truth out of an amorphous mass of details.

*Denmark Vesey's Rebellion* cannot be advertised as the only true story of the Charleston slave conspiracy. No filmmaker can honestly promote his or her production as such an achievement. Interpreting history through drama is a profoundly subjective enterprise. Other artists could examine the same historical materials and come up with very different dramas about the events of 1822. "Truth" is a matter of debate. It is constantly challenged and reconsidered. Different interpreters, communicating in different eras, may draw lessons that are quite distinct from the ones we advanced in our film.

My experience working on *Denmark Vesey's Rebellion* also revealed that contentiousness about history presented on the screen has its roots in the divisions that animate scholarship. I enlisted a blue-ribbon panel of scholarly experts to assist the production, yet those academic giants conflicted strongly when interpreting key elements of the story. On issues as vital as the personal motivation of the conspirators, their fundamental goals, and their chances of success, our advisers disagreed vehemently. The scholars were not even of one mind in assessing Denmark Vesey's character or his place in history. In all these matters, the professionals had to settle for a form of compromise that is not unlike the conclusions they draw in traditional scholarship. They had to accept a story that attempted to tell the truth as best as we could judge it. And in filmmaking, that truth is often a collective judgment.

Despite considerable manipulation, fictionalization, invention, and speculation in *Denmark Vesey's Rebellion,* I am proud of the drama's overall achievement. Its historical interpretations are supported by numerous works of scholarship. Accomplished historians vetted its design from the earliest conceptualization to the crafting of several script drafts. A talented production team worked hard to create intelligent and multidimensional views of slavery, while keeping in mind practices of genre that help make cinematic history artistically appealing. We did as much as we reasonably could to establish a delicate balance between responsible instruction and appealing entertainment.

If this educational production supported by the National Endowment for the Humanities and designed for broadcast on PBS Television required a great deal of creativity, we should not be surprised that feature films involve enormous exercises of artistic license. Hollywood filmmakers are certainly under much greater pressure to take liberties. Their big-budget movies have to reach much larger audiences than do PBS productions. Feature films need to appeal to less educated audiences, communicating interpretations of history in ways that all viewers can understand. Their messages about history usually feature less complexity than did our story about the Charleston conspiracy of 1822. Hollywood's cinematic historians need to paint their history with broad strokes, greatly simplifying the portrayal of situations, characters, events, and ideas.

My experiences in filmmaking have led to considerable sympathy for the cinematic historians who confront these difficulties. After working in film's production trenches, I better appreciate the challenges that Hollywood artists face when they attempt to bring the past to life on the screen. I am more tolerant of their efforts to compress, invent, and speculate than I was before I produced a cinematic drama myself. The fascinating but complicated effort to render history on the screen made me much more aware that all attempts to interpret the past, including serious works of scholarship, call for a good deal of creative imagination.

# CHAPTER FIVE

# The Study of Cinematic History

In 1990, John E. O'Connor, one of the historians who pioneered research on the use of film for the study of history, observed that a chasm existed
between historians and film studies specialists. He noted that individuals in
each field seemed to work at a distance from each other and paid little attention to scholarship outside their own fields. Some responsibility for this lack of
communication could be traced to the historians, said O'Connor. History professionals resisted the theoretical apparatus that film studies specialists employed in their research. Evidently, said O'Connor, historians needed to learn
more about the theoretical basis of recent film scholarship.[1]

The chasm O'Connor identified in 1990 remains impressively large today.
On one side stand scholars who employ standard approaches of the history
profession when examining film. On the other side are film professionals who
raise different questions, address different issues, and speak and write in a language that is quite distinct. Occasionally a representative of one or the other
group suggests the value of constructing a bridge that can bring the two groups
together. Bridge building requires cooperation among many participants,
however, and colleagues in each group demonstrate little enthusiasm for the
effort. Most prefer to shout epithets across the chasm. In these scornful comments, they draw attention to the shoddy work of researchers on the other side
who do not share their perspective or methods. Then they return to their own
professional activities, speaking and writing for the benefit of colleagues who
inhabit their particular side of the chasm.

Who is represented in these two groups? Generally, on one side are individuals who conduct most of their teaching, research, and writing within the field
of history. Most do not consider themselves "traditional" historians, and indeed, many of them are at the cutting edge of new developments in their
profession's research on race, class, gender, and other subjects broadly associated with social and cultural history. When called on to discuss documentary
and dramatic films, however, they are not given to reading the literature on
film generated by academics working outside their discipline. On the other
side are scholars from diverse backgrounds: professionals from cinema studies

programs, specialists in literature, and individuals from philosophy, psychology, and other fields who are interested in the connections between film and history. There are also some professional historians in this group, individuals who agree with the general outlook of cinema studies specialists.

Cinema scholars complain that most historians take ad hoc approaches when analyzing motion pictures. They say that historians tend not to bring big ideas, theories, or techniques to their investigations. Film specialists complain that historians look at each production individually, consider its interpretation of the past, and then render judgments about the soundness of its treatment based on their own knowledge of the historical scholarship. Film scholars criticize historians for failing to view each film in the context of larger cinematic developments. Many of the historians' criticisms of motion pictures are irrelevant, say the film scholars, because the historians' observations lack this broader perspective.

Film scholars often object to the way historians go searching for an accurate, truthful, or representative picture of the past in the cinema. Hollywood movies are not a mirror of the past, argue the film specialists; movies cannot recreate actual conditions of history. Nor are Hollywood movies a window on the past, a clear and accurate image of the way life was in an earlier age.[2] *Everything* in a dramatic film is fictitious—the physical appearance of the actors, the way they dress and walk, the words they speak, the gestures they make. All these elements are more or less a director's speculation about the way people appeared and acted in the past.[3]

More important, film scholars argue that a completely truthful presentation of the past is impossible, because there is no single truth to uncover. No historical interpretation is the real or correct one; all explanations of history are constructed. The narrative itself is a construction, formed out of the interests and ideological inclinations of the storyteller. Even history texts are interpretive dramatizations. Linda Hutcheon, for example, welcomes the postmodern intellectual's challenge to history's "truth claim, both by questioning the ground of that claim in historiography and by asserting that both history and fiction are discourses, human constructs, and both derive their major claim to truth from that identity."[4] Even traditional historical interpretations involve a great deal of artistic creativity, says Hutcheon. The distinction between history and fiction is often exaggerated, she argues.[5] Janet Staiger makes a related point, noting that postmodern writers such as Hayden White, Michel Foucault, and Peter Gay "all stress that no scholar comes 'objectively,' 'neutrally,' or 'innocently' before his or her evidence."[6] Film scholars often point out that dramatic film cannot offer a total judgment on history that represents an objective or true picture of the past. Stressing the relativity of truth claims, they praise postmodernist, anti-narrative approaches to storytelling, experimental movies that recognize that truth is always contested.[7] Films may help us think differently about the past, says Robert A. Rosenstone, a historian who endorses much of the new film scholarship.[8] He appreciates directors who employ imaginative, anti-narrative techniques that refuse to sum up through single-minded conclusions. The filmmakers who win Rosenstone's applause remind audiences that historical understanding involves an open-ended investigation rather than a closed and certain judgment.

Many film scholars reference Hayden White in their discussions about this relativistic perspective. White, who has taught at the University of California–Santa Cruz and at Stanford University, is the author of a number of influential books. He argues that historical interpretation involves the arranging and telling of stories, not the objective presentation of truth. All historical explanations constitute forms of fiction, White points out, and we must be cautious about promoting false distinctions between fact and fiction. There is no single authoritative story about the past. Commentators who attempt to explain the French Revolution or the murder of President John F. Kennedy, for example, may tell very different stories. Whatever coherence we find in their explanation of events is a function of the narrators' determined efforts to shape interpretations. These storytellers do not find evidence lying in the archives that naturally suggest explanations. Instead, they privilege a few facts from the many they encounter and connect them in a narrative that constructs a specific reading of the material's significance. This process is strongly subjective; it hardly constitutes an objective search for the truth. White praises movies that, in a postmodernist style, reveal that the meaning of the past is contested. He appreciates films that suggest we cannot answer questions about the past comprehensively and with certainty.[9]

Film scholars stress that we do not necessarily have to abandon the search for historical truth when we recognize the impossibility of presenting history objectively. Although moviemakers manipulate evidence, misrepresent facts, and configure details in a manner that irritates historians, they can nevertheless communicate thoughtful viewpoints on the past. Filmmakers may get specific representations wrong, but they can address broader or higher truths in their productions.[10] Rosenstone stated this case eloquently when he said, "the Hollywood history film will always include images that are invented and yet may still be considered true; true in that they symbolize, condense, or summarize larger amounts of data; true in that they carry out the overall meaning of the past that can be verified, documented, or reasonably argued."[11]

*In* Walker *(1987), Ed Harris (on horseback) plays William Walker, an American adventurer who tried to become president of Nicaragua in the 1850s. Some film enthusiasts praised* Walker *for its break from familiar narrative conventions. (Museum of Modern Art Film Archive)*

Some film scholars use these insights to take aim at efforts to judge the validity of cinematic history. They criticize historians for viewing movies traditionally. Cinema specialists complain that historians act as if they can find true history lessons in Hollywood dramas. Their attempts to point out errors, misrepresentations, and fictional flourishes in these films are often misdirected, say these cinema scholars. Robert Burgoyne notes, for example, that historians frequently protest the mixing of fact and fiction, expressing much "anguished commentary" about filmmakers' employment of artistic license. When historians assess movies such as *JFK, Malcolm X, Jefferson in Paris,* and *Nixon,* they appear to hold the movies "to standards of authenticity and verifiability that nearly equal the standards applied to scholarly texts," notes Burgoyne.[12]

Attention to cinematic interpretations of the past "misses the point" and obscures more important issues.[13] Similarly, Sumiko Higashi finds historians and the public heavily invested in "traditional concepts about the past." Observing that historians, including myself, drew attention to fabrications and misrepresentations in *Mississippi Burning* (1988), Higashi asked, "Why did academics not simply dismiss *Mississippi Burning* as just another movie?"[14]

Higashi and Rosenstone urge students of cinematic history to consider film in a different way. They suggest that historians expend less energy fretting about the historical interpretations in popular movies and give greater attention to more radically conceived productions that boldly challenge the public's ideas about the past. Both Higashi and Rosenstone cite *Walker* (1987) for its achievement in breaking from familiar conventions. *Walker* deals with the adventures of William Walker, the filibusterer who succeeded briefly in taking control of Nicaragua in the 1850s (he was later executed by Honduran authorities). The movie includes, however, some modern-day references in its imagery, such as a Mercedes-Benz, a Zippo lighter, a computer, a helicopter, and copies of *Time, Newsweek,* and *People* magazines. In these and other scenes, *Walker* references both the Vietnam War and the Sandinista-Contra conflict in Nicaragua and suggests critical questions about the impact of U.S. economic and military interventions in Latin America and the world. Both Higashi and Rosenstone praise Oliver Stone's *JFK* (1991), too, for its lively experimentation. Rosenstone acknowledges that the motion picture fudges some details about the Kennedy assassination, but he argues that it effectively questions official "truths." He points out that the film confronts audiences with a provocative and important question: Has something gone wrong with America since the 1960s? Whatever the movie's flaws, says Rosenstone, "*JFK* has to be among the most important works of American history ever to appear on the screen."[15]

Both authors appreciate *Walker, JFK,* and other avant-garde movies that eschew traditional storytelling techniques. They applaud filmmakers' panache in mixing genres, presenting odd juxtapositions, incorporating sarcasm and humor, creating temporal jumps, and generally promoting postmodern perspectives.[16] Movies that explore new modes of communication confront audiences with a "multiplicity of viewpoints," says Rosenstone. These films challenge audiences to think differently, to "revision" the past.[17]

Film scholars and historians who sympathize with this point of view raise important issues for the study of cinematic history, but their arguments call for critical analysis. Significant questions regarding the application of their concepts need to be addressed. Just as many historians need to confront the questions raised by cinema specialists, cinema specialists need to deal with important questions addressed by historians.

First, movies that experiment with radically different narrative structures are rarely among the popular productions that attract huge audiences and revenues. Artistic films, with their fragmented narrative styles, usually appeal to niche audiences, not the multiple millions reached by major Hollywood productions (*JFK*, with its fast-changing MTV-style presentation, is a notable exception). The films that excite enthusiasm from film scholars because of their postmodernist, counternarrative strategies are minority entries within the

*In JFK (1991), New Orleans district attorney Jim Garrison (Kevin Costner) excites controversy with his claims of a conspiracy in the assassination of President John F. Kennedy. Historian Robert A. Rosenstone acknowledges that the movie fudges a number of details regarding the assassination, but he believes that the movie imaginatively challenges official "truths." (Museum of Modern Art Film Archive)*

broad field of cinematic history. Film scholars' analyses of these unconventional films are interestingly suggestive, but they do not speak to a broader need. A more important task remains: providing historians and the public with insights that are useful for dealing with mainstream Hollywood-style cinematic history.

Second, despite film scholars' frequent references to Hayden White's argument that films should demonstrate that truth is not knowable, many of the movies that film scholars applaud do, in fact, suggest a specific, knowable past. These motion pictures—even the postmodern, avant-garde ones—are not as balanced in the presentation of multiple perspectives or open-ended inquiries as film scholars suggest in their commentaries. This is certainly the case with *JFK* and *Walker*. Despite Stone's reported attempt to turn *JFK* into a *Rashomon*-like study that shows clashing viewpoints, the movie has a strongly opinionated perspective on the key events. *JFK* delivers a hard-hitting attack on the Warren Commission's conclusions about the Kennedy assassination and a sharp criticism of U.S. policy in Vietnam. *Walker* is strongly critical of U.S.

intervention in Nicaragua in the nineteenth century, and by implication, it lambastes the Reagan administration's policies in Central America in the 1980s.

The appeal of these movies to film scholars may relate to ideology as well as to the directors' artistic skills. If Stone had produced an experimental, boldly designed motion picture defending the Warren Commission and supporting U.S. intervention in Vietnam, would Higashi, Rosenstone, and others have praised the director for his panache? Similarly, if Alex Cox had produced a movie that applauded William Walker's involvement in Nicaragua in the nineteenth century and, by implication, supported Reagan's intervention in Central American affairs, would the authors have celebrated the director's artistry? This question can be addressed more broadly as well. Is the film scholars' demand for more movies that raise questions and challenge familiar truths only a general appeal for more sophisticated engagements with history? Or does it reveal a discontent with the political perspectives they encounter in mainstream movies? Do their suggestions communicate an interest in more agreeable political messages rather than just a demand for multiple perspectives and open-ended structures?

The film scholars' enthusiasm for White's ideas about the relativity of historical truths creates another problem. It leaves open for discussion questions about the limits of such relativism. Scholars who advance White's theories tend to defend many different cinematic experiments involving historical evidence. They support directors' manipulation of historical details in the interest of communicating symbolic or higher truths. When historians protest the way filmmakers deal with the historical record, the familiar response from film scholars is essentially, "Be careful about throwing stones. You, too, live in glass houses." But acknowledgment that written history is also a "constructed" narrative should not be used to dismiss demands for greater truthfulness in cinematic history. Certainly we can excuse some of the filmmakers' manipulations, for as we have seen, creative design is inherent in motion picture composition. But are all manipulations defendable? Are any of them problematic? Is every invention a praiseworthy example of creative filmmaking? In what situations is criticism of historical depictions appropriate? Are questions about historical representation, by their very nature, irrelevant? It is not enough to make a relativist case, citing White's deconstructionist reminder that scholars of the printed word also invent. Are there no limits to White's model? Can it be taken to extremes?

In dealing with this question of extremes, some historians acknowledge the value of the questions that White and others have raised, but they nevertheless hold moviemakers accountable to *some* standards of truth telling. In speaking about *JFK*, for example, historian Alan Brinkley recognized that skepticism about claims of objectivity is healthy. There may be no completely objective or "absolute truth," Brinkley acknowledged, "but there are such things as untruths." He continued, "There are things that simply are not true, that are lies. . . . We do not always find [truth], but we seek it. And in seeking truth, we also have to seek untruth and attempt to avoid it or discredit it." Brinkley warned that "if we abandon any notion of truth then we are entering very serious ground, indeed." One way to identify historians, he claimed, is to call them "people who are seeking truth."[18] Eric Foner, another prominent historian, also raised questions about artistic license in connection with *JFK*. Foner recognized that all people who examine history have an agenda or a point of view. He noted, however, that the public does not welcome any expression of a personal perspective. If an individual's point of view is "completely divorced from the evidence" and serious historians view the argument as implausible, other historians "would point that out because the evidence is there and there are standards."[19] Brinkley and Foner alerted fellow historians to the danger of extreme subjectivity, to the hazard of claiming that since all truths are contestable, we can privilege none.

The dangers that Brinkley and Foner allude to are illustrated in David Irving's attempt to present a sharply distorted view of the Holocaust. If a filmmaker tried to dramatize Irving's argument, maintaining in a Hollywood production that Auschwitz was essentially a labor camp where Jews died chiefly from typhus rather than from planned extermination, observers would face questions about objectivity, subjectivity, and judgment in stark form. In such a circumstance, many historians (and, it is hoped, film scholars, too) would strongly denounce the interpretation as a lie. Like the British judge who threw out Irving's suit against Deborah Lipstadt—the historian who called Irving "one of the most dangerous spokesmen for Holocaust denial"—these scholars would likely affirm that there are, as Brinkley maintained, "untruths" that ought to be discredited. The postmodernist claim that all narratives about history are subjective and constructed would not excuse such a motion picture's fooling with the evidence. As Tony Judt notes, the Irving verdict reminds us that "some statements are true, some are false. Some writers have integrity and are to be believed, however outlandish their opinions. Others are knowingly disseminating seductive falsehoods. Some people are good. And some are evil."[20]

There is another question regarding White's argument that needs consideration by film scholars. In many respects, the fundamental thrust of White's thesis is quite familiar to professional historians. Historiography, the study of evolving and conflicting interpretations of the past, is fundamental in the graduate training of history professionals. By reading Edward Hallett Carr's

*What Is History?* and Gerald N. Grob and George Athan Billias's *Interpretations of American History: Patterns and Perspectives,* as well as other books that introduce this perspective, historians in training learn that so-called truths about the past are actually very much in dispute.[21] Conclusions are always subject to argument and reinterpretation. Students learn to appreciate the way current intellectual trends, recent events, and present-day political outlooks affect the way historians view the past. As Carr points out, historians do not approach their subjects neutrally. They bring a personal political philosophy to the research table, and their outlook often has an impact on their choice of topics, their interest in specific evidence, and their efforts to draw conclusions. Hence, the fashionable relativist argument of film scholars does not come as a revelation to historians; questioning truths and examining the bias of authors who create historical narratives is central to their scholarship. Historians are not naïve about the truth claims of either authors or filmmakers. They are quite familiar with the argument that complete objectivity is an impossible goal and that all interpretations, whether in print or on film, are constructed and contestable. They are therefore quite amused by film scholars' excitement in making this discovery and lecturing historians about its importance.

Another difficulty associated with film scholarship relates to its heavy association with Marxist ideology. Especially in the 1980s and early 1990s, homage to perspectives of the ideological Left appeared abundantly in the film studies literature. The problem with this is a question of degree rather than presence. Open-minded inquiry welcomes all points of view; censorship is repugnant. The references to such theories became so prevalent in the film studies literature of the 1980s and 1990s, however, that they appeared to achieve a status of political correctness. Film scholars attached themselves to a troubled intellectual tradition when they privileged Marxist and neo–Marxist outlooks. By the late twentieth century, Marxist perspectives were nearly bankrupt as guides for understanding the economic and psychological foundations of human behavior. The growing intellectual disaffection with Marxism in America and the world also had a significant impact on interpretations in traditional fields of study such as history, economics, political science, and sociology. Film studies, however, was among the slowest disciplines to respond to these developments.

In the late twentieth century, Marxist ideas became quite fashionable in the professional literature on film. Authors frequently cited the neo–Marxian viewpoints of Louis Althusser and Antonio Gramsci as a means of explaining why the masses failed to recognize that their own interests were exploited under capitalism. Theorists argued that the public had become mystified, confused, and fooled by false beliefs. The theorists claimed that a predominantly conservative, pro-capitalist outlook had been promoted through many outlets.

In religious training, formal education, the law, and popular culture (including novels, theater, and film) the public learned to accept an ideology of the ruling class. In this respect, Hollywood looked like a good target for Marxist analysis, because a few gigantic corporations (studios run by business moguls) dominated production and distribution.[22] Film scholars also eagerly employed psychoanalytic concepts from Jacques Lacan and other writers to explain why audiences were psychologically predisposed to accept capitalist hegemony. These scholars became sympathetic to the view that ideological beliefs can develop through unconscious processes.[23] The masses absorbed the ruling class's propaganda, said the film scholars, and were, in a sense, under a form of mind control. Audiences believed they were free agents but were, in fact, greatly influenced by the hegemonic powers. Movies created this impression in subtle but powerful ways, the scholars observed. Hence, capitalism's influence needed to be understood in cultural as well as economic terms.[24]

There was an obvious problem with this outlook. It made the masses appear to be passive figures who demonstrated little potential to defend their interests. Some film scholars began to resist this pathetic portrait of the public as duped receptors and victims. Eventually, a new wave of research and theorizing emerged that contradicted the earlier characterizations. Notions of "agency" became popular in the revised literature. Film scholars were now less likely to characterize the masses as passive recipients of capitalist propaganda. Instead, they claimed that citizens worked to shape their own destinies. Moviegoers did not simply absorb what Hollywood moguls produced for them, argued the film scholars. Audiences achieved power at the box office and in other commercial outlets by accepting or rejecting various dramas, forcing the Hollywood executives to revise their production plans.[25] Furthermore, film scholars focused on the works of a new generation of directors who made unusually provocative movies in the 1960s and 1970s, such as Martin Scorsese, Arthur Penn, Francis Ford Coppola, and Stanley Kubrick. The scholars praised these unconventional filmmakers for designing a new kind of cinema that challenged the earlier celebratory accounts of American society.

These rather abrupt shifts in the arguments of leftist film specialists suggested that ideological needs of the moment had a substantial impact on scholarly interpretations. A good deal of Marxist research during the 1960s, 1970s, and 1980s maintained that cinema failed to perform an emancipating role in the class struggle, thwarting the development of revolutionary consciousness. By the 1990s, when notions of agency had become trendy, film specialists were busy demonstrating something quite different: that moviegoers resisted the conservative values communicated on the screen. Although audiences had not become revolutionaries, at least they seemed to be more in control of their affairs than the masses described in earlier writings had been. Such a rapid change in interpretive direction hinted of a research agenda that was highly politicized. Evidently, many film scholars decided what they were going to discover well before they undertook their research. Inspired by the concepts of Lacan, Althusser, and Gramsci, they looked for the power of ideology in popular culture and found it. Later, motivated by the new literature on agency, they searched for evidence of resistance to ideology and found that, too. Whether such agenda-laden investigations truly constituted scholarship is a subject worthy of debate. The process of research in film studies certainly does not resemble university models of scientific inquiry and experimentation, investigations in which researchers establish hypotheses and create rigorous experiments to see if the evidence supports their hunches.

The argument of ideologically inclined scholars that Hollywood movies rarely show collective solutions to social difficulties is also problematic. Many leftist observers criticize American cinema for almost always viewing great economic and social issues at the personal level, portraying specific individuals struggling against society's problems. Large groups, especially classes, rarely appear as the movers and shakers in these stories, they note. The crowd, so much a factor in Sergei Eisenstein's early motion pictures produced in the Soviet Union, is much less a force in American-made dramas. The Hollywood approach is a cop-out, these writers suggest. It refuses to address a need for collective action.[26] The scholars also criticize Hollywood's tradition of producing happy endings for its stories. Too frequently, say these scholars, movies hint that all problems can be settled within the capitalist system. In the final minutes, cinema almost always presents solutions to the characters' difficulties. This practice suggests a positive view of American society, one that seems smugly comfortable with the way things are.

This familiar claim that Hollywood's storytelling promotes conservative values is fundamentally wrong. It reflects little appreciation for the power of genre. As discussed earlier, moviemaking in the United States has developed a number of conventions, techniques of dramatic presentation that have worked over the years in creating profitable cinema. Among the most important generic elements are the two aspects that film scholars criticize: emphasis on individual action, and upbeat conclusions. Audiences respond favorably to movies that feature one or two heroic figures and to narratives that, in the end, provide some sort of triumph or symbolic redemption for the main characters. If audiences preferred class struggles rather than individual heroics and depressing endings rather than inspiring ones, studio executives and filmmakers would, no doubt, rush to give them what they wanted. Hollywood, which invests tens of millions of dollars in new productions, responds sensitively to the public's taste. Charges that the cinema's storytelling techniques reflect capitalist ideology or timidity in recognizing the need for collective action represent irrelevant grumbling.

Furthermore, the leftist scholars' assumption that the powerful people behind Hollywood productions are strong defenders of conservative values lacks merit. The authors of an important study, *Hollywood's America: Social and Political Themes in Motion Pictures*, reveal the error of this assumption by gathering a great deal of statistical information on artistic and business talent in Hollywood. Stephen Powers, David J. Rothman, and Stanley Rothman tested the film theorists' claims that a conservative elite controls Hollywood and uses movies to promote the values of the nation's ruling classes. Unlike the many film scholars who characterize Hollywood leaders on the basis of speculation, Powers, Rothman, and Rothman conducted detailed research. They surveyed Hollywood artists and business executives on a number of subjects and found that they were significantly more liberal than the American public on social, economic, racial, religious, gender, and military issues. The authors acknowledge that Hollywood turned somewhat cautious in the 1940s and 1950s, during the years of big-studio control, House Un-American Activities Committee hearings, and competition from television. They note, however, that in the 1960s and after, when conservative pressures on the motion picture community began to disintegrate, story themes increasingly suggested more critical views of American society. The new movies communicated greater antagonism toward authority figures, the U.S. government bureaucracy, and the military. Hollywood filmmakers were hardly the conservative elite that film scholars made them out to be, and Hollywood productions, especially those from the 1960s and after, were not simply appeals for complacency or veiled propaganda for a conservative ideology.[27]

Powers, Rothman, and Rothman build their case on a great deal of evidence, and by implication, they castigate film scholars for dipping too deeply into theory. Their research demonstrates a need for documenting ideas rather than borrowing them liberally from the works of prominent theorists (many of them European) who have philosophized widely on issues related to language, literature, film, and society in general. The authors score an important point in this regard, for scholarship on film is replete with theoretical references that are unsupported by evidence. The professional stakes in citing these concepts are quite high, as evidenced by the numerous efforts of film scholars to reference the esteemed theorists in articles and books. Evidently, these scholars learned in college and graduate school that they would face academic penalties if they left out the exalted names. Scholarship on film, including analysis of cinematic history, frequently cites Michel Foucault, Christian Metz,

Louis Althusser, Claude Levi-Strauss, Jacques Derrida, Jean-Louis Baudry, Raymond Bellour, and Ferdinand de Saussure, as well as the concepts of Karl Marx and Sigmund Freud.[28] Often the quotations are so brief or obscure that the relevance of a theorist's idea to the film scholar's interpretation is not immediately clear. In many cases, the scholars seem to be unsure of the concept's pertinence themselves, but they recognize the professional value of citing fashionable luminaries in their discussions.

A historian who wades through these vague abstractions may feel a sense of wonderment at the pervasiveness of this language. A reader from outside the field is inclined to ask: Is no one willing to challenge the relevance of much of this work? Are not some film scholars troubled by so much unsubstantiated theorizing? Is anyone willing to question the many vague abstractions in the literature? Does someone in the field have the professional courage to challenge these works for their lack of clarity?

There is such a figure: Noel Carroll. Carroll deserves accolades for publishing an unusually bold criticism of this literature. In *Mystifying Movies: Fads and Fallacies in Contemporary Film Theory*, Carroll draws attention to the "shoddy thinking" and "slapdash scholarship" in many of the film studies publications. He claims that many film specialists support a form of self-censorship, restraining frank criticism of writings in the field. Those who question the fashionable interpretations are summarily dismissed as neoconservatives. Many film scholars demand the expression of politically correct views, says Carroll, a practice that "protects bad scholarship."[29] He maintains that too many concepts central to modern film theory are "systematically ambiguous" and represent "extended exercises in equivocation."[30] The field's explanatory metaphors are abstract and vague, and concepts are not rigorously defined. Film scholars need to frame their questions more explicitly and clearly so that manageable answers can be created for them.[31] "The problem with this language," says Carroll, "is that it says virtually nothing. It has impeded research and reduced film analysis to the repetition of fashionable slogans and unexamined assumptions."[32]

Historians who investigate film scholarship must certainly be prepared to deal with the dense, mystifying language that Carroll describes. Jargon is a staple in the literature. Nebulous, uncommitted statements are abundant, and clear, crisp phrases are in short supply. Straightforward language that articulates a firm opinion is frustratingly absent in key sections of the literature where a thesis needs to be communicated. For instance, early in *Film, Politics and Gramsci*, Marcia Landy identifies the heart of her thesis. She announces: "I wish to address the efficacy of Gramsci's insights into the dynamic nature of capitalist formations, into the contradictory positions that constitute subalternity, and into the importance of arriving at a sense of the multivalent relations between economic, cultural, and political phenomena."[33] What was that again? Near the beginning of *Film Nation: Hollywood Looks at U.S. History,* Robert Burgoyne attempts to set up the foundations of his thesis. He explains: "Social identity, as conceived in these films, originates neither from 'above,' in alignment with the nation-state, nor from below, with ethnicity or race, but rather from 'across,' through horizontal relations whose antagonistic and transitive character is left represented in terms of 'inside' and 'outside.'"[34] Is this the language that will illuminate the book's thesis? In her introduction to *The Persistence of History: Cinema, Television, and the Modern Event,* Vivian C. Sobchack opens with a discussion of the 1994 movie *Forrest Gump.* She writes: "The complexity of diverse individual trajectories and their nodal coalescence in the massive 'historical events' we see foregrounded as the film's background are ironically revealed as nothing less (while something more) than confusion: that is, notions of both rationality and system are undermined by the visible evidence that 'History' is the concatenated and reified effect of incoherent motives and chance convergences."[35] This statement hardly establishes a clear basis for the book's principal arguments. Sobchack offered much clearer commentary on film in a book she published with Thomas Sobchack sixteen years earlier, *An Introduction to Film.*[36] Evidently, lengthy exposure to film studies literature over subsequent years effected an enormous embellishment of language.

These statements do not represent a few unusual examples of obfuscation in the film literature. Unfortunately, similarly dense writing can be found in much of the film scholarship about movies generally and cinematic history specifically. The scholars' commentaries are replete with multisyllable words, vague references, and cloudy arguments.

There is a simple remedy for this communication problem: authors in cinema studies can read a few issues of *Foreign Affairs* before they commence writing. That distinguished journal, the source of many influential articles on international affairs, provides a useful model for clarity. The editors of *Foreign Affairs* insist that their contributors reach out to audiences in comprehensible and lively language that engages readers from diverse disciplines. They expect authors to deal with complex issues, but they demand that the authors present their theses in language that is interesting and understandable to all readers. A professional in history, political science, or international relations can easily pick up a copy of the journal and profit from the reading experience. For that matter, a nonprofessional can examine *Foreign Affairs* and find considerable intellectual stimulation. The lesson is valuable. Film scholars do not have to write like James Joyce in *Ulysses* to prove their capability of addressing the subject with intelligence and insight.

Film scholars can also learn from the example of Robert A. Rosenstone, a professional historian who expresses considerable interest in the research and ideas of film professionals. Rosenstone writes in clear, comprehensible language; he does not avoid judgment by hiding his opinions in a muddle of multisyllable words. Rosenstone attempts to communicate the theoretical arguments of film scholars in prose that can be appreciated by fellow historians as well as by individuals from other disciplines. Furthermore, he recognizes that a moving image can present ideas in unique and highly stimulating ways. Through his own experiments in innovative modes of presentation, Rosenstone hints that all students of history can profit from postmodern perspectives. In his book *Visions of the Past*, Rosenstone offers the reader radical shifts in thought, brief explorations of tangential issues, observations on his personal relationship to the material, and penetrating questions about issues that sometimes challenge the thesis he is advancing. Through these imaginative techniques, Rosenstone attempts breakthroughs in communication similar to the ones he hopes filmmakers will achieve. He practices what he preaches. Rosenstone shows concern not only for addressing ideas but also for finding effective modes of presenting them.[37]

Rosenstone effectively prods his fellow historians to think more imaginatively than do those who are obsessed with factual errors or artistic liberties in films. He reminds readers that a film is not a book. Pointing to the generic conventions of cinematic history such as the ones described in this book, Rosenstone emphasizes that film can never provide "some mirror of a vanished past." Still, the medium can offer important insights in unique ways. "Rather than lamenting the supposed sins of film," argues Rosenstone, "we need to investigate its strengths."[38] At its best, film can contest and revision our notions of history. Film can deliver insights that are as important as those found in books (but in a different manner). Rosenstone's perspective lifts our consideration of historical film to a higher level, above narrow questions about whether a filmmaker got the hats right or left out a speech. To better appreciate the medium's possibilities, says Rosenstone, historians need to give greater attention to the ideas developed in film studies scholarship. Like John E. O'Connor, cited at the beginning of this chapter, Rosenstone urges his history colleagues to become acquainted with the conceptual and theoretical works published by scholars in cinema studies and literature, as well as with the work of the few historians who have been thinking differently about film.

But is there not a correlative to consider as well? If we accept the conclusion that historians need to become better versed in the literature of film studies, must we also insist that film scholars develop greater sensitivity to issues that concern historians? Film studies specialists are very demanding, claiming that historians ought to read their literature and become familiar with their paradigms. But are they eager to listen to historians, to ponder the issues that interest them? Indeed, are they willing to read the historians' publications and become aware of the principal trends in their scholarship?

Many individuals writing from the perspective of film studies give relatively little attention to historical scholarship. Generally, their footnotes in articles and books about history and film contain few references to research in history. Surprisingly, when they cite a work in history, often the reference is to a textbook or general survey of history rather than to a scholarly monograph. For the most part, instead of referring to historical scholarship, the authors refer to other motion pictures or to ideas about cinema articulated by various film theorists. These writers pay little attention to scholarship in history because they do not believe that it is pertinent to the issues that interest them. In fact, some of them consider the question that intrigues history professionals—how well does cinema deal with the past?—pretty much irrelevant.

Disagreements about which questions are important sometimes produce friction between historians and film specialists. Cinema scholars often give a cold reception to historians' interest in assessing filmmakers' presentations of history. Some film specialists have crusaded so strongly for the idea that cinema is art and entertainment and communication and business that they appear rather uncomfortable with discussions about cinema as history. When film professionals encounter historians criticizing the treatment of history in Hollywood productions, they consider the observations unjustified.

This kind of reaction does not help advance a dialogue. A number of historians sense that cinematic history can have a significant impact on the public's perceptions about the past, and these historians believe that the popular productions coming out of Hollywood deserve serious discussion. They are also aware of the caveats film scholars mention in their essays and books. Historians recognize that a film is not the same as a book and that students of film must learn about its distinctive means of communication. Still, these historians want to know what kind of history film does provide, and how it can be judged.

There are perils in trying to combine an interest in investigating cinematic interpretations of history with an interest in addressing the issues raised by film scholars. I have experienced these difficulties firsthand. Sometimes even a brief reference to historians' criticisms of film draws angry fire. For example, Maureen Ogle, also a historian, complained about an article I wrote for the American Historical Association's newsletter *Perspectives*. My essay referred to the way criticisms by historians and journalists had undermined some Hollywood movies' chances for an Academy Award. Ogle's letter to the editor expressed outrage: "Let me get this straight," she wrote. "According to Robert Brent Toplin, historians have taken it upon themselves to function as monitors and watchdogs of the film industry." Ogle went on to question whether there are "*any* limitations to historians' professional arrogance."[39]

The question is ridiculous, yet historians who suggest that we need to assess the treatment of history in film are likely to encounter charges like it. Some critics seem wedded to the misguided notion that historians are proposing gatekeeping, turf protection, thought policing, or censorship when they express judgments about filmmakers' treatments of the past.

In sum, we face a significant challenge. It relates to the important issue that Robert A. Rosenstone and John E. O'Connor raised, but the implications are more complex. The challenge involves the difficult task of not only exposing historians to ideas from film scholarship but also making scholars in cinema studies aware of the concerns of professional historians. Enthusiasts of the perspectives promoted in film studies need to face the *C* word—*content*—to acknowledge that historians care a great deal about it and to explain (forthrightly and in intelligible language) how they propose to deal with it. Much more than film scholars, historians want to talk about the historical substance of films—the words, pictures, sounds, structures, narratives, and other elements that communicate interpretations of the past.

Historians should play an important role in judging historical presentations that turn up on the screen. When making these judgments, historians need to be broad-minded and informed about the issues addressed in film scholarship, but they should not be timid. Classroom teachers, scholars, and public historians do not need to apologize for taking filmed interpretations seriously and should not be silenced by claims that the stuff on the screen is just art. Politicians, TV talk-show commentators, and newspaper and magazine pundits take cinematic history seriously, frequently discussing and disputing its messages in the popular media. Historians need stronger voices in these debates. They should not remain hidden in their classrooms, libraries, museums, and archives, separated from the important discussions going on outside their institutions.

What, then, can historians or anyone interested in cinematic history gain from explorations into film scholarship? Surely, there is much of value in the professional literature. The scholarship awakens readers to the way film conveys messages differently from the printed word. It encourages readers to think about the medium's unique characteristics, to ponder the language and signs by which motion pictures communicate. Cinema scholarship teaches readers to examine the structure of film and encourages them to advance discussions beyond an ad hoc consideration of individual movies. By exploring the elements of genre and positing theoretical concepts related to cinema, the new scholarship can lift discussions of the subject to a higher level. Above all, the research challenges history-minded students of film to raise new questions about Hollywood's productions, to go beyond stale and pedantic discussions about whether a war movie depicts troop movements properly or a drama set in the nineteenth century uses the correct type of furniture. Film scholarship encourages audiences to recognize that movies convey both literal and symbolic truths. It can assist them, too, in thinking differently about the subject of history. Film scholarship demonstrates how innovative movies can raise provocative questions, forcing students of history to view the subject in new ways, to "revision" the past.

At the same time, a historian cannot help but express disappointment with some characteristics of the emerging film scholarship. In a number of respects, the literature fails to live up to the achievements enthusiastically advertised by its practitioners. A good deal of film analysis appears in impenetrable, jargon-laden language; discussions are heavy on theory and light on detailed research. The literature also displays considerable intellectual timidity. Authors bow frequently to favored theorists, and few writers are courageous enough to suggest that the supposed gurus do not offer much relevant commentary about the subject or that they might be seriously mistaken in some of their observations. Critical spirit, celebrated in words, turns up much less in deed. Oft-repeated references to Hayden White's questions about objectivity and truth rarely include considerations of the limits of White's relativism. Particularly surprising is the legitimacy given to Marxist and Freudian analysis. Scholars in many disciplines now recognize that Freud's interpretations were often wildly speculative and lacking in experimental confirmation, yet film scholars remain eager to invoke his name and apply his ideas about psychoanalysis to film. Similarly, researchers around the world have come to view Marxist theories as so mistaken in their fundamental assumptions that they are of questionable value, yet many film scholars continue to discuss these concepts as if they still had a good deal of intellectual clout. Disappointing, too, is the inattention to historical scholarship. A number of film scholars who write about cinematic history delve very little into the publications of historians. In fact, many of them display little interest in the most fundamental question historians raise about cinematic history: How well do films deal with the past?

In years to come, these difficulties may be surmounted. The dialogue between professionals in the disciplines of history and cinema studies may improve substantially, and each will generously fertilize the understanding of the other. Unfortunately, that day of familiarity and appreciation is still far off. Much important work remains to be done in both camps to deal with the still-present chasm.

# CHAPTER SIX

# Impact

"I haven't read the book, but I have seen the movie," said Commandant Alfonso Cano, "and we are the last of the Mohicans." The guerrilla was speaking about the Marxist group that he led in the jungle and mountain regions of Colombia. Evidently, Hollywood's view of eighteenth-century American history had made an impact on the way Cano thought about himself, his comrades, and the condition of his society.[1]

Is Cano's example representative of a larger pattern? Do many people in the United States and around the world draw lessons from the history they see enacted on the silver screen? Do Hollywood's stories excite, inspire, and anger viewers, influencing their attitudes and actions well after they leave the theaters or turn off their videos?

These questions have long interested the public, but attempts to answer them remain speculative. The responses involve guesswork, because only fragmented and anecdotal evidence about the impact of movies is available. We lack a broad statistical picture of public reactions to cinematic history, and not much evidence is available regarding the influence of specific films. This analysis of impact must begin, then, with a caveat: examples presented here represent only bits and pieces of evidence, samplings that seem to demonstrate that the messages contained in the movies sometimes affect the audience's thinking and behavior.

There are, of course, many popular anecdotes that suggest that movies affect audiences beyond the few hours they sit in a theater. Back in the mid-1930s, for example, the American clothing industry took a financial beating when Clark Gable took off his shirt in Frank Capra's *It Happened One Night* (1934). Male moviegoers noticed that the handsome star wore no undershirt, and they soon imitated his example, sending sales of men's undershirts plummeting. Later in that decade, actor Don Ameche achieved fame by playing the inventor of the telephone in *The Story of Alexander Graham Bell* (1939). Soon after the movie's release, the actor's name became part of the nation's household vocabulary when Americans said to friends and family, "I'll call you on the Ameche." In more recent years, isolated evidence has continued to suggest that some audiences react strongly to what they see on the screen. Reactions to 1989's *Field of Dreams,* a popular baseball movie, have been intriguing. Many baseball fans and movie buffs expressed a strong emotional attachment to the mythical story about an Iowa farmer who knocks down his corn crop to create a playing field, where ghosts of the Chicago Black Sox baseball team appear. About 50,000 people a year now visit the cornfield in northeastern Iowa where *Field of Dreams* was filmed.[2] Another popular movie, *Free Willy* (1993), inspired a tremendous outpouring of sympathy for the film's huge star, a killer whale named Keiko. *Free Willy* is about a boy who befriends the orca in a theme park and helps him escape to the sea. The movie displayed a toll-free number at the end so viewers could call and make contributions to help release the real killer whale. More than 300,000 viewers placed phone calls, and Keiko eventually got his freedom.[3]

Leaders of some of the twentieth century's worst totalitarian regimes have acted in the belief that movies can have a strong impact on people's attitudes. Sometimes these tyrants employed movies for propaganda purposes. Vladimir Ilyich Lenin, who dominated the early history of the Soviet Union, said, "Of all the arts, cinema is the most important."[4] Lenin recognized the power of film, proclaiming, "This is the medium for the masses."[5] Joseph Stalin, Lenin's successor, arranged to have banners hung over Moscow's theaters featuring Lenin's comments on the subject. Fascists also employed drama for propaganda purposes. For example, Hitler's minister of propaganda, Joseph Goebbels, released a dramatic film that showed veteran movie star Werner Kraus playing a dozen unappealing Jewish characters. This anti-Semitic presentation was loosely based on the life of Josef Suss Oppenheimer, an influential German tax adviser in the eighteenth century.[6] Of course, Germany's fascists also feared the power of dramatic film. In the early 1930s, before they controlled the government, the Nazis reacted vigorously to *All Quiet on the Western Front,* which presented a strong message about the senselessness of war. Fascist thugs smashed into theaters and tried to terrorize audiences by releasing snakes and mice, as well as stink bombs and sneezing powder. Later, when Hitler became chancellor of Germany, he banned the film, as did Italy's fascist dictator Benito Mussolini.

Leaders of totalitarian regimes in the Middle East and the Far East have also expressed anxiety about docudramas, especially films that cast their societies in an unfavorable light. Movies that raise questions about the social conditions in conservative Arab countries seem especially mischievous. In 1980, for example, officials in Saudi Arabia's government complained about the release of the British TV movie *Death of a Princess,* the story of a Middle Eastern princess and her lover who were publicly executed in 1977 for the crime of adultery.[7]

When the Saudi government threatened to cut trade and diplomatic links with Britain because of the supposedly offensive production, some English leaders expressed concern about the likely diplomatic and economic repercussions. Speaking in the House of Commons, Sir Ian Gilmour said, "the so-called dramatization or fictionalization of alleged history is extremely dangerous and misleading, and is something to which the broadcasting authorities must give close attention." Lord Carrington echoed these sentiments in the House of Lords, advising producers of the program "to have a good look at the consequences of what they are doing."[8] In a related way, authorities in China threatened economic and political consequences if the Disney Company went forward with its plans for worldwide release of Martin Scorsese's *Kundun* (1997). A Chinese official complained that the movie, which deals with China's takeover of Tibet and the consequent exile of the Dalai Lama, was highly biased and could damage China's international image. The movie "is intended to glorify the Dalai Lama," argued the official, "so it is an interference in China's internal affairs." He warned that Disney's provocation might wreck the entertainment company's plans to build a theme park in China, distribute movies in the country, and market entertainment merchandise.[9]

Anecdotal evidence suggests that movies can influence attitudes and behavior in more democratic environments as well. The easing of censorship in Russia in the 1990s, for instance, allowed Sergei Bodrov to release a provocative dramatization about one of his country's most controversial political problems. Bodrov's *Prisoner of the Mountains* sympathizes with both sides in Russia's struggle in Chechnya but is generally opposed to the war. Boris Yeltsin, the Russian president at the time, screened the film in his private dacha and then changed his position on the controversy a few days later. An agreement followed that temporarily brought the eighteen-month war in Chechnya to a halt. Bodrov claimed that his movie had influenced Yeltsin's important decision. "Before, he called [the guerrillas in Chechnya] bandits and said no to negotiations," noted Bodrov. "A few days later he suddenly decided to push for negotiations. I'm sure he was watching this movie with his family and his grandkids and it moved him."[10] Much more well-known is the impact of a work of cinematic history on an American president. In 1970, when President Richard M. Nixon was contemplating an invasion of Cambodia, he viewed the newly released *Patton* in the White House. Nixon was greatly impressed with the bold and courageous general depicted in the movie, and a few days after his second viewing, the president ordered U.S. and South Vietnamese troops to invade the southeast Asian nation. With Patton-like pride, he insisted that the action had to be taken, for when the chips were down, "the world's most powerful nation" should not "act like a pitiful helpless giant."[11]

Some films appear to have affected opinions on sensitive political issues. *Braveheart* (1995), for example, inspired the Scots, who saw their forebears depicted heroically on the big screen, while the English leaders who exploited them were portrayed as degenerate sadists. *Braveheart* excited Scottish interest in the separatist-minded Scottish National Party. At its annual convention, the party's member of Parliament, Alex Salmon, scolded his countrymen for their slow recognition of the nationalist cause. "We should be ashamed," said Salmon, "that it has taken Hollywood to give so many Scots back their history."[12]

A made-for-television docudrama may have influenced opinion and action in England as well. *Who Bombed Birmingham?* excited interest because it cast doubt on the conviction of six men in the bombing of two British pubs. After the program appeared on television, Prime Minister Margaret Thatcher expressed contempt for the story's message and claimed that it would have little public impact. Thatcher insisted that "a television program alters nothing." She was mistaken in her judgment, for the controversial movie aroused demands for a new inquiry into the Birmingham bombing case. Eventually, the two convicted men were released from prison.[13]

Docudramas may have affected elections, too. In 1948, for example, the Italian Communist Party seemed likely to win an important election, and American policy makers were fearful that such a victory could mean a setback for U.S. interests in Europe. Consequently, they arranged for the distribution of *Ninotchka*, a 1939 film starring Greta Garbo in which communists are easily seduced by the materialistic splendors of Paris. Italian communists lost the critical election, and a pro-communist worker concluded, "What defeated us was *Ninotchka*."[14] In the United States, a Hollywood movie's appearance during the close presidential contest in 1976 may have had a significant impact as well. Early in the race, Democratic candidate Jimmy Carter held a strong lead, but then Republican incumbent Gerald Ford began to close in. The release of Alan Pakula's *All the President's Men* in the spring of 1976 represented bad news for President Ford, however. The film, starring Robert Redford and Dustin Hoffman, showed determined young journalists uncovering important information about the Watergate scandal. *All the President's Men* reminded audiences (millions of them voters) about the wide-ranging corruption that had brought down the Nixon administration just a short time before. In the November 1976 voting, Ford lost the presidential election by a small margin.[15]

These movies represent only one element among many that influenced the Italian and American voters, and it is not possible to identify the films as the principal determining factors in the election outcomes. It seems reasonable to conclude, however, that the films affected the attitudes of at least some voters in these close campaigns. If the number of people influenced represents thousands or perhaps millions of those who went to the polls, the movies' impact may have been significant.

Cinematic history's power in influencing opinions is also suggested by the angry reactions of prominent people to highly controversial films. In 1998, for instance, Barbra Streisand produced a drama for television that presented a strong case against handguns generally and the National Rifle Association (NRA) specifically. *The Long Island Incident* portrays the real-life ordeal of Carolyn McCarthy, whose husband was killed and her son seriously wounded by a deranged gunman on a crowded commuter train. McCarthy responded to her family's tragedy by campaigning against guns and running successfully for Congress. In the course of dramatizing this story about struggle and redemption, *The Long Island Incident* negatively depicts the NRA leader who opposed McCarthy's fight for gun legislation. Through its sympathetic treatment of McCarthy's activities, the film also makes a strong case for legislation to regulate gun sales. Not surprisingly, spokesmen for the NRA denounced the film, and the association's incoming president, actor Charlton Heston, criticized Streisand publicly, saying that she was "extraordinarily liberal." Heston and NRA spokesman Bill Powers argued that it was "inappropriate and dangerous" for a major television network and production company to broadcast a drama that advances a specific political opinion. They complained that Streisand's film mixes fact and fiction so thoroughly that it complicates viewers' efforts "to sift through what's true and what's not."[16]

Another prominent figure, Alexander Haig, also registered public protests against a made-for-television movie. He objected to TNT's *Kissinger and Nixon* (1995), complaining that the film left impressions that were contrary to fact. Haig, a prominent leader in the last months of the Nixon administration, argued in a letter to the *New York Times* that the film made President Nixon look bad by frequently showing him drinking on the job. "To my knowledge," wrote Haig, "the President was at worst a modest social drinker." Haig also objected to the movie's treatment of a more weighty political issue. He complained that *Kissinger and Nixon* seemed to create a sympathetic case for the North Vietnamese's cause while displaying almost no sympathy for America's wartime allies, the South Vietnamese.[17]

Another public figure, Mike Wallace of CBS's *60 Minutes*, was apprehensive about the appearance of the Hollywood feature film *The Insider* (1999). Michael Mann's movie takes a sympathetic view of the efforts of former tobacco company executive Jeffrey S. Wigand to reveal secret information that the cigarette companies had about the dangers of smoking, including an interview he did with *60 Minutes*. *The Insider* enacts behind-the-scenes discussions at CBS regarding the controversial nature of Wigand's recorded interview and

*Lowell Bergman (Al Pacino, left), a* 60 Minutes *television producer, tries to convince tobacco company insider Jeffrey Wigand (Russell Crowe) to reveal the truth about industry practices in* The Insider *(1999). The presence of Wigand's daughter in his arms suggests that cooperating is likely to create serious problems for his career and family.* Sixty Minutes *anchor Mike Wallace was reportedly apprehensive about the movie's portrayals. (Museum of Modern Art Film Archive)*

suggests that CBS executives were so worried about the legal risks associated with broadcasting his most contentious comments that they tried to excise those remarks from the report. Wallace found the movie portrayal troubling because it raises questions about his role in these decisions; it makes him look weak-willed and shows him initially supporting the cuts out of concern that the entire CBS News organization could fall victim to an expensive legal assault by the tobacco company. Later in the story, the character representing Wallace shows greater fortitude and commitment to the principles of free speech. CBS News president Andrew Heyward defended Wallace's behavior in the Wigand case in an internal memo to his staff, asserting that *The Insider* "casts a very misleading light" on the distinguished CBS newsman. Later, Wallace's friends viewed *The Insider* and brought him the good news that Hollywood's portrayal did not make him look nearly as bad as anticipated.[18]

Each of these prominent individuals was concerned about the power of cinematic history to influence viewers' attitudes. They believed that docudramas could advance persuasive arguments about people and events. Heston, Haig, and Wallace worried that movie and television entertainment could, from their point of view, create a negative impact. Through both subtle and direct arguments communicated by the medium of drama, these films seemed capable of undermining their positions in the public eye.

Criticism regarding the impact of cinematic history has, of course, been evident since the dawn of motion picture development. One of the earliest cases occurred back in 1915, when D. W. Griffith's *Birth of a Nation* (1915) was the source of public debate. In view of its central place in the debate about film's impact and its power as an interpreter of history, *Birth of a Nation* deserves a closer look.

Griffith's hit film was tremendously innovative. It was lengthier than typical films of its time, developing its story in several reels, and it presented history in soap opera fashion. Griffith brilliantly touched the audience's emotions, using melodrama to follow the experiences of key characters. *Birth of a Nation* was also technically innovative, featuring close-ups; wipes; bold angles; lively mixtures of long, medium, and close shots; and various other techniques that were new at the time. While Griffith's storytelling skills and artistic virtuosity give the movie extraordinary appeal, his interpretation of American history provides the controversy.

*Birth of a Nation* communicates strong opinions about the Civil War and Reconstruction in the United States. It begins with rather cheerful views of both Northern and Southern societies on the eve of the conflict, suggesting that the impending war is an unfortunate calamity that will temporarily destroy the national family. When identifying the cause of the great conflict, *Birth of a Nation* points to Northern agitation over slavery. It shows Yankee slave traders introducing slavery to America and observes that the Africans' substantial presence in the Union is the eventual source of its breakup. The war comes, and the Southern hero of the drama, Ben Cameron, fights bravely, but he struggles in a lost cause. Abraham Lincoln makes some appearances, serving as a magnanimous leader who understands the South's difficulties and seeks a fair and generous settlement of the sectional disagreements. The president's tragic death creates opportunities for venal Northern carpetbaggers and their corrupt African-American partners to take forceful control of the South during the postwar period of Reconstruction, and a dark period of oppressive rule begins. In some of the most memorable scenes depicting these times, black leaders shove whites off the sidewalk, uneducated black politicians chew on chicken bones as they preside over meetings of the state government, and a lust-driven black man chases Ben Cameron's sister into the woods. Fearing rape, the girl leaps off a cliff and dies. Throughout this frightening picture of the early Reconstruction period, *Birth of a Nation* argues strongly, in captions and in imagery, against integration of the races and miscegenation.

*Silas Lynch (George Seigmann) displays his amorous interests while Austin Stoneman (Ralph Lewis) looks on in D. W. Griffith's* Birth of a Nation *(1915). This sharply biased view of the Reconstruction era came under strong criticism for promoting racial prejudice. (Museum of Modern Art Film Archive)*

Eventually, Cameron, the hero, creates a secret order of the Ku Klux Klan. Hooded knights race through the countryside and into the town, frightening blacks and their Republican supporters. Cameron and the Klan finally succeed in freeing the South from the domination of the white Yankee aggressors and their black partners. In view of this sharply biased presentation of history, it is not surprising that *Birth of a Nation* became the target of numerous protests soon after its release.

Griffith should have expected angry reactions, for he based his drama on episodes from *The Clansman,* a highly prejudiced novel written by North Carolinian Thomas Dixon. In fact, the director called his movie *The Clansman* up to the time of its opening in Los Angeles in 1915. But sensing the provocative nature of the title and its association with the controversial author, Griffith renamed the film *Birth of a Nation* before it opened in New York City. Thomas Dixon also attempted to promote the movie with the press, fueling the public controversy. Dixon's most significant action was arranging a screening for his old friend from graduate school days, Virginia-born President Woodrow Wilson. The author reported that Wilson was enthusiastic about the film and exclaimed, "It is like writing history with lightning." When a newspaper editor asked Dixon what he hoped could be accomplished by the production of *Birth of a Nation,* the North Carolinian said that he wanted whites, especially women, to develop feelings of abhorrence toward Negro men. Dixon suggested that such reactions to the movie could help prevent the mixture of white and Negro blood through intermarriage.[19] Griffith tried to steer clear of Dixon's most strident and controversial observations, emphasizing instead the historical authenticity of his production. But Griffith, along with Dixon, took the brunt of many criticisms regarding the movie's emotion-laden characterization of blacks.

Leaders in the newly formed National Association for the Advancement of Colored People (NAACP) and their liberal white allies were especially vocal in denouncing the movie. An editorial in the NAACP's *Crisis* called Dixon's book a "sordid and lurid melodrama" that "brutally" falsified history.[20] Under the title "Capitalizing Race Hatred," a *New York Globe* editorial criticized the film's message. "To make a few dirty dollars," said the editorial, "men are willing to pander to the depraved tastes and to foment a race antipathy that is the most sinister and dangerous feature of American life."[21] Some of the most aggressive protests occurred in Boston, where groups circulated petitions and demonstrated by the hundreds, demanding that screenings of the movie be closed down. Politicians in Massachusetts expressed their agreement with these calls for censorship, and the governor promised to seek legislation aimed at prohibiting movies with highly prejudiced content related to race and religion.

Authorities in Chicago managed to close the production, and the state of Illinois later banned it.[22] For the most part, however, efforts to censor *Birth of a Nation* were unsuccessful. In 1915, political leaders in communities around the country were considerably less enamored of censorship than they had been earlier in the Progressive Era, when motion pictures first became popular. *Birth of a Nation* was shown in many theaters around the country without difficulty, and generally the film proved both popular and profitable.

How great was *Birth of a Nation*'s impact? Did the movie influence ideas about American history? Did it affect racial attitudes? As in the case of other examples of cinematic history, evidence is fragmentary and certainly not substantial enough to warrant sweeping or confident conclusions. The details do reveal, however, that a number of people looked seriously on the public debate about impact and suspected that the motion picture could influence the perspectives of its audience.

When controversies over the movie became public, Griffith energetically defended his film's interpretation of history. He declared the movie's depictions authentic, and he tried to enlist testimonials from authorities to back up his claims. The director published letters and articles in leading newspapers, explaining that he drew information about the Civil War and Reconstruction from Woodrow Wilson's respected history of the United States and other authoritative sources. Griffith also announced that three clergymen "have given us permission to use their names in approval of this picture in its entirety."[23]

Even though Griffith affirmed his confidence in the truthfulness and fairness of his portrayals, his decision to release a big-budget movie about prejudice just a year after the release of *Birth of a Nation* suggested that the public criticisms troubled him. Griffith's *Intolerance* (1916) portrayed examples of prejudice through the ages. His elaborate, expensive production was a flop at the box office (relative to the cost), but the movie did help somewhat in disassociating Griffith from the illiberal sentiments of Thomas Dixon. Woodrow Wilson also attempted to distance himself from Dixon. Following the outburst of major protests against *Birth of a Nation* and Dixon's public efforts to accentuate the movie's message against miscegenation, the president backed away from the positive references to the movie that had been attributed to him.

The most suggestive evidence of *Birth of a Nation*'s impact relates to the re-emergence of the Ku Klux Klan. After the film received a strong public reception in Los Angeles and New York, it was scheduled for screening in theaters around the nation, including in the South. A week before the film's premier in Atlanta, Colonel William J. Simmons gathered friends in the region (including two members of the original KKK of Reconstruction years) and created a ceremonial beginning for a new organization at Stone Mountain, Georgia.

*The Ku Klux Klan attacks an African American in* Birth of a Nation *(1915). A week before the film's premier in Atlanta, Colonel William J. Simmons created a new Klan organization at Stone Mountain, Georgia. (Museum of Modern Art Film Archive)*

Simmons's Klan stressed 100 percent Americanism, supremacy of the Caucasian race, and keeping the Negro in his place. By 1919, the organization had several thousand members, and in the 1920s, membership numbered in the millions. The KKK's influence spread across much of the nation, but many who joined the Klan outside the South were more concerned about Catholics and Jews (especially immigrants) than they were about African Americans.[24]

If *Birth of a Nation* represents one of the most impressive examples of cinematic history's unfortunate impact, *Holocaust,* a TV miniseries of the late 1970s, represents one of the notable examples of a positive impact. In the United States and Europe, many viewers found the drama's revelations about Nazi-led genocide during World War II shocking. Touched emotionally by *Holocaust*'s personalization of a historic tragedy, millions who saw the program became more knowledgeable about the Jews' suffering. As Peter Novick reports in his book *The Holocaust in American Life,* "Without doubt the most important moment in the entry of the Holocaust into general American consciousness was NBC's presentation, in April 1978, of the miniseries *Holocaust.*"[25] A German journalist suggested an even more powerful influence in his society when he wrote, "'Holocaust' has shaken up post-Hitler Germany in a way that German intellectuals have been unable to do. No other film has ever made the Jews' road of suffering leading to the gas chambers so vivid. . . . Only since and as a result of 'Holocaust' does a majority of the nation know what lay behind the horrible and vacuous formula, 'Final Solution of the Jewish Question.'"[26]

*Holocaust* presents its story over nine and a half hours by following the experiences of two fictional families, one of which is Jewish. That family's central character is a generous and likable medical doctor, Josef Weiss (Fritz Weaver). At the beginning of the film, it is 1935, and Weiss's son (James Woods) is marrying a gentile (Meryl Streep). Present at the wedding ceremony are some prejudiced Germans who speak critically of marriage with Jews and hint of Nazi efforts against such unions. After introducing other attractive Jewish characters from the Weiss family, the film looks at the troubled life of Erik Dorf (Michael Moriarty), an unemployed lawyer who is encouraged by his ambitious wife to join the Nazi Party and advance his career. Dorf eventually attains a good position within the party under Reinhard Heydrich (David Warner), a cold and calculating mass murderer who helps organize Hitler's campaign against the Jews. At various points in the story, members of the Weiss and Dorf families interact with each other. Dr. Weiss, for example, is Mrs. Dorf's doctor, but she later turns against him and supports the arrests of Jews. Over the course of the drama, virtually all the significant historical developments related to the Holocaust affect members of the Weiss family. By viewing their ordeal, the audience learns about the Nuremberg laws; Kristallnacht; the concentration camps at Buchenwald, Sobibor, and Auschwitz; and the Warsaw ghetto uprising. By the end of the series (representing a ten-year span of history), all key members of the Weiss family have suffered terribly or died. One of the most memorable scenes involves the suicide of a grandfather who is proud of the Iron Cross he received from the kaiser for gallant service in the German infantry during the First World War. In the final episode, a handsome survivor from the Weiss family who fought in the underground resistance goes off to begin a new life in Israel.

NBC executives hoped that their miniseries would provide an effective network response to ABC's marvelously successful miniseries of the previous year, *Roots,* which broke television records. *Holocaust* did not surpass the extraordinary reception for *Roots,* but it certainly scored impressively in audience appeal: 120 millions Americans watched the program, enough to make it a notable financial success.

NBC had to deal with some vociferous objections from unexpected quarters, however, for several prominent Jews criticized the program. The most influential protester was Elie Wiesel, an articulate survivor of Hitler's extermination programs who had written important books on the Holocaust and given a number of impressive public addresses about it. Writing in the *New York Times*, Wiesel protested the commercial dramatization of a story about the Holocaust, insisting that the tragedy was a unique subject that required a different kind of treatment. "Auschwitz cannot be explained nor can it be visualized," he wrote. "Only those who were there will know what it was; the others will never know." Remember the Holocaust, he urged, "but not as a show." Additionally, Wiesel identified factual errors in the popular dramatization and complained that many of the details were wrong. Jewish refugees who crossed the Russian border before the German invasion were not allowed to move freely, as shown in the film, and Auschwitz inmates could not keep their suitcases, family pictures, and music sheets. Jews did not wear their prayer shawls at night, he noted, and the rabbi in the film recites the wrong blessing for Torah readings and for a wedding. In reviewing these mistakes, Wiesel also took issue with the series' entire dramatic format. Fictional characters in the story were made to appear quite real to the audience, he complained. The movie made no clear distinction between fact and fiction, between actual personalities from history and invented ones. Furthermore, major characters in the story were involved in every salient historical event of the Holocaust. These were implausible coincidences, Wiesel protested, and most of the scenes did not ring true. *Holocaust* offered "too much 'drama,' not enough 'documentary.'"[27]

Wiesel's sharp attack quickly excited a spirited debate in the pages of the *New York Times*. A number of comments and letters appeared in support of Wiesel's critical position. Wolfe Kelman, executive vice president of the Rabbinical Assembly in New York City, said that NBC lost a "once-in-a-generation opportunity to reach and teach a mass audience," and Mark S. Golub, executive director of Jewish Education in the Media, complained that the drama failed to show viewers the sadism of the Nazi high command. The TV series did not adequately display the Nazis as the diabolical lunatics they were, said Golub.[28] John O'Connor, who reviewed the series for the *New York Times*, offered criticisms of the dramatization that were similar to Wiesel's. He claimed that the drama was fatally flawed because it trivialized history. "The incomprehensible is nearly always made trite," wrote O'Connor. He lambasted *Holocaust*'s "shameful history," which was "regurgitated as soap opera."[29] Abraham Brumberg took a similar position, complaining about the story's "idiotic dialogues, simplistic characterizations, implausible situations and fraudulent history." Brumberg was repulsed by the filmmakers' attempt to "distort, prevaricate, dilute, vulgarize and misrepresent reality," and he concluded that the series offered "putrid nonsense!"[30]

Others who participated in this debate in the *New York Times* defended the program. Rabbi Marc Tannenbaum, director of national interreligious affairs for the American Jewish Committee and a consultant for the series, emphasized that a principal goal of the filmmakers was to reach non-Jews who knew almost nothing about the Holocaust. In that aim, the series' creators succeeded, Tannenbaum declared.[31] Dore Schary, a screenwriter, drew attention to this educational purpose too, observing that "Mr. Wiesel overlooks the impact that the program is having on people who have forgotten or never knew about the horror of the Holocaust."[32] Another defender, letter-writer Evelyn Gerter, challenged the critics to come up with a more accurate drama of their own. For the moment, wrote Gerter, *Holocaust* provides a good means to help young Americans understand what Hitler stood for.[33]

This brouhaha inspired Gerald Green, the screenwriter, to defend his production in the *Times*. First, Green responded to claims that the historical subject was too special to be represented in a dramatic film. He said that Elie Wiesel was attempting to establish a monopoly as the "self-anointed and the only voice on the Holocaust." Wiesel failed to understand that the popular miniseries was likely to excite public interest in learning more about the Holocaust. In fact, wrote Green, Wiesel was likely to sell more books and receive more speaking engagements because of the program's success. Regarding the complaints about dramatization advanced by Wiesel and others, Green pointed out that such artistic license was long familiar in great literature. Tolstoy invented many of the major characters that appear in *War and Peace*, and his story about these figures' experiences is considered a fascinating and memorable literary work about history. The Weiss and the Dorf families are fictitious, Green admitted, but their presence in the story helps bring to life an important chapter from the past.[34]

Looking back on this controversy many years later, it is evident that Green held the stronger ground in the debate. He was defending an art form that was somewhat new at the time but is much more familiar to audiences of the twenty-first century. In the 1970s, television was just beginning to broadcast history-based miniseries such as *Thirteen Days* (1974), *Eleanor and Franklin* (1976), and *Roots* (1977). Elie Wiesel and other critics were unable to see these programs as representations of a genre, as modes of storytelling with their own traditions of mixing fact and fiction. Artistic invention is fundamentally important in this craft. Certainly *Holocaust*'s practice of placing a few characters at the scene of many important historical events is much less controversial today; this dramatic strategy is now a familiar element in cinematic history. Wiesel and others also failed to understand that cinematic history frequently puts fictitious characters at the center of its story. The appearance of invented figures such as Josef Weiss and Erik Dorf does not, by itself, suggest that the film generates only flawed history. Weiss and Dorf serve as stereotypes, and through an examination of their invented personalities and experiences, the audience encounters conditions that affected the lives of many people in the period. These stereotypes also confront the audience with significant questions about the causes of European anti-Semitism and the popularity of the Nazis in pre–World War II Germany. Furthermore, Wiesel failed to understand the broad potential of the mass media to make people around the world aware of this tragic history. *Holocaust*'s tremendous impact in Germany, as well as the influence of the 1993 film *Schindler's List,* shows that cinematic reflections on genocide can arouse, provoke, and educate in significant ways.

When *Holocaust* moved to European television after its American debut, the series attracted an enormous audience. In Britain, it drew very high ratings and helped sell many paperback books about the history of Nazi atrocities. A record 52 percent of French TV viewers watched the series' first episode. In Sweden, over half the nation's population of 8 million watched some parts of the program. The most interesting European audience response, however, came from the region where many of the historic crimes took place.

West Germany needed a historical awakening at the time, for the Holocaust had received little public attention. In German high schools, teachers often gave the subject only cursory treatment, and by the late 1960s, some Germans were protesting the oversight. The Frankfurt psychoanalysts Alexander and Margarete Mitscherlich discussed the problem in a best-selling book published in 1967. They noted that many Germans had maintained relative silence on this sensitive subject. By avoiding a mental confrontation with this disturbing history, they displayed an "inability to mourn." Citizens of the Federal Republic were unable to work through their troubled thoughts about wartime events because of such wide-ranging denial, said the Mitscherlichs.[35]

German TV executives appeared to be in no position to begin the mourning process when a dubbed version of *Holocaust* became available. At first, they put their noses in the air when given an opportunity to broadcast the series. They complained that *Holocaust* represented "cheap commercialism" in a soap opera format. Peter Schultz-Rohr, program director for Sudwestfunk, called the program "garbage." Focusing on inaccuracies in the small details, he complained that *Holocaust* showed members of Hitler's youth organization wearing summer uniforms in the middle of winter and that the drama showed the unlikely situation of Jewish relatives visiting inmates at Buchenwald. "We have had enough of bald obligatory exercises in digesting our past," complained Schultz-Rohr.[36] Heimut Oeller, program director of Bayerischer Rundfunk, also debunked the production. He thought the series delivered typical Hollywood entertainment, "not quite real, not quite truth." Another

TV official, Peter Mertisheimer, concluded cynically, "Hollywood remains Hollywood, no matter what the subject."[37]

At first, the hostile reception from German TV executives delayed broadcast of the series. Media leaders reported that their network program schedules were unusually tight for the months ahead. Then the executives managed to treat the series as second-class entertainment. They chose not to feature it as part of regular network programming. Instead, they fed the series to the nine regional stations of West Germany, allowing each local unit to choose how to deal with it.

Did the executives' reactions suggest an effort to undermine the film's impact in Germany? Did their frequent complaints about melodrama and commercialism constitute rationales for keeping the program off the air? Did their excuses, including references to busy program schedules, mean that these Germans did not want to expose their audiences to a drama that dealt with a controversial subject? Were the executives fearful that the movie could inflame emotions? (Indeed, a bomb did knock out a big regional antenna. It had evidently been planted to prevent the broadcast of a documentary about the Holocaust scheduled to precede the dramatic series.) The executives' motivation is not entirely clear. Their public remarks concentrated on the film's artistic value and the network schedules. In view of the series' popularity in the United States and the eagerness of TV executives in other European nations to broadcast *Holocaust*, the behavior of the Germans appears suspect.

Despite the executives' resistance, *Holocaust* became an instant hit in Germany. Thirty-two to 39 percent of the TV audience in West Germany tuned in to the various episodes, and about 15 million West Germans (roughly half the adult population) watched one or more installments. The ratings were not as high as for major soccer games and some popular mystery programs, but they indicated surprisingly strong audience interest. Furthermore, about 30,000 calls came in to the local stations from viewers who wished to comment on what they had seen or to request more information. The viewers' comments ran approximately two to one in favor of the series. Many callers asked: How could it happen? How many people knew?[38] An official associated with the main broadcast stations in Cologne and West Berlin said, "We have never had this kind of reaction before. . . . This is an absolute record."[39] Even though *Holocaust* was not broadcast in communist East Germany, citizens there managed to catch the series on their antennas. One report indicated that about 85 percent of the TV sets in the east were tuned in to the first episode of the series.

*Holocaust* seems to have had a substantial impact on the debates in West Germany over the statute of limitations for Nazi war crimes. The laws guiding punishment for such capital offenses were scheduled to expire at the end of 1979, the year of *Holocaust*'s broadcast in West Germany. Excitement about the

*Dr. Josef Weiss and his wife Berta (Fritz Weaver and Rosemary Harris, left-center) and Lowy and his wife (George Rose and Kate Jaenicke, foreground) are herded onto boxcars bound for concentration camps. Broadcast of the TV miniseries* Holocaust *in Germany provoked new interest in World War II–era history. (Photofest)*

TV series changed the political environment in the Federal Republic. *Holocaust* communicated a powerful moral indictment of the Nazis' actions, pushing discussions of the horrible past to the front of the national political dialogue. Eventually, legislators in the Bundestag voted to extend the statute of limitations, and many Germans attributed the decision to public reaction to the TV drama. The media event also excited a colorful *Historikerstreit* ("historians' debate"), the term German scholars gave to the intellectual clashes that animated academics in their country during the 1980s. This clash of interpretations was related to the lessons that could be drawn from the study of twentieth-century German history. Some scholars sought to capitalize on the surge in public interest in the Holocaust by giving the subject much more prominence in exchanges on German history. They sought a deeper understanding of why German society allowed such heinous crimes to take place. Other scholars complained that enthusiasm for the television series had led to exaggerated attention to Nazi atrocities. They claimed that most Germans were not deeply prejudiced or advocates of genocide against the Jews. Besides, they argued, people in other countries had participated in different forms of atrocity;

German society was not uniquely evil, they insisted. Unfortunately, the increased public attention to Nazi war crimes, publicized by *Holocaust,* made the society appear distinctly evil.[40]

Indirectly, a talented German filmmaker walked into this debate by composing a lengthy TV series that gives little attention to the Nazis or their atrocities. Edgar Reitz's *Heimut* examines life in a small German village over many years. His dramatic program communicates a love for the simple life of the small town and the countryside, stressing the values of home, family, and community. *Heimut* suggests a critical view of life in the rootless, soulless urban environment. Nazi activities intrude little in the day-to-day lives of the people portrayed in Reitz's television series. There are occasional references to the well-known history of the Third Reich, but Reitz keeps most of the references to Hitler, fascism, and the Holocaust at the margins.

Reitz's popular program became the object of considerable scholarly debate. Some praised him for showing that there were important stories to tell about modern German history that had little to do with the familiar textbook accounts of Nazi oppression. Others criticized the series for attempting to whitewash modern German history. *Heimut,* they said, reinforces the familiar postwar German efforts to hide from the unpleasant past.[41]

*In* Schindler's List *(1993), German industrialist Oskar Schindler (Liam Neeson, on the platform) welcomes workers to the safety of his new factory at Brinnlitz. Steven Spielberg's film may have been an important catalyst when a Swiss bank guard acted on behalf of Holocaust victims. (Museum of Modern Art Film Archive)*

By the time *Schindler's List* arrived in Germany in 1993, new generations of Germans were already accustomed to public discussions of the Holocaust, and Spielberg's movie amplified their interest. The German media gave a great deal of attention to the Holocaust in the weeks surrounding the movie's opening across the country. Newspapers, magazines, and television talk shows featured discussions about the persecution of the Jews, as well as commentaries on the record of Oskar Schindler. The media also focused on director Steven Spielberg, noting how creating the movie had helped put him in touch with his Jewish roots. Emma Schindler, widow of the story's hero, received media attention as well. She came to Germany from Argentina and did a number of interviews with TV and print journalists. Germany's overall reception of *Schindler's List* was impressive. Nearly 100,000 saw the film in its first four days, even though there were only forty-five copies available in the country at the time. *Schindler's List* eventually attracted some of the largest German movie audiences of the late twentieth century.[42]

Spielberg's film also may have served as an important catalyst in Switzerland, where a bank guard recalled the movie's message and acted on behalf of Holocaust victims. Christophe Meili was a security guard at the Union Bank of Switzerland when he came across two carts filled with Holocaust-era documents that were headed for the shredder. Destruction of the documents would have violated a recently passed Swiss bank law designed to protect information regarding Jewish clients, and Meili recovered the documents. News reports of his discovery put international pressure on Switzerland to release all records pertaining to the Jews' bank accounts. Explaining the motivation for his important action, Meili said, "I . . . knew that I had to do something, that I could not just turn my head and look the other way." He explained that he "suddenly saw visions of Holocaust victims" when he came across the papers. "I remembered the movie *Schindler's List*," said Meili.[43]

We may never have completely convincing and quantifiable information about the impact of cinematic history on its audiences, but the anecdotal evidence presented here suggests that the effect can be significant. In the specific cases of *Birth of a Nation* and *Holocaust*, we encounter intriguing evidence of a rather substantial stimulus. In numerous other examples from film and television drama, researchers can find additional details suggesting that audiences take ideas away from their viewing experiences. These fragments of information indicate that viewers do not always consider cinematic history merely mindless escapism that has no relevance to their lives. Evidently, the genre can have an impact on attitudes, and sometimes it influences personal and public actions as well.

# Conclusion

When *Birth of a Nation* revolutionized motion pictures in 1915 by demonstrating the drawing power of a lengthy and well-crafted movie drama, D. W. Griffith waxed eloquent about the potential of film to change the way people learned about history. He delivered three principal messages about the educational benefits of motion pictures. First, Griffith imagined that the day was not far off when citizens would obtain much of their knowledge about the past by watching movies. Second, he spoke of movies' value in presenting stories about the past that had a greater emotional and intellectual impact on audiences than did descriptions presented in traditional ways. Finally, Griffith maintained that intelligently designed and well-researched films could give audiences authentic pictures of history.[1] The noted director was extraordinarily prescient in making his first two judgments about movies' potential to play an educational role, but his third conclusion was grossly simplistic.

Griffith put his finger on significant contradictions associated with cinematic history that continue to animate debates today. History-oriented films have become familiar sources of entertainment, and they often excite audiences' interest in their subjects. Yet these productions communicate in a highly personal and politicized manner. They are hardly the nonpartisan, balanced, and truth-based interpretations that Griffith described in his enthusiastic remarks of 1915. In many ways, then, Griffith helped introduce the debate that has provoked arguments among historians, film scholars, media pundits, and the public ever since. In speaking of cinematic history's future utility and impact, he identified its importance, and in claiming that these influential portrayals were true, he invited a lively battle over its messages.

Griffith effectively anticipated the modern era when he imagined that classrooms and libraries would someday have the technological capacity to offer instructive motion pictures about "practically everything."[2] He predicted that educational institutions would feature devices that allowed individuals to seat themselves "at a properly adjusted window, in a scientifically prepared room, press the button, and actually see what happened."[3] Of course, that potential has been realized in both public and private settings. In the twenty-first century, history is abundantly available in movie theaters, on home television sets, and through a variety of video, DVD, and Internet devices. Screenings in schools and universities are familiar components of classroom instruction. College and community libraries contain numerous booths at which visitors can view films on monitors. Today, the technology Griffith envisioned in 1915 easily delivers cinematic history to the masses.

Griffith was among the first to articulate an insightful view of film's advantages over books and stage plays. He observed, for example, that a story about the Civil War could take several days to read, but the essential elements of that history could be portrayed on the screen in just three hours. Motion picture production had progressed to new levels of sophistication, he pointed out. "It is capable of conveying a given image in many ways enormously more effectively than any mode of expression the world has ever possessed."[4] A film director had distinct advantages over a stage director, Griffith argued. Portrayals on a stage were "confined and limited" by three walls. For background, a stage director could provide only a few painted and manufactured effects, "which are, after all, only miserable imitations of natural objects." Movie directors, in contrast, could use "poetic simulation." When portraying a shipwreck, said Griffith, "we show the angry sea and the restless waves." A story about a secret encounter between lovers could take place outdoors in "some sylvan dell," with roses blooming in natural sunlight and real mountains in the background. These advantages lifted motion pictures to a higher plane. Movies were "the newest and most powerful form of dramatic expression," and they tended to make a more enduring impression on the public than books or stage plays did. Weeks and months after seeing a movie, audiences were likely to forget the details of specific stories, "but the ideas and the recollections go on as long as life lasts."[5]

Griffith identified the emotional power of movies, a quality that draws much attention today. Commentators speak frequently about the extraordinary impact of motion pictures on the sentiments of viewers. They note that *Gandhi* inspired interest in nonviolent protest, *JFK* aroused concerns about conspiracy, *Braveheart* excited Scottish patriotism, and *Titanic* stirred tremendous interest in the 1912 tragedy at sea. The images and interpretations of motion pictures have, as Griffith predicted, deeply affected our modern perspectives of history. For many Americans, and for people around the world, visions of the past emerge from scenes in Hollywood productions. When imagining conditions in ancient Rome, life in the American West, social relationships in the antebellum South, scenes from the royal court of England, or conditions at a World War II battlefront, individuals often conjure up images and words from the movies.

Because of dramatic film's extraordinary power over audiences, today's debates about cinematic history frequently become intense. Participants in the discussions believe that the stakes are high, and they recognize that cinema weighs heavily in audiences' thinking. As Griffith noted in 1915, dramatic film has a "silent power." Its mode of communication seems more subtle, concealed, and complex than that in other forms of presentation. Through the manipulation of many stimuli not available to a writer, speaker, or stage director, motion picture artists can turn their interpretations into what Griffith called an emotional "tour de force."[6]

Although Griffith astutely gave early recognition to cinematic history's potential for popularity and influence, he was certainly mistaken when rhapsodizing about its veracity. Griffith suggested that movies could present images on the screen that re-created authentic pictures of the past. Through careful research, he argued, a movie director could design stories that were free of bias, which viewers could watch with perfect confidence. In future productions, "there will be no opinions expressed," wrote Griffith. "You will merely be present at the making of history." Thanks to careful preparation of the portrayal by "recognized experts," movies will deliver "a vivid and complete expression." Thirty-two years after the release of *Birth of a Nation*, Griffith continued to speak confidently about the authenticity of motion picture portrayals. In a letter written to *Sight and Sound* in 1947, he claimed that *Birth of a Nation* offered "to the best of my knowledge the proven facts and presented the known truth about the Reconstruction period in the American South." The film's portrayal had support from an abundance of "authentic evidence and testimony," Griffith said. Its picture of history required "no apology, no defence, no 'explanations.'"[7]

Did D. W. Griffith genuinely believe these arguments about the objectivity and truthfulness of cinematic history when he first made them to promote his 1915 film? Did he continue to believe as late as 1947 that *Birth of a Nation* offered an authentic and unbiased view of the Civil War and Reconstruction? Or was he making a calculated effort in both instances to deflect criticisms of the film? Did he, perhaps, recognize the absurdity of these claims but make them anyway, to defend his production against attackers?

Whatever Griffith's purpose, his remarks addressed a contradiction that is at the core of modern-day debates about cinematic history. Historians, media critics, and the public often demand that filmmakers create fair and representative pictures of the past. This demand is hardly realistic, for the individuals who express it fail to take into account the medium's fundamental nature. Hollywood movies do not present balanced and objective perspectives such as Griffith idealized. Modern-day cinematic history does not usually look as transparently biased as *Birth of a Nation,* but it is nevertheless a highly opinionated and strongly manipulated perspective on the past. Today's artists apply almost as much partisan spin to their topics as did the controversial director who was criticized in 1915 for pandering a strongly prejudiced view of Reconstruction.

Reactions to the controversial nature of cinematic history have been diverse. Many observers complain that movies serve primarily as instruments for communicating the directors' personal agendas. They do not believe that cinema provides sophisticated commentaries on weighty topics. Some, who are wedded to traditional print-oriented approaches to history, consider motion picture entertainment largely irrelevant. They do not find much educational value in productions that manipulate and distort evidence excessively. Moviemakers cavalierly violate scholarly standards for the handling of evidence, they note. Hollywood filmmakers readily bend, distort, and invent facts to create appealing stories. Because filmmakers exhibit little concern for discovering truths about the past, their productions should not be considered serious commentaries on history. Others, viewing these films from the perspective of cinema studies, agree that Hollywood productions are not historical works, but they take a different tack. Many of them view these films not as portraits of the past but as metaphorical statements, experiments in artistic imagination, allegories referring to the present, and other forms of creative expression. Because scholars in cinema studies see the productions as largely symbolic stories rather than representational ones, they are far more tolerant of the manipulation of historical evidence than the first group is. Tradition-minded critics are given to lambasting filmmakers for getting the details wrong and for exercising artistic license excessively. Observers from cinema studies are more likely to praise filmmakers for their imaginative and insightful artistic flourishes.

This book has attempted to find a middle ground between the two. It demonstrates an appreciation of the demand for sophisticated portrayals of the past in dramatic film, yet it also suggests that moviemakers must deal with history in ways that are very different from the techniques authors apply when they write nonfiction books.

Hollywood artists can never present as broad-minded a view of history as the authors of nonfiction analyses do. Moviemakers cannot deliver as comprehensive a picture of diverse developments, provide as much abstract analysis of events, explore the impact of impersonal forces in history (such as important economic, political, social, and intellectual changes), or expose audiences to as many conflicting interpretations of the past as authors do. Writing is almost always a better medium for achieving such broad understandings.

This book also recognizes that Hollywood filmmakers are always influenced to a considerable degree by practices of their craft. Cinematic history constitutes a genre. Moviemakers adopt elements of style to enhance the entertainment value and profitability of their productions. In many respects, they employ techniques that D. W. Griffith demonstrated in primitive form in *Birth of a Nation*. Filmmakers collapse several historical characters into a few, condense the time sequence of events, focus on only a few moments of crisis, and leave out a great deal of peripheral information. Their stories focus on personalities rather than issues, examining great events in terms of the experiences of a few heroes or heroines. Heinous villains also populate their dramas, antagonists who rather starkly stand in for the forces of evil. Hollywood's storytellers privilege tales about conflict, about confrontations over power and rights. They usually sympathize with the poor and humble, and their villains are often in positions of power and wealth. Moviemakers frequently deliver a democratic message when focusing on the common people's struggle, leaving audiences with uplifting moral lessons. With the exception of some war stories, the genre usually features romance to enhance audience interest. The principal characters' love affair is often threatened by the troubling historical events that swirl around them.

Invention is fundamental in this genre. To simplify detailed and complicated information and make it understandable to audiences, cinematic historians fictionalize. Often they invent the movie's principal characters, which ensures that key figures in the film participate in many important historical events (certainly far more events than real-life figures encountered). This device also protects filmmakers from attacks by detail-minded critics. Historians and media reviewers frequently lambaste filmmakers for simplifying or distorting details associated with specific figures from history. If a story purports only to symbolize the behavior of many people or to represent a combination of actions by several different individuals, it makes a less tempting target for the fact checkers. Fictionalizing also helps moviemakers account for aspects of behavior that are generally unknowable. Cinema needs to take audiences behind closed doors and expose them to the thoughts and actions of people living in the past, but evidence of those thoughts and actions is rarely recorded in the history archives. Invention helps remedy this problem. The movie's fictional scenes offer informed speculation—educated guesses about how ideas and behavior found expression in those unrecorded settings. Thus, dramatic invention is a critical component of the filmmaker's craft. It is employed abundantly, even in the most sophisticated productions, including those with serious educational purposes.

A great deal of ink and airtime are wasted on angry indictments of cinematic history for engaging in practices of the genre or for inventing and manipulating evidence. These criticisms would not seem irrelevant if they were framed with an understanding of the way Hollywood drama works. If the commentators recognized at the outset that *all* cinematic history conforms in some ways to traditional practices of the genre and that *all* such productions call for degrees of fictionalization, their criticisms would reflect greater sophistication. Unfortunately, such awareness is not evident in many of the familiar remarks about history from Hollywood. Critics often act as if Hollywood artists should make their interpretations conform to scholarly standards. They blast the filmmakers for simplifying complex historical events, complain about the characterization of heroes and villains, and rail about information that is left out. Critics grumble about attention to romantic trysts, arguing that the movies should focus instead on major political or historical developments; they complain that the dramas provide only one explanation of events, ignoring other factors that deserve attention as well. Most frequently, they argue that characters and situations in Hollywood's stories are adjusted for entertainment purposes, that filmmakers invent portrayals rather than attempting to render them authentically. All these complaints lose their punch, however, if the individuals making them do not recognize that such adjustments are, to some degree, essential in all dramatic depictions of history.

Cinematic history needs to be addressed with a different vision of achievement and failure. Discussions about its value ought to be couched in language that takes into account the distinctive conditions under which commercial filmmakers operate. Hollywood artists always borrow from the traditions of successful film presentation; to enhance their prospects for financial success, they must employ the techniques of storytelling that have proved effective over the past century. Often they tweak the genre, challenging some of its traditions to arouse audience interest, but they can ill afford to turn completely away from practices of the craft. They must also resort to fictionalization. Historical evidence is too fragmentary to provide a neat, seamless tale for screenwriters to dramatize, and no specific individual's experience perfectly touches all the major historical events an artist wants to depict. A cinematic historian's work necessarily involves creative license. Effective communication of history on the big screen is virtually impossible without it. But how much creative license? When do manipulation and invention become problematic, raising valid questions about a production's relationship to history?

As we have seen in the preceding discussion, the task of addressing these questions is more difficult than many of the eager critics of cinematic history imagine. All Hollywood portrayals of the past can come under attack for distorting evidence and manufacturing facts. Even a sophisticated historical epic such as *Glory* contains a number of creative adjustments that raise the eyebrows of history enthusiasts. Yet *Glory*'s manipulations are not employed cavalierly; they are not designed solely to enhance the movie's entertainment value. Most of the film's distortions serve the purpose of communicating broader truths about the Civil War experiences of African Americans. *Glory* fudges some of the details but presents its big picture quite effectively. In contrast is the more troublesome record of three other works: *Mississippi Burning, Amistad,* and *The Hurricane*. Each of these films offers riveting drama, and like *Glory,* each deals with important questions about racial injustice. Yet these motion pictures contain so many elements of fictional excess and gross simplification that they deservedly were attacked by historians and pundits in the media. And these films demonstrate that moviemakers do pay a price for irritating the followers of Clio, because the buzz in Hollywood was that these films were less-than-attractive candidates for Academy Awards. The movies fell short not only because of questions about their dramatic quality but also because their historical portrayals had been criticized by many people who expressed a serious interest in history. Some worked in educational institutions, but many critics wrote and spoke from outside the academy.

The challenge of assessing cinematic history involves more than just raising complaints about the handling of evidence. It involves praise as well as criticism. A sophisticated response also calls for recognition of the distinctive ways that movies can stir the public's thinking about history. To appreciate these contributions, we must think differently about the medium. Film cannot view the past in the fashion of the printed word, but it can serve as a powerful stimulus to historical thinking.

Cinematic history has evolved considerably since the days of *Birth of a Nation,* but it remains, as in D. W. Griffith's time, more notable for its emotional impact on audiences than for the detailed historical information it imparts. Audiences remember Hollywood's productions for their style, not their statistics; for their flair, not their facts. Many of the great motion pictures of recent decades give audiences only limited information about historic events, yet they leave viewers with memorable portraits of the past. This irony is certainly evident in the contributions of some notable war films. *Saving Private Ryan* presents little factual detail about the issues in America's fight against the Nazis, but it effectively portrays the *experience* of war. *Schindler's List* provides little general information about the Third Reich's extermination policy, but it presents a damning and compelling indictment of it. A few paragraphs in a textbook could relate more specific information about the Union army's employment of black troops in the Civil War than *Glory* does, yet the film manages to communicate a forceful statement about the *significance* of that participation. *The Execution of Private Slovik* relates only one soldier's tragic story, yet it leaves viewers with deeply troubling and meaningful questions about the military's treatment of its soldiers during wartime.

In these and many other successful examples of cinematic history, audiences receive a modicum of information about broad historical events but are, nevertheless, emotionally and conceptually rewarded. Memorable films address important questions about the past and attach viewers' emotions to the debates about them. Hollywood gives life and personality to individuals and groups that often appear rather sterilely in the pages of history books. Cinema helps transform stale, one-dimensional stories into lively, two-dimensional experiences to which audiences can relate.

We have seen, too, that cinematic history often makes an impact on its audiences. A controversial historical treatment such as *Birth of a Nation* or *JFK* can stimulate lively debates across the country. Films such as *Holocaust* and *Schindler's List* can arouse disgust for ethnic intolerance and stir young Germans to dig into their dark history and examine the crimes of their predecessors. In recent years, historians, politicians, media commentators, and others have commented on the influence of notable Hollywood films in their lives. For many, the images in cinema serve as impressive models for attitudes and behavior. How broad is this influence? We can only speculate, because this fascinating question about impact has received little scholarly attention to date.

I close, then, with an invitation for critics at the poles to move closer to the middle of debates about cinematic history. At one pole are tradition-minded enthusiasts of history who are eager to dismiss Hollywood productions as only commercial entertainment. Sounding complaints about distortions and artistic liberties, they project an excessively negative outlook on these productions. When suggesting how Hollywood could please them, they hold up scholarly standards for the presentation of evidence. Their recommendations are idealistic, not realistic, for they demonstrate little understanding of the different rules under which Hollywood filmmakers operate. At the other pole are cinema specialists who often look askance at the historians' interest in finding important elements of historical understanding in Hollywood dramas. Preoccupied with claims about the relativity of all historical interpretations, and fascinated by discussions about film's potential for symbolic, partisan, and experimental communication, they demonstrate only limited interest in the issues that excite history scholars, media critics, and the public. Many are engaged in insular dialogues that involve only professional colleagues. By devoting great attention to issues that have little appeal outside their disciplines, they fail to apply their considerable insights on film to a new and more complex public understanding of its relationship with history.

The challenge of reaching that understanding is exciting as cinematic history moves into its second century of activity. In many ways, D. W. Griffith's vision has been realized. The genre is now ubiquitous, and it has the potential to sway the thoughts of millions of people when they contemplate history and draw conclusions about its lessons. Hollywood artists have become enormously influential interpreters of the past. To judge their work and appreciate their contributions, it behooves us to think imaginatively about their distinctive role as cinematic historians.

# Notes

## INTRODUCTION

1 There are, of course, a number of important analyses that deal either directly or in a related way with this subject. A useful introduction appears in the special forum on film in the December 1988 issue of *American Historical Review*. Among the many broadly interpretive works on cinematic history are Robert A. Rosenstone, *Visions of the Past: The Challenge of Film to Our Idea of History* (Cambridge: Harvard University Press, 1996); Robert Brent Toplin, *History by Hollywood: The Use and Abuse of the American Past* (Champaign-Urbana: University of Illinois Press, 1996); Mark C. Carnes, ed., *Past Imperfect: History According to the Movies* (New York: Henry Holt, 1995); Robert Burgoyne, *Film Nation: Hollywood Looks at U.S. History* (Minneapolis: University of Minnesota Press, 1997); Natalie Zemon Davis, *Slaves on Screen: Film and Historical Vision* (Cambridge: Harvard University Press, 2000); Leger Grindon, *Shadows on the Past: Studies in the Historical Fiction Film* (Philadelphia: Temple University Press, 1994). Useful anthologies that address important theoretical issues include John E. O'Connor, *The Image as Artifact: The Historical Analysis of Film and Television* (Malabar, Fla.: Robert E. Krieger, 1990); Tony Barta, ed., *Screening the Past: Film and the Representation of History* (Westport, Conn.: Praeger, 1998); Alan Rosenthal, ed., *Why Docudrama? Fact-Fiction on Film and TV* (Carbondale: Southern Illinois University Press, 1999); Vivian Sobchack, ed., *The Persistence of History: Cinema, Television, and the Modern Event* (New York: Routledge, 1996); Robert A. Rosenstone, ed., *Revisioning History: Film and the Construction of a New Past* (Princeton, N.J.: Princeton University Press, 1995); James Combs, ed., *Movies and Politics: The Dynamic Relationship* (New York: Garland, 1993); Marcia Landy, ed., *The Historical Film: History and Memory in Media* (New Brunswick, N.J.: Rutgers University Press, 2000). Pierre Sorlin gets credit for creating one of the earliest book-length examinations of the topic in *The Film in History: Restaging the Past* (New York: Barnes and Noble Books, 1980). Interesting comments on the historical treatments of individual movies appear in Joseph Roquemore, *History Goes to the Movies: A Viewer's Guide to the Best (and Some of the Worst) Historical Movies Ever Made* (New York: Doubleday-Mainstreet Books, 1999).

## 1. CINEMATIC HISTORY AS GENRE

1 Quoted in Colin McArthur, "*Braveheart* and the Scottish Aesthetic Dementia," in Barta, *Screening the Past*, 168.

2 Walter Goodman, "History as a Springboard in the Service of Fun," *New York Times*, December 9, 1995.

3 Quoted in Rosenthal, *Why Docudrama*, 7–8.

4 Jerry Kuehl, "Lies about Real People," in Rosenthal, *Why Docudrama*, 124.

5 See Ken Burns's commentary in Sean B. Dolan, ed., *Telling the Story: The Media, the Public, and American History* (Boston: New England Foundation for the Humanities, 1994), 109.

6 I discuss Burns's approach to history in this series in Robert Brent Toplin, ed., *Ken Burns's* The Civil War: *Historians Respond* (New York: Oxford University Press, 1996), xv–xxvi, 19–36.

7 Expressions of concern about the impact of poor cinematic history on impressionable children appear in Rosenthal, *Why Docudrama*, 351 (with regard to *JFK*), and in Joe Queenan, "Compensate History's Reel Victims," *Wall Street Journal*, April 17, 1998, A4 (with regard to *Titanic*). Educators have addressed the concern, too. John E. O'Connor says that "it appears that even well-educated Americans are learning most of their history from film and television" ("History in Images/Images in History: Reflections on the Impact of Film and Television Study for an Understanding of the Past," *American Historical Review* 93, no. 5 [December 1988]: 1201).

8 Referenced in Hayden White, "The Modernist Event," in Sobchack, *Persistence of History*, 20.

9 Dolan, *Telling the Story*, 33.

10 Quoted in Barta, *Screening the Past*, 46.

11 David J. Belin, "History According to Hollywood," *Wall Street Journal*, February 14, 1996.

12 The series was based on Alex Haley, *Roots* (Garden City, N.Y.: Doubleday, 1976). For an excellent discussion of the TV series' handling of history and its popularity, see Leslie Fishbein, "*Roots*: Docudrama and the Interpretation of History," in Rosenthal, *Why Docudrama*, 271–295.

13 Harold Schecter and Jonna G. Semeiks, "Leatherstocking in 'Nam: *Rambo, Platoon*, and the American Frontier," in Combs, *Movies and Politics*, 116.

14 Thomas Schatz, *Old Hollywood/New Hollywood: Ritual, Art, and Industry* (Ann Arbor, Mich.: UMI Research Press, 1983), 48, 74. See also Pam Cook and Mieke Bernink, *The Cinema Book*, 2d ed. (London: BFI Publishing, 1999), 137–141; Thomas Schatz, *Hollywood Genres: Formulas, Filmmaking, and the Studio System* (New York: Random House, 1984).

15 See also Tom Ryall, "Genre and Hollywood," in *American Cinema and Hollywood: Critical Approaches*, ed. John Hill, Pamela Church Gibson, Richard Dyer, E. Ann Kaplan, and Paul Willemen (New York: Oxford University Press, 2000), 102–104; Wes D. Gehring, ed., *Handbook of American Film Genres* (Westport Conn.: Greenwood Press, 1988); Barry Keith Grant, ed., *Film Genre Reader II* (Austin: University of Texas Press, 1995).

16 Richard Slotkin offers an intriguing interpretation of the western in *Gunfighter Nation: The Myth of the Frontier in Twentieth Century America* (New York: Atheneum, 1992). See also Richard A. Blake, *Screening America: Reflections on Classic Films* (New York: Paulist Press, 1991), 84–85; David Bordwell and Kristin Thompson, *Film Art: An Introduction*, 5th ed. (New York: McGraw-Hill, 1997), 56; Grant, *Film Genre Reader*, 92, 98–99; Combs, *Movies and Politics*, 14–20.

17 Ryall, "Genre and Hollywood," 105, 107, 109; Cook and Bernink, *The Cinema Book*, 140. See also the introduction in Wheeler Winston Dixon, *Film Genre 2000: New Critical Essays* (Albany: State University of New York Press, 2000), 2; Bordwell and Thompson, *Film Art*, 53.

18 *Gladiator* (2000) contained many of these elements but lacked the attention to Christianity that was a familiar feature of 1950s movies that dealt with antiquity.

19 Jeanine Basinger, *The World War II Combat Film: Anatomy of a Genre* (New York: Columbia University Press, 1986).

20 John Sayles discusses his use of muted colors in *Thinking in Pictures: The Making of the Movie* Matewan (Boston: Houghton Mifflin, 1987), 57.

21 Robert A. Rosenstone, *Visions of the Past: The Challenge of Film to Our Idea of History* (Cambridge: Harvard University Press, 1996), 55–60.

22 Grindon, *Shadows on the Past*; Burgoyne, *Film Nation*.

23 Basinger, *World War II Combat Film*.

24 Schatz, *Hollywood Genres*, vii.

25 Quoted in Michiko Kakutani, "So Captain Bligh Wasn't that Bad?" *New York Times*, November 14, 1995, B2.

26 Quoted in David Platt, *Celluloid Power: Social Film Criticism from* Birth of a Nation *to* Judgment at Nuremberg (Metuchen, N.J.: Scarecrow Press, 1992), 410.

27 Excellent examples of the diverse responses to *JFK* can be found in Oliver Stone and Zachary Sklar, eds., *JFK: The Book of the Film* (New York: Applause Theater Books, 1992).

28 Wells Root, *Writing the Script: A Practical Guide for Film and Television* (New York: Holt, Rinehart and Winston, 1980).

29 Schatz, *Old Hollywood/New Hollywood*, 47–48.

30 Author's interview with Bruce Robinson, July 2, 2000.

31 Ibid.

32 Paul J. Vanderwood, "*Viva Zapata!* (1952)," in *American History/American Film: Interpreting the Hollywood Image*, ed. John E. O'Connor and Martin Jackson (New York: Frederick Ungar, 1979), 183–200.

33 Davis, *Slaves on Screen*, 17–40.

34 Toplin, *History by Hollywood*, 104–124.

35 Davis, *Slaves on Screen*, 136.

36 Richard Grenier, "The Gandhi Nobody Knows," *Commentary* (March 1983): 59–72; quote on p. 60.

37 John F. Burns, "Gandhi on the Pedestal: All Too Human as Well as Great Guru," *New York Times*, May 2, 1998, A13.

38 Brock Yates, "Don't Believe Everything You See at the Movies," *Washington Post Magazine*, May 8, 1988, W45.

39 H. Gordon Frost and John H. Jenkins, *I'm Frank Hamer: The Real Life of a Texas Police Officer* (Austin, Tex.: Pemberton Press, 1968), 179, 187–195; John Toland, "Sad Ballad of the Real Bonnie and Clyde," *New York Times Magazine*, February 18, 1969; John Toland, *The Dillinger Days* (1963; reprint, New York: De Capo Press, 1969), 281–283.

40 William Ross St. George, "The Patriot," *Journal of American History* 87, no. 3 (December 2000): 1146–1148.

41  Michael Shaara, *The Killer Angels: A Novel* (New York: McKay, 1974).

42  James M. McPherson, a Civil War historian, gives the movie a generally positive review in Carnes, *Past Imperfect,* 128–131.

43  Maria Wyke, *Projecting the Past: Ancient Rome, Cinema, and History* (New York: Routledge, 1997), 11–13, 23–24; Edward Maeder, ed., *Hollywood and History: Costume Design in Film* (New York: Thames and Hudson; Los Angeles County Museum of Art, 1997).

44  George F. Custen, *Bio/Pics: How Hollywood Constructed Public History* (New Brunswick, N.J.: Rutgers University Press, 1992), 3–7.

45  Edward D. C. Campbell, *The Celluloid South: Hollywood and the Southern Myth* (Knoxville: University of Tennessee Press, 1981); Jack Temple Kirby, *Media-made Dixie: The South in the American Imagination* (Baton Rouge: Louisiana State University Press, 1978).

46  Frank Capra, *The Name above the Title: An Autobiography* (New York: Macmillan, 1971), 304–305.

47  Christine Hanley, "Hit Movie Pulls Plaintiff for New Suit against Utility," *Wilmington (N.C.) Star-News,* March 28, 2000, 6C.

48  Randy Roberts and David Welky, "A Sacred Mission: Oliver Stone and Vietnam," in *Oliver Stone's USA: Film, History, and Controversy,* ed. Robert Brent Toplin (Lawrence: University Press of Kansas, 2000), 66–92.

49  For criticism of the filmmaker's strategy in representing the Canadians, see Selwyn Raab, "Separating Truth from Fiction in 'The Hurricane,'" *New York Times,* December 28, 1999, E1.

50  William Leuchtenburg criticizes some aspects of *All the President's Men* in Carnes, *Past Imperfect,* 288–292.

51  Sayles, *Thinking in Pictures,* 4, 17–20, 30.

52  Grindon, *Shadows on the Past,* 155–156.

53  Ibid., 178.

54  Ibid.

55  Richard Marius, "*A Man for All Seasons,*" in Carnes, *Past Imperfect,* 70–73.

56  Elie Wiesel, "Trivializing the Holocaust: Semi-Fact and Semi-Fiction," *New York Times,* April 16, 1978, sec. 2, p. 1.

57  *The Sea Hawk* shows King Phillip II of Spain throwing his shadow across a large map of the sixteenth-century world. Audiences of 1940 could not miss the message that, like Hitler, the movie's character threatened to dominate England and all of Europe.

58  Combs, *Movies and Politics,* 4–5, 69; Stephen Prince, *Visions of Empire: Political Imagery in Contemporary American Film* (New York: Praeger, 1992), 1–2; Grindon, *Shadows on the Past,* 1–2.

59  John E. O'Connor, "The Moving Image as Representation of History," in O'Connor, *Image as Artifact,* 34.

60  Toplin, *History by Hollywood,* 142.

61  William Goldman, *Adventures in the Screen Trade: A Personal View of Hollywood and Screenwriting* (New York: Warner Books, 1983), 237–239.

62  See, for example, Peter C. Rollins and John E. O'Connor, eds., *Hollywood's Indian: The Portrayal of the Native American in Film* (Lexington: University Press of Kentucky, 1998).

63  Slotkin, *Gunfighter Nation*. See also Robert Warsow on westerns in Grant, *Film Genre Reader*, 98 – 99; Gretchen M. Bataille and Charles L. P. Silet, eds., *The Pretend Indians: Images of Native Americans in the Movies* (Ames: Iowa State University Press, 1980); Jacquelyn Kilpatrick, *Celluloid Indians: Native Americans in Film* (Lincoln: University of Nebraska Press, 1999).

64  Grindon, *Shadows on the Past*, 179 – 184.

65  Sorlin, *Film in History*, 208.

66  For a fascinating review of how such movie plots took liberties with the historical record, see Roquemore, *History Goes to the Movies*.

67  Robert Lang, ed., *The Birth of a Nation: D. W. Griffith, Director* (New Brunswick, N.J.: Rutgers University Press, 1994), 13 – 14.

68  Daniel Walkowitz, "Visual History: The Craft of the Historian-Filmmaker," *Public Historian* 7 (1985): 1193 – 1199.

69  Gordon Bowker, "Bertolucci Brings Back Imperial China," *New York Times*, February 1, 1987, sec. 2, p. 21.

70  Toplin, *History by Hollywood*, 151–152.

71  Thomas E. Curran, "Capturing Missouri History on Film: The Thrill of 'Devil' Is in the Details," *St. Louis Post-Dispatch*, December 12, 1999, F1; Robert W. Butler, "Screen Notes," *Kansas City Star*, December 19, 1999, J4.; Robert W. Butler, "History Challenged? Try This 'Devil' for Dummies," *Kansas City Star*, November 21, 1999, J3.

72  Robert W. Butler, "Speaking of the 'Devil,'" *Kansas City Star*, November 21, 1999, J1.

73  Stephen Holden, "Far from Gettysburg: A Heartland Torn Apart," *New York Times*, November 24, 1999, E1.

74  Engel Ringel Gillespie, "A Devilish Ride into America's Paradox," *Atlanta Constitution*, December 17, 1999, 3Q.

## 2. JUDGING CINEMATIC HISTORY

1  Carlos Villa Flor, "Intertextuality in *Shadowlands:* From the Essay to the Love Story," *Literature Film Quarterly* 27, no. 3 (1999): 97.

2  James M. McPherson, "The 'Glory' Story," *New Republic*, January 8 and 15, 1990, 22 – 27.

3  Ibid. McPherson also discusses these issues in *"Glory,"* in Carnes, *Past Imperfect*, 128 – 131.

4  Rosenstone, *Visions of the Past*, 55 – 60.

5  *Titanic* production information, Paramount Pictures, 1997; Andy Seller, "Director Pours His Soul into Film," *USA Today*, December 19, 1997, D1 – D2. For an extensive commentary on the movie, see Kevin S. Sandler and Gaylyn Studlar, Titanic: *Anatomy of a Blockbuster* (New Brunswick, N.J.: Rutgers University Press, 1999).

6  Richard Corliss, "Down to a Watery Grave," *Time*, December 8, 1997, 91.

7  Ibid.

8  Ken Ringle, "*Titanic*'s Sloppiness with Facts Is Typical Big Budget, No-Brain Cinema," reprinted in *Wilmington (N.C.) Star-News*, April 12, 1997. For a good example of complaints about the movie's dramatic quality, see Kenneth Turan, "*Titanic* Sinks Again (Spectacularly)," *Los Angeles Times*, December 19, 1997, F2.

9  I discuss these issues in "*Titanic:* Did the Maker of *True Lies* Tell the Truth about

History?" *Perspectives* (newsletter of the American Historical Association), March 1998, 1, 29–31.

10  Ibid. For a good cultural history of the tragedy and the way it has been interpreted, see Steven Biel, *Down with the Old Canoe: A Cultural History of the* Titanic *Disaster* (New York: Norton, 1996).

11  Biel, *Down with the Old Canoe,* 38; Steven Biel, "*Titanic,*" *Journal of American History* 45, no. 7 (December 1998): 1177–1179.

12  Janet Maslin, "A Spectacle as Sweeping as the Sea," *New York Times,* December 19, 1997, E1.

13  Sally Hadden has written an informative and detailed criticism in "*Amistad,*" *H-Net Film Review,* http://www.h-net.msu.edu/~law/amistad.htm.

14  Broad criticisms of the characterizations and suggestions about history appear in Jesse Lemish, "Film: Black Agency in the *Amistad* Uprising: or, You've Taken Our Cinque and Home," *Souls: A Critical Journal of Black Politics, Culture and Society* (Winter 1999): 57–70; Eric McKitrick, JQA: For the Defense," *New York Review of Books,* April 23, 1998, 53–54; John Thornton, "Liberty or License?" *History Today* 48, no. 4 (April 1998): 58–59.

15  McKitrick, "JQA: For the Defense."

16  Richard S. Newman, "Not the Only Story in 'Amistad': The Fictional Joadson and the Real James Forten" (essay in the author's possession, 1998).

17  Eric Foner, "Hollywood Invades the Classroom," *New York Times,* December 20, 1997, A13. See also Gary Trudeau, "*Amistad* Is Important: Discuss," *Time,* December 29, 1997, 170.

18  Clifton H. Johnson, "*Amistad:* Steven Spielberg as Historian" (presented at the conference of the Historical Society, Boston, May 29, 1999).

19  Arthur Abraham, "*Amistad:* Steven Spielberg as Historian" (presented at the conference of the Historical Society, Boston, May 29, 1999).

20  Bertram Wyatt-Brown, "*Amistad,*" *Journal of American History* 85, no. 3 (December 1998), 1174–1177; quote on p. 1176.

21  Howard Jones, *Mutiny on the* Amistad: *The Saga of a Slave Revolt and Its Impact on American Abolition, Law and Diplomacy* (New York: Oxford University Press, 1987).

22  Howard Jones, "History and Hollywood: 'Amistad,' Movie as History" (essay in author's possession, December 29, 1997). Jones has also written about the historical background to the movie; see "Cinque of the *Amistad* a Slave Trader? Perpetuation of a Myth," *Journal of American History* 87, no. 3 (December 2000): 923–940; "All We Want Is Make Us Free!" *American History* 32, no. 6 (January/February 1998): 22–30.

23  Davis, *Slaves on Screen,* 70–81.

24  Joseph McBride, *Steven Spielberg: A Biography* (New York: Simon and Schuster, 1997), 414–448; Philip M. Taylor, *Steven Spielberg: The Man, His Movies, and Their Meaning* (New York: Continuum, 1992), 113–123.

25  Natalie Zemon Davis intelligently assesses these strengths and weaknesses in *Slaves on Screen,* 70–93.

26  Seth Cagin and Phillip Day, *We Are Not Afraid: The Story of Goodman, Schwerner, and Chaney and the Civil Rights Campaign in Mississippi* (New York: Macmillan, 1988); William Bradford Huie, *Three Lives for Mississippi* (Oxford: University Press

of Mississippi, 2000); Don Whitehead, *Attack on Terror: The FBI against the Ku Klux Klan in Mississippi* (New York: Funk and Wagnalls, 1970).

27  Author's interview with Chris Gerolmo, November 18, 1991.

28  Harvard Sitcoff, "*Mississippi Burning*," *Journal of American History* (December 1989): 1019.

29  Author's interview with Fred Zollo, November 19, 1991.

30  Toplin, *History by Hollywood*, 25–44.

31  James S. Hirsch, *Hurricane: The Miraculous Journey of Rubin Carter* (Boston: Houghton Mifflin, 2000); Rubin Carter, *The Sixteenth Round* (New York: Warner Books, 1975); Sam Chaiton and Terry Swinton, *Lazarus and the Hurricane: The Freeing of Rubin "Hurricane" Carter* (New York: St. Martin's Press, 2000).

32  Raab, "Separating Truth from Fiction in 'The Hurricane.'"

33  Lewis M. Steel, "*The Hurricane*," *Nation*, January 3, 2000, 8–9.

34  Alison Gray and Jason Kerrigan, "Storm over *The Hurricane* May Blow away Oscar Chances," *Scotsman*, February 11, 2000.

35  "Ring of Truth," *Sports Illustrated*, February 28, 2000, 26.

36  Raab, "Separating Truth from Fiction in 'The Hurricane.'"

### 3. AWARDING THE HARRY AND THE BROOKS

1  Foner, "Hollywood Invades the Classroom."

2  Wyatt-Brown, "*Amistad*," 1176.

3  "I Maximus!" *Crisis* 18 (July/August 2000): 49–50.

4  For information on the origins of *Gladiator*'s story, including speculation about concepts and techniques borrowed from earlier movies about the ancient world, see "*Gladiator*," *Rolling Stone*, May 25, 2000, 81–82.

5  Anne Billson, "How Hollywood Won the War," *Sunday Telegram* (London), June 4, 2000, 4.

6  Clay Blair, *Hitler's U-boat War: The Hunters, 1939–1942* (New York: Random House, 1996), 683–684; David Syrett, *The Defeat of the German U-boats. The Battle of the Atlantic* (Columbia: University of South Carolina Press, 1994), 257–258. Details of German experiences in World War II submarines that resemble those of the characters in *Das Boot* can be found in Herbert A. Werner, *Iron Coffins: A Personal Account of the German U-boat Battles of World War II* (New York: Holt, Rinehart and Winston, 1969).

7  Information about the operation of convoys and wolf packs appears throughout Blair, *Hitler's U-boat War*.

8  Kevin Phillips, "'Patriot's' Skirmish with Truth," *Los Angeles Times*, July 7, 2000, F2.

9  Anne Billson, "History Debunked Cinema," *Sunday Telegraph* (London), July 16, 2000, 8.

10  Reported by Gary Gallagher in a conversation with the author, summer 2000.

11  For details on Brown, see Stephen B. Oates, *To Purge this Land in Blood: A Biography of John Brown* (New York: Harper and Row, 1970); Richard Warch, ed., *John Brown* (Englewood Cliffs, N.J.: Prentice-Hall, 1973).

12  For criticism of the movie's treatment of history, see Larry J. Easley, "*The Santa Fe Trail*, John Brown, and the Coming of the Civil War," *Film and History* 13, no. 2 (May 1983): 25–33.

13   For details on Custer, see Stephen E. Ambrose, *Crazy Horse and Custer: The Parallel Lives of Two American Warriors* (Garden City, N.Y.: Doubleday, 1975); Jeffrey D. Wert, *Custer: The Controversial Life of George Armstrong Custer* (New York: Simon and Schuster, 1996).

14   Stephen E. Ambrose emphasizes the complexity of judging clashes between whites and Native Americans; see *Crazy Horse and Custer,* 298.

15   See Fred E. Hoxie, *A Final Promise: The Campaign to Assimilate the Indians, 1880–1920* (New York: Cambridge University Press, 1989).

16   Toland, *Dillinger Days.*

17   For ciriticisms of *JFK*'s treatment of history, see, for example, Edward J. Epstein, "The Second Coming of Jim Garrison," *Atlantic Monthly,* March, 1993, 90; Gerald Ford and David W. Belin, "The Kennedy Assassination: How about the Truth?" *Washington Post,* December 17, 1991, A21.

18   J. M. Lawrence, "Documents Renew Questions about Oswald Probe; Feds May Have Hid JFK Assassination Evidence," *Boston Herald,* November 22, 1999, 1; Ian Brodie, "Hidden Kennedy Files Feed Conspiracy Theories," *Times* (London), September 30, 1998.

19   Jim Marrs, *Crossfire: The Plot that Killed Kennedy* (New York: Carroll and Graf, 1990).

20   Robert A. Rosenstone, *"JFK,"* in Rosenthal, *Why Docudrama,* 339.

21   Robert S. McNamara with Brian VanDeMart, *In Retrospect: The Tragedy and Lessons of Vietnam* (New York: Times Books, 1995); Arthur Schlesinger, Jr., "On *JFK* and *Nixon,"* in Toplin, *Oliver Stone's USA,* 213.

22   Robert A. Rosenstone, *"JFK,"* *American Historical Review* 97, no. 2 (April 1992): 506–512.

23   For a sampling of scathing reviews of *Heaven's Gate,* see *Film Review Annual: 1981* (Englewood, N.J.: James S. Ozer, 1982), 410–416.

24   Mark C. Carnes, *"Fat Man and Little Boy,"* in Carnes, *Past Imperfect,* 246–249.

25   Criticism of the drama appears in Joe Morganstern, "Black and White in Color," *Wall Street Journal,* February 2, 1998. For an interesting personal account of involvement in the movie, see Willie Morris, *The Ghosts of Medgar Evers: A Tale of Race, Murder, Mississippi and Hollywood* (New York: Random House, 1998).

26   Werner, *Iron Coffins,* xv–xvii.

27   Jeanine Basinger, "Translating War: The Combat Film Genre and *Saving Private Ryan,"* *Perspectives,* October 1998.

28   Stephen Ambrose, *Citizen Soldiers: The U.S. Army from the Normandy Beaches to the Bulge to the Surrender of Germany, June 7, 1944–May 7, 1945* (New York: Simon and Schuster, 1997), 74–76.

29   Stephen E. Ambrose, *"The Longest Day,"* in Carnes, *Past Imperfect,* 236–241.

30   Cornelius Ryan, *The Longest Day: June 6, 1944* (New York: Simon and Schuster, 1994).

31   Ambrose, *"The Longest Day,"* 239.

32   Kenneth Turan, "Restraint from the Master of Razzmatazz," *Los Angeles Times,* December 15, 1993, F1.

33   Mirium Bratu Hansen, *"Schindler's List* Is Not *Shoah,"* in *Spielberg's Holocaust: Critical Perspectives on* Schindler's List, ed. Yosefa Loshitzky (Bloomington: Indiana University Press, 1997), 83.

34 Quoted in Natasha Lehrer, "Between Obsession and Amnesia: Reflections on the French Reception of *Schindler's List*," in Loshitzky, *Spielberg's Holocaust*, 216.

35 Hansen, "*Schindler's List* Is Not *Shoah*," 84.

36 Lehrer, "Between Obsession and Amnesia," 215.

37 Bryan Cheyette, "The Uncertain Certainty of *Schindler's List*," in Loshitzky, *Spielberg's Holocaust*, 63.

38 Sara R. Horowitz, "But Is It Good for the Jews? Spielberg's Schindler and the Aesthetics of Atrocity," in Loshitzky, *Spielberg's Holocaust*, 125–137.

39 Andrew Nagorski, "*Schindler's List*," *Foreign Affairs* (July/August 1994): 152–156.

40 Joseph P. Lash, *Eleanor and Franklin: The Story of Their Relationship, Based on Eleanor Roosevelt's Private Papers* (New York: Norton, 1971).

41 For an example of the positive reception, see Karl E. Meyer, "Portrait of a Lady," *Saturday Review,* January 10, 1976, 8. *Eleanor and Franklin* won an Emmy for the 1975–1976 season for Outstanding Special—Drama or Comedy.

42 William Bradford Huie, *The Execution of Private Slovik* (1954; reprint, New York: Delacorte Press, 1970).

43 Stephen E. Ambrose, *The Victors: Eisenhower and His Boys: The Men of World War II* (New York: Simon and Schuster, 1998), 266–271.

44 Huie, *The Execution of Private Slovik*, 164.

45 Benedict B. Kimmelman, "The Example of Private Slovik," *American Heritage* (September/October 1987): 97–104.

46 Lawrence Suid, *Guts and Glory: Great American War Movies* (Reading, Mass.: Addison-Wesley, 1978), 244–245.

47 Toplin, *History by Hollywood*, 171.

48 Quoted in Henry J. Taylor, "Film on Patton Captures Life and Times in World War II" (clipping in the *Patton* file, American Academy of Motion Picture Arts and Sciences, Los Angeles).

49 Francis O. Beeman, "The Real Blood and Guts to Stand in Twentieth's 'Patton,'" October 8, 1968 (microfiche file, Academy of Motion Picture Arts and Sciences, Los Angeles).

50 John J. O'Connor, "Viewing Patton: Pick Your Angle," *Wall Street Journal,* May 3, 1970; "Left, Right Hail War Picture," *Variety,* February 11, 1970; Richard Cuskelly, "*Patton:* Reaction Divided," *Los Angeles Herald-Examiner,* July 1, 1970.

51 "The Man Who Loved War," *New Yorker,* January 31, 1970, 73.

52 Allen Weinstein, *Perjury: The Hiss-Chambers Case* (New York: Random House, 1978); Sam Tenenhaus, *Whittaker Chambers: A Biography* (New York: Random House, 1997).

53 Dolan, *Telling the Story,* 151; Arthur Unger, "'Concealed Enemies': Disturbing but Enlightening Confrontation with Truth," *Christian Science Monitor,* May 4, 1984, 21; Stephen Farber, "Director Sacrifices for a Vision," *New York Times,* May 22, 1984, C16; "Hiss-Chambers Case Dramatized on WNET," *New York Times,* May 7, 1984, C17; Fox Butterfield, "TV Plays the Hiss Case Down the Middle," *New York Times,* May 6, 1984, sec. 2, p. 1.

54 Jonathan R. Cohen, "A Decent Son—But Also a Confused One," *Chicago Sun-Times,* July 4, 1999, 13.

## 4. SCREENING HISTORY: A TEST CASE

1 I give a briefer report of my work on this film in Robert Brent Toplin, "The Making of *Denmark Vesey's Rebellion,*" *Film and History* (September 1982): 48 –51.

2 The most important foundation for our work on Solomon Northup was Sue Eatkin and Joseph Logsdon, eds., *Twelve Years a Slave* (Baton Rouge: Louisiana State University Press, 1968). Useful for the film on Charlotte Forten was Charlotte L. Forten, *The Journal of Charlotte Forten: A Free Negro in the Slave Era,* ed. Ray Allen Billington (New York: Collier Books, 1961), and Thomas Wentworth Higginson, *Army Life in a Black Regiment* (East Lansing: Michigan State University Press, 1960). The script about Moncure Conway benefited from the excellent research of John D'Entremont, whose biography of Conway was published later; see John D'Entremont, *Southern Emancipation: Moncure Conway, the American Years, 1832–1865* (New York: Oxford University Press, 1987).

3 Willie Lee Rose, *Rehearsal for Reconstruction: The Port Royal Experiment* (New York: Oxford University Press, 1976).

4 Robert S. Starobin, *Denmark Vesey: The Slave Conspiracy of 1822* (Englewood Cliffs, N.J.: Prentice-Hall, 1970); the footnote is on pp. 30 –31. For additional information on Vesey and the conspiracy, see *The Trial Record of Denmark Vesey,* introduction by John Oliver Killens (Boston: Beacon Press, 1970); Edward A. Pearson, ed., *Designs against Charleston: The Trial Record of the Denmark Vesey Conspiracy of 1822* (Chapel Hill: University of North Carolina Press, 1999); Douglas R. Egerton, *He Shall Go out Free: The Lives of Denmark Vesey* (Madison, Wis.: Madison House, 1999); David Robertson, *Denmark Vesey* (New York: Alfred A. Knopf, 2000).

5 William W. Freehling, "History and Television," *Southern Studies* 22, no. 1 (1983): 76 –81. Freehling intelligently placed the Vesey rebellion in the context of antebellum politics in *Prelude to Civil War: The Nullification Controversy in South Carolina, 1816–1836* (Magnolia, Mass.: Peter Smith Publishers, 1995). For an understanding of connections with the Civil War, see Stephen A. Channing, *Crisis of Fear: Secession in South Carolina* (New York: Simon and Schuster, 1970).

6 Quoted in Toplin, "The Making of *Denmark Vesey's Rebellion,*" 53 –54.

7 Richard Wade, "The Vesey Plot: A Reconsideration," *Journal of Southern History* 30, no. 2 (May 1964): 143 –161.

8 Michael P. Johnson, "Denmark Vesey and His Co-Conspirators," *William and Mary Quarterly* (October 2001): 915 –962.

## 5. THE STUDY OF CINEMATIC HISTORY

1 O'Connor, *Image as Artifact,* 7 –8.

2 Rosenstone, "*JFK,*" in Rosenthal, *Why Docudrama,* 337.

3 Rosenstone, *Visions of the Past,* 67 –69.

4 Linda Hutcheon, *The Poetics of Postmodernism: History, Theory, Fiction* (New York: Routledge, 1988), 93.

5 Janet Staiger, "Cinematic Shots," in Sobchack, *Persistence of History,* 51.

6 Janet Staiger, "This Moving Image I Have before Me," in O'Connor, *Image as Artifact,* 101.

7 Rosenstone, *Visions of the Past,* 61–64; Robert Burgoyne, "Modernism and the Narrative of Nation in *JFK,*" in Sobchack, *Persistence of History,* 113–115.

8 Robert A. Rosenstone, The Future of the Past: Film and the Beginnings of Postmodern History," in Sobchack, *Persistence of History,* 206.

9 Hayden White, "The Modernist Event," in Sobchack, *Persistence of History,* 17–32. See also Hayden White, "Historiography and Historiophoty," *American Historical Review* 93, no. 5 (December 1988): 1193–1199. White develops his ideas more broadly in *The Content of the Form: Narrative Discourse and Historical Representation* (Baltimore: Johns Hopkins University Press, 1987) and *Tropics of Discourse: Essays on Cultural Criticism* (Baltimore: Johns Hopkins University Press, 1978). Robert Burgoyne employs some of White's ideas in an analysis of *JFK* in "Modernism and the Narrative of Nation in *JFK,*" 118.

10 Jerry Kuehl, "Lies about Real People," in Rosenthal, *Why Docudrama,* 161.

11 Rosenstone, *"JFK,"* in Rosenthal, *Why Docudrama,* 337. The original essay appears in *American Historical Review* 97, no. 2 (April 1992): 506–512.

12 Burgoyne, *Film Nation,* 5.

13 Ibid., 3, 6.

14 Sumiko Higashi, "*Walker* and *Mississippi Burning:* Postmodernism versus Illusionist Narrative," in Rosenthal, *Why Docudrama,* 351–352.

15 Rosenstone, *"JFK,"* in Rosenthal, *Why Docudrama,* 339.

16 Rosenstone, "The Future of the Past," 205.

17 Ibid., 206.

18 Quoted in Dolan, *Telling the Story,* 118.

19 Eric Foner, "A Conversation between Eric Foner and John Sayles," in Carnes, *Past Imperfect,* 25.

20 Tony Judt, "Writing History, Facts Optional," *New York Times,* April 13, 2000, A31.

21 Edward Hallett Carr, *What Is History?* (New York: Vintage, 1961); Gerald N. Grob and George Athan Billias, *Interpretations of American History: Patterns and Perspectives* (New York: Free Press, 1987).

22 The main outlines of the Marxist critique of film are outlined in Robert C. Allen and Douglas Gomery, *Film History: Theory and Practice* (New York: Alfred A. Knopf, 1985), 132–140.

23 David Bordwell and Noel Carroll, *Post-Theory: Reconstructing Film Studies* (Madison: University of Wisconsin Press, 1996), 48.

24 Combs, *Movies and Politics,* 11–12, 33; Douglas Kellner, "Film, Politics, and Ideology: Toward a Multiperspectional Theory," in Combs, *Movies and Politics,* 56–57, 70–84; Robert Sklar, "Oh Althusser! Historiography and the Rise of Cinema Studies," in *Resisting Images: Essays on Cinema and History,* ed. Robert Sklar and Charles Musser (Philadelphia: Temple University Press, 1990), 18–32 (see also the introduction by Sklar and Musser, 3–5); Noel Carroll, *Mystifying Movies: Fads and Fallacies in Contemporary Film Theory* (New York: Columbia University Press, 1988), 52–58. For commentary on audiences getting a false image of reality, see Marc Ferro, *Cinema and History,* trans. Naomi Greene (Detroit: Wayne State University Press, 1988), 28; Prince, *Visions of Empire,* 41.

25 Combs, *"Movies and Politics,"* 11–12; introduction to Sklar and Musser, *Resisting Images,* 5.

26 Leger Grindon, in an analysis of *Reds,* contrasts Warren Beatty's focus on the actions of individuals and Sergei Eisenstein's emphasis on the power of the crowd. "In *Reds,*" writes Grindon, "the personal experience of the protagonists confines the historical treatment of the film. Beatty fails to gain a generalized, social understanding of events and prevents the film from reaching beyond the emotional sensibility of his characters to comprehend the historical circumstances in which they find themselves" (Grindon, *Shadows on the Past,* 205, 210). Douglas Kellner complains that Hollywood posits individual solutions to social problems, "thus reinforcing the conservative appeal to individualism and the attack on statism" ("Hollywood Film and Society," in Hill et al., *American Cinema and Hollywood,* 134.

27 Stephen Powers, David J. Rothman, and Stanley Rothman, *Hollywood's America: Social and Political Themes in Motion Pictures* (Boulder, Colo.: Westview Press, 1996).

28 For a good example of name-dropping, see Patricia Mellencamp and Phillip Rosen, *Cinema Histories, Cinema Practices* (Westport, Conn.: Greenwood, 1984), ix–xiii. See also the introduction to Landy, *Historical Film,* 1–24.

29 Noel Carroll, "Prospects for Film Theory: A Personal Assessment," in Bordwell and Carroll, *Post-Theory,* 37–38, 45–46.

30 Carroll, *Mystifying Movies,* 226.

31 Ibid., 232–234.

32 Ibid., 234.

33 Marcia Landy, *Film, Politics and Gramsci* (Minneapolis: University of Minnesota Press, 1994), 2.

34 Burgoyne, *Film Nation,* 3; see also the comments on pp. 3, 5, 21, 45.

35 Sobchack, *Persistence of History,* 2.

36 Thomas Sobchack and Vivian C. Sobchack, *An Introduction to Film* (Boston: Little, Brown, 1980).

37 Rosenstone, *Visions of the Past,* 226–246.

38 Ibid., 21–22.

39 Letter from Maureen Ogle, received by the American Historical Association April 6, 1999, and subsequently published in *Perspectives.* Also relevant are letters sent to the AHA from Marshall Poe and Christopher Moon, published in the May 1999 issue of *Perspectives.*

## 6. IMPACT

1 "Colombia's Rebels Keep the Marxist Faith," *New York Times,* July 25, 2000, 1.

2 Pam Belluck, "A Battlefield of Dreams for Iowa Farmers," *New York Times,* August 6, 1999, 1

3 "'Free Willy' Whale Is Nearer to Freedom," *San Diego Union-Tribune,* March 4, 2000, A19; Julia Preston, "Willie the Whale Is Free! Well, Moved, Anyway," *New York Times,* January 8, 1999.

4 Roquemore, *History Goes to the Movies,* xv.

5 Phillip W. D. Martin, Shaking up the World, or Shaped by It?" *New York Times,* February 2, 1997, H15.

6 For an appeal to analyze films of the Nazi era, including anti-Semitic works, in a new way, see Scott Specter, "Was the Third Reich Movie-made? Interdisciplinarity

and the Reframing of 'Ideology,'" *American Historical Review* 106, no. 2 (April 2001): 460–484.

7   David Edgar, "Theater of Fact: A Dramatist's Viewpoint," in Rosenthal, *Why Docudrama,* 175.

8   Leslie Woodhead, "The Guardian Lecture: Dramatized Documentary," in Rosenthal, *Why Docudrama,* 101–102.

9   Jean Nathan, "What China Would Bury in the Moroccan Sand," *New York Times,* December 22, 1996; "Dalai Lama Movie Imperils Disney's Future in China," *New York Times,* November 26, 1996, 1.

10   Martin, "Shaking up the World, or Shaped by It?"

11   Stephen E. Ambrose, *Nixon: The Triumph of a Politician, 1962–1972,* 3 vols. (New York: Simon and Schuster, 1989), 2:322, 345.

12   Quoted in McArthur, "*Braveheart* and the Scottish Aesthetic Dementia," in Barta, *Screening the Past,* 180–181.

13   Ian McBride, "Where Are We Going and How and Why?" in Rosenthal, *Why Docudrama,* 116.

14   Martin, Shaking up the World, or Shaped by It?"

15   Toplin, *History by Hollywood,* 197–198.

16   Will Joyner, "After Massacre, Facts Meet Memory," *New York Times,* May 2, 1998.

17   Walter Goodman, "History as a Springboard in the Service of Fun," *New York Times,* December 9, 1995; Alexander Haig, Jr., letter to the editor, *New York Times,* December 15, 1995, A18.

18   "Mike Wallace Getting over It," *New York Times,* November 3, 1999.

19   Thomas Dixon, "Reply to the *New York Globe,*" in Fred Silva, ed., *Focus on* Birth of a Nation (Englewood Cliffs, N.J.: Prentice-Hall, 1971).

20   Silva, *Focus on* Birth of a Nation, 65.

21   Ibid., 75.

22   Garth Jowett, *Film: The Democratic Art* (Boston: Little, Brown, 1976), 103; Joel Williamson, *The Crucible of Race: Black-White Relations in the American South since Emancipation* (New York: Oxford University Press, 1984), 175–176; Thomas Cripps, "The Reaction of the Negro to the Motion Picture *Birth of a Nation,*" in Silva, *Focus on* Birth of a Nation, 111–124.

23   Lang, *Birth of a Nation: D. W. Griffith, Director,* 169.

24   David Mark Chambers, *Hooded Americanism: The First Century of the Ku Klux Klan, 1865–1965* (Garden City, N.Y.: Doubleday, 1965), 25–32; Kenneth T. Jackson, *The Ku Klux Klan in the City, 1915–1930* (New York: Oxford University Press, 1967), 3–4. For a discussion of the movie's quality as a film and its unfortunate message about race relations, see William Grimes, "Can a Film Be Both Racist and Classic?" *New York Times,* April 27, 1994, B1.

25   Peter Novick, *The Holocaust in American Life* (Boston: Houghton Mifflin, 1999), 209.

26   Quoted in ibid., 213.

27   Elie Wiesel, "Trivializing the Holocaust: Semi-Fact and Semi-Fiction," *New York Times,* April 16, 1978, sec. 2, p. 1. See also Ilan Avisar, *Screening the Holocaust: Cinema's Images of the Unimaginable* (Bloomington: Indiana University Press, 1995), 129. For related criticisms regarding the dramatization of Anne Frank's story, see

Cynthia Ozick, "Who Owns Anne Frank?" *New Yorker,* October 6, 1997, 76–82. See also Saul Friedlander, ed., *Probing the Limits of Representation: Nazism and the "Final Solution"* (Cambridge: Harvard University Press, 1992); "Forum on Representing the Holocaust," *History and Theory* 33, no. 2 (1994).

28  Rabbi Mark S. Golub, letter to the editor, *New York Times,* April 28, 1978, 26.

29  John O'Connor, "TV Weekend," *New York Times,* April 14, 1978, sec. 3, p. 26.

30  Abraham Brumberg, letter to the editor, *New York Times,* May 4, 1978, 22. See also Avisar, *Screening the Holocaust,* 139–140.

31  "Ethnic Leaders React to Impact of 'Holocaust,'" *New York Times,* April 16, 1978.

32  Dore Schary, letter to the editor, *New York Times,* April 30, 1978, 31.

33  Evelyn Gerter, letter to the editor, *New York Times,* April 30, 1978, 31.

34  Gerald Green, "In Defense of *Holocaust,*" *New York Times,* April 23, 1978, sec. 2, p. 1.

35  Loshitzky, *Spielberg's Holocaust,* 175.

36  John Vinocur, "'Holocaust' TV Series Criticized, Is Sidelined by West Germans," *New York Times,* July 3, 1978, 2.

37  Ibid., 55.

38  "'Holocaust' Audience Far Bigger than West Germans Anticipated," *New York Times,* January 25, 1979, 15; Ellen Lentz, "Effects of 'Holocaust' on West German TV Cross Border into East," *New York Times,* January 28, 1979, 11.

39  Lentz, "Effects of 'Holocaust' Cross Border," 11.

40  Charles R. Maier, *The Unmasterable Past: History, Holocaust, and German National Identity* (Cambridge: Harvard University Press, 1988), 1–8, 44, 47–56, 118.

41  Anton Kaes, *From Hitler to Heimut: The Return of History as Film* (Cambridge: Harvard University Press, 1989), 3–35, 164–189. See also Geoffrey H. Hartman, ed., *Holocaust Remembrance: The Shapes of Memory* (Oxford, England: Blackwell, 1994).

42  Liliane Weissberg, "The Tale of a Good German: Reflections on the German Reception of *Schindler's List,*" in Loshitzky, *Spielberg's Holocaust,* 177–178, 184.

43  "Swiss Bank Guard Seeks Asylum in U.S.," *Wilmington (N.C.) Star-News,* May 21, 1997, 1.

## CONCLUSION

1  D. W. Griffith, "The Motion Picture and the Witch Hunters," and 1947 letter to *Sight and Sound,* in Lang, *Birth of a Nation: D. W. Griffith, Director,* 4; D. W. Griffith, "The Future of the Two Dollar Movie," in Silva, *Focus on* Birth of a Nation, 100–101.

2  Griffith, letter to *Sight and Sound,* 4.

3  Ibid.

4  Griffith, "The Motion Picture and the Witch Hunters," 97.

5  Griffith, "The Future of the Two Dollar Movie," 100–101.

6  Ibid., 100.

7  Griffith, letter to *Sight and Sound,* 3.

# Index